Low and Lower Fertility

Ronald R. Rindfuss • Minja Kim Choe
Editors

Low and Lower Fertility

Variations across Developed Countries

Editors
Ronald R. Rindfuss
Department of Sociology and Carolina
  Population Center
University of North Carolina
Chapel Hill, NC, USA

East-West Center
Honolulu, HI, USA

Minja Kim Choe
East-West Center
Honolulu, HI, USA

ISBN 978-3-319-21481-8   ISBN 978-3-319-21482-5 (eBook)
DOI 10.1007/978-3-319-21482-5

Library of Congress Control Number: 2015952636

Springer Cham Heidelberg New York Dordrecht London
© Springer International Publishing Switzerland 2015
This work is subject to copyright. All rights are reserved by the Publisher, whether the whole or part of the material is concerned, specifically the rights of translation, reprinting, reuse of illustrations, recitation, broadcasting, reproduction on microfilms or in any other physical way, and transmission or information storage and retrieval, electronic adaptation, computer software, or by similar or dissimilar methodology now known or hereafter developed.
The use of general descriptive names, registered names, trademarks, service marks, etc. in this publication does not imply, even in the absence of a specific statement, that such names are exempt from the relevant protective laws and regulations and therefore free for general use.
The publisher, the authors and the editors are safe to assume that the advice and information in this book are believed to be true and accurate at the date of publication. Neither the publisher nor the authors or the editors give a warranty, express or implied, with respect to the material contained herein or for any errors or omissions that may have been made.

Printed on acid-free paper

Springer International Publishing AG Switzerland is part of Springer Science+Business Media (www.springer.com)

Foreword

Over the past few decades, countries around the world have experienced rapid economic growth along with far-reaching changes in social and political conditions. In many countries, these developments have been accompanied by fertility declines to very low levels. Today, the total fertility rates (TFR) for most economically developed countries range from less than 1.0 to 2.1 children per woman. As recently as 20–30 years ago, women in some of these countries were having, on average, four or more children.

Within the general trend toward lower fertility, current fertility levels and the pace of fertility decline have been widely diverse. This diversity is important because total fertility rates of 1.2 or 2.1 children per woman have very different effects on population age structure and population growth, as well as important implications for institutions and policies. As a result, fertility levels and trends have captured the attention of demographers and policymakers alike. Research, however, has yet to produce a comprehensive understanding of fertility behavior across low-fertility countries.

Early in 2013, the Korea Institute for Health and Social Affairs (KIHASA) and the East-West Center agreed to collaborate on a project to improve understanding of the patterns and causes of fertility decline in various social, economic, cultural, and political settings and to consider the associated policy implications. The project identified low-fertility countries with varying fertility levels and trends, cultural backgrounds, social patterns, and economic conditions. For each country selected, an expert scholar was invited to write a country paper and participate in a series of workshops for discussions with experts from other countries.

The essays in this volume are revised versions of the papers presented at the first workshop of the project, held at the East-West Center in December 2013. The papers in this first volume address the fertility situation in Australia, China, Hong Kong, Japan, South Korea, the Netherlands, Singapore, and the United States. The second volume, based on papers presented at a second workshop that was held at the East-West Center in August 2014, will discuss the factors that are influencing fertility in Austria, Canada, the Czech Republic, France, Hungary, Italy, Norway, Spain, Taiwan, and the United Kingdom. It is hoped that the collection of papers presented in these two volumes will serve as an important reference point for all those interested in fertility variation across economically advanced countries.

The Ministry of Health and Social Affairs of the Government of the Republic of Korea provided generous funding for the project. Thanks are due to East-west Center's Research Program for project coordination and institutional support. On behalf of KIHASA, I am grateful to East-west Center Senior Fellows Minja Kim Choe, Sang-Hyop Lee, and Ronald R. Rindfuss for coordinating project activities, to Sidney B. Westley for expert editorial management, and to Ki-Tae Park for research assistance.

Korea Institute for Health and Social Affairs Byong-ho Tchoe
Seoul, South Korea

Contents

1   **Diversity across Low-Fertility Countries: An Overview** 1
Ronald R. Rindfuss and Minja Kim Choe

2   **China's Long Road toward Recognition
of Below-Replacement Fertility** 15
Wang Feng

3   **Singapore's Pro-natalist Policies: To What Extent
Have They Worked?** 33
Gavin W. Jones and Wajihah Hamid

4   **Understanding Ultra-Low Fertility in Hong Kong** 63
Stuart Basten

5   **Below-Replacement Fertility in Japan: Patterns,
Factors, and Policy Implications** 87
Noriko O. Tsuya

6   **Lowest-Low Fertility and Policy Responses in South Korea** 107
Samsik Lee and Hyojin Choi

7   **Variation in U.S. Fertility: Low and Not so Low,
but Not Lowest-Low** 125
S. Philip Morgan

8   **The Evolution of Population and Family Policy in Australia** 143
Peter McDonald

9   **The Dutch Fertility Paradox: How the Netherlands
Has Managed to Sustain Near-Replacement Fertility** 161
Melinda C. Mills

Chapter 1
Diversity across Low-Fertility Countries: An Overview

Ronald R. Rindfuss and Minja Kim Choe

The low fertility "problem" in economically advanced countries has captured the attention of fertility researchers in a way that high fertility did in an earlier generation. Painting with a broad brush, what has emerged are two low-fertility regimes. In some countries, fertility is at or just a little below the replacement level of 2.1 children per woman. In these countries, either there is limited discussion of fertility or self-congratulations that policies put in place to stabilize fertility near the replacement level have worked. In other countries, fertility is well below replacement level. In these countries, there is active discussion among policymakers and the general public about the consequences of low fertility and what can be done about it. In Japan, for example, where fertility has been well below replacement level since 1974, each spring, when the national statistical office releases the fertility rate for the previous year, it is a front-page story in the newspapers and widely discussed in social media.

That countries with advanced economies and highly educated populations can differ so widely on something as basic as the number of children women have suggests that country-level factors are operating—including institutions, history, culture, and policies—factors that tend to be stable within a country but vary across countries. The chapters in this volume discuss trends in fertility levels and the factors that have likely shaped fertility in eight diverse settings around the world: Australia, China, Hong Kong,[1] Japan, South Korea, the Netherlands, Singapore, and the United States. This is the first of two volumes with country-specific reviews of

---

[1] Hong Kong is technically not a country, but rather a territory of China with considerable autonomy. For linguistic ease, we refer to it as a country.

R.R. Rindfuss (✉)
Department of Sociology and Carolina Population Center, University of North Carolina, Chapel Hill, NC, USA

East-West Center, Honolulu, HI, USA
e-mail: ron_rindfuss@unc.edu

M.K. Choe
East-West Center, Honolulu, HI, USA

© Springer International Publishing Switzerland 2015
R.R. Rindfuss, M.K. Choe (eds.), *Low and Lower Fertility*,
DOI 10.1007/978-3-319-21482-5_1

the institutional, cultural, historic, and policy factors affecting fertility. The second volume will discuss the factors influencing fertility in Austria, Canada, Czech Republic, France, Hungary, Italy, Norway, Spain, Taiwan, and the United Kingdom. Together these volumes describe a broadly diverse set of countries – spanning different geographies, histories, political systems, institutional arrangements, and fertility regimes.

The trend in total fertility rates (TFRs) for the countries in this volume is shown in Fig. 1.1 for 1980–2010.[2] Australia, the Netherlands, and the United States have experienced moderately high fertility, especially since 2000, while the rest—all in Asia—have had TFRs below 1.5 children per woman since at least 2001.

The papers in this volume were initially presented at a conference with all the authors present. The authors were asked to describe the institutions, history, culture, and policies of their countries that might be affecting fertility, negatively or positively, intentionally or inadvertently. Discussions of each country paper as well as cross-country comparisons revealed that what is seen every day may not be noticed. And if noticed, the implications and ramifications may not be evident, especially if the effects are inadvertent or "it is the way it always has been." The chance for "outsiders" to probe country "insiders" about why fertility might be as high or low as it is resulted in insights that would not have been possible without such exchanges. The revised papers in this volume and this introductory chapter reflect the rich discussion that occurred, filling a gap in the literature by contextualizing the childbearing choices that women, and couples, make within the environment of a particular country. There are many illustrations in these chapters of one general hypothesis: Any factor that makes it easier to combine parenting, and particularly mothering, with other roles leads to higher fertility, and conversely, any factor that makes such role combinations more difficult results in lower fertility.

In this introductory chapter, we explain a few technical terms that run throughout the papers and then highlight some of the factors that support or constrain fertility across countries. Throughout this introduction, we use country names to refer to the chapters that follow.

First, Some Definitions

We begin by noting a few issues of definition that permeate the chapters. We address these issues in non-technical language. Readers interested in technical details are urged to consult standard demographic texts (such as Preston et al. 2001 or Wachter 2014) or journal articles on specialized topics (such as Bongaarts and Feeney 1998 on tempo distortion in period total fertility rates).

---

[2] As Wang Feng (this volume) notes, the actual TFR levels for China have been a matter of dispute among Chinese government agencies and demographers. The rates shown in Fig. 1.1, beginning in 1994, are from the National Bureau of Statistics and are widely accepted among demographers.

1 Diversity across Low-Fertility Countries: An Overview

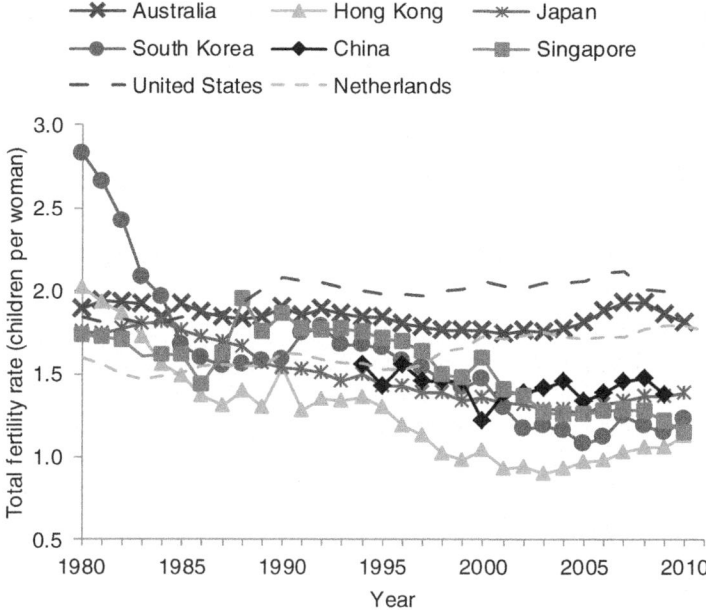

Fig. 1.1 Trends in total fertility rates in selected countries, 1980–2010 (For China, National Bureau of Statistics data in China chapter, this volume; for other countries, World Bank 2013)

The *total fertility rate* (TFR) is a measure of fertility for a particular time period, usually a year. It has the useful property of not being distorted by the age structure of a population in a particular year. The TFR is the number of children a woman would have in her lifetime if she experienced the age-specific fertility rates that existed in the year for which the TFR was calculated. As such, it is expressed in an easily understood metric: number of children per woman.

Replacement-level fertility is the TFR that would produce a population growth rate of 0.0 if it were experienced for a long time and there were no change in mortality and no in- or out-migration. For most purposes, 2.1 is a reasonable approximation of replacement-level fertility. It is larger than 2.0 because some female births do not survive to childbearing age.

Tempo distortion occurs whenever women are having children at either earlier or later ages than they had previously. If births are occurring earlier, tempo distortion will result in a higher TFR even if women are not having more births throughout their lives. And conversely, if women are postponing births, the TFR will be lower even if women are having the same number of births as previously. To intuitively see this, imagine a population where all women had twins at age 25 year after year—the TFR in that population would be 2.0. If for some reason these women postponed having their twins until age 26, during the postponing year the TFR would drop to 0.0 even though the actual number of children women in this population were having over their lifetimes would not change.

Although the language of *causality* is frequently used in these chapters, the papers do not represent empirical tests of causal hypotheses. Rather, the authors were asked to describe the institutions, history, culture, and policies of a country that might be affecting fertility. As such, it is important to recognize that what is being presented is a series of hypotheses rather than causal analyses.

Why the Concern about Low Fertility?

Why should we be concerned about very low fertility, that is, total fertility rates of 1.5 or below? The main reasons are that sustained very low fertility leads to population aging and eventually to population decline. To see this intuitively,[3] imagine a population where couples are having fewer than two children; that is, they are not replacing themselves. As this continues, and in the absence of extremely large-scale immigration, the number of children in the population becomes smaller and smaller. The shrinking is occurring at the youngest ages, and hence the average age of the population becomes older. As these smaller numbers of children grow up, the number of working-age adults also decreases. To put the population decline in perspective, a "stable" population (a population with no in- or out-migration as well as unchanging fertility and mortality rates for several generations) with a total fertility rate of 1.5 will be reduced by half in 64 years. If the total fertility rate is 1.9, it takes 230 years for the population to shrink by half (Toulemon 2011). To put the aging issue in perspective, in South Korea (Chap. 6, this volume) the proportion of the population age 65 and above is expected to climb from 10 % in 2009 to 30 % in 2037.

Why care about population aging? The principal concern here involves the mechanisms countries use to fund their social security and social welfare systems, and especially the provision of support to the elderly. With rare exceptions,[4] benefits for the elderly are funded by taxing the working-age population. As the elderly become a larger share of the population and the working-age population that pays taxes shrinks, governments are faced with reducing benefits for the elderly, increasing taxes on the working-age population, or some combination of the two. All these options are unpopular with the electorate. If a country has not yet put in place an income and benefits plan for its elderly, as is the case with China (Chap. 2, this volume), adult children who need to support their aging parents might be unwilling to take on the extra burden of raising children, creating a positive feedback loop that leads to further fertility decline. Another concern, sometimes mentioned, is that

---

[3] For an excellent formal discussion of how different fertility and mortality rates affect the age structure of a population see Coale (1972).

[4] Norway is an interesting exception with its large and growing Sovereign Wealth Fund, based upon its oil revenue. Some of the proceeds will be used for Norway's elderly pension system. Currently, the fund has assets of more than US$ 900 billion or more than US$ 175,000 per Norwegian.

young adults bring creativity, inventiveness, and vigor to a society, and that aging societies will experience a loss of vitality.

Why be concerned about a shrinking population? One reason, and perhaps the worst reason, is nationalism. There is a nationalistic pride in having a growing population, although this sentiment is typically left unspoken. Additionally, there are economic concerns. Typically, the domestic market is responsible for the largest share of a country's economy, and as the number of consumers declines the economy is also likely to decline. There are also military concerns related to having a sufficient number of able-bodied young people to staff an army. Stephen (2011) estimates that by 2020 South Korea may not have enough 20 year olds to maintain the size of its armed forces. On the other hand, many environmentalists would be pleased to see the population of their country shrink. This is mentioned in the Netherlands chapter in connection with concerns about the very high Dutch population density.

Work

Numerous aspects of work and work settings influence childbearing decisions. The long work hours for employed women and men in Hong Kong, Japan, Singapore, and South Korea make it difficult to be in the mother and father roles. Both employers and co-workers commonly expect a worker to be on the job for long hours, often with little regard for the family responsibilities a worker might have. And a long commute can increase the hours devoted to a job. In many cases, mothers of young children are forced to leave the labor force. In Japan especially, but also to some extent in the other three countries, married women find it difficult to obtain a regular job, with benefits and opportunities for career advancement, when they return to the labor force after their children reach school age. Instead, they are likely to find jobs with little security, few (if any) benefits, and relativity low pay.

In these East Asian societies, cultural expectations are that women are fully responsible for housework and childcare regardless of whether or not they are employed outside the home. Long hours at work plus commuting time also make it difficult for men to help with domestic tasks, even if they wished to. There are signs that some of these problems related to work and family life are starting to occur in China as well. The double burden of work and domestic responsibilities makes the "marriage package" particularly unattractive for women.

The Netherlands provides a contrasting example. Women and men have a government-protected right to work part time, with no wage discrimination and with the same benefits as full-time workers, including healthcare, pensions, and related benefits. In a situation characterized as "unequal pay for unequal work," 61 % of women and 15 % of men were working part time in 2005, clearly indicating the popularity of part-time jobs. The Netherlands still has a male-breadwinner model, maternity leave is short, and childcare is generally only used on a part-time basis. Yet fertility levels in the Netherlands are fairly close to replacement.

In Australia and the United States, which also have fertility near replacement level, labor markets tend to be more flexible than in East Asia. Part-time positions are available, although not with the guarantees and benefits found in the Netherlands, and re-entry into the labor force is easier than in Japan or South Korea.

Job insecurity and precarious work is a growing issue in all the countries covered in this book, mostly due to the forces of globalization. The current situation is more of a shock in countries such as Japan and South Korea—which had a system of lifetime employment, seniority-based pay raises, and company-provided on-the-job training—than in countries such as the United States and Australia, which never had such a high level of job security. There is evidence from the Netherlands (Chap. 9, this volume) and Japan (Chap. 5, this volume and Piotrowski et al. 2014) that uncertainties regarding employment lead to a substantial postponement of marriage and childbearing.

The Marriage-Childbearing Link

The contrast in the levels of non-marital fertility among the countries described in this volume is sharp. In Singapore, South Korea, and Japan, about 2 % of births occur outside marriage, while in Hong Kong it is about 5 %. In these Asian settings, the marriage-fertility link is strong, and a principal purpose of marriage is to have children. Indeed, marriage is frequently postponed because young women and men are not ready to have children. Marriage and fertility are linked together as a "package," and social norms and legal systems tend to disadvantage children not born within a marital union,[5] keeping non-marital fertility low.

In the Netherlands (Chap. 9, this volume), by contrast, about 20 % of births occur outside of marriage. In the United States and Australia, the percentage is closer to 40 (Carmichael 2014; Monte and Ellis 2014). To the extent that the flexibility of having births within or outside marriage results in higher fertility, then the strong norms against non-marital fertility in the Asian countries are likely one factor contributing to their low fertility levels.

Gender Equity

Gender equity, both in the domestic realm and in the labor force, is hypothesized as an important factor differentiating economically advanced countries that have fertility levels close to replacement from those whose fertility is much lower (Esping-Anderson 2009; McDonald 2006). China, Hong Kong, Japan, and South Korea all have a patriarchal culture, with considerable gender inequality within families.

---

[5] We note that recent political and judicial decisions in Japan and South Korea are changing the legal status of children born outside a marital union.

Wives have primary, almost exclusive, responsibility for household tasks and child-rearing duties, while husbands tend to spend relatively little time on either. In these Asian countries, there is also overt and inadvertent discrimination against women in the work force. Although patterns vary, employers tend to hire men for key jobs in their companies because it is expected that women will leave the workplace when they become mothers. And given the very long work hours in Asian companies, the lengthy work day tends to discriminate inadvertently against mothers of young children. Fertility in Asia's developed economies is much lower than in Australia or the United States, where the women's movement has been stronger, there is more equitable sharing of domestic tasks, and there is less discrimination against women in the work place—all consistent with theoretical arguments about gender equity.

The Netherlands, where promoting gender equity has not been a particularly salient issue, is an interesting case from the gender-equity perspective. It still has a male-breadwinner model, or perhaps a "one-and-one-half-earner" model, as Mills (Chap. 9, this volume) notes. There are strong norms for the mother to stay at home and care for her young children. Feminist voices have been comparatively mild. Women with the highest education levels and most successful careers are likely to remain childless. Yet fertility in the Netherlands approaches replacement level. This seeming anomaly has been described as the "Dutch fertility paradox."

Childcare and Time Off for Working Parents

Given that virtually all work places in today's economically advanced countries are not appropriate for infants or young children, an incompatibility arises between being a worker and a mother. Organized childcare centers are a common strategy to reduce this incompatibility, yet it is noteworthy that this collection of moderate- and low-fertility countries does not contain a single example of high enrollment rates in government-subsidized childcare centers. Singapore has a limited number of facilities, which are private and expensive. Japan has been trying to increase the availability of government-supported childcare centers, but the supply is still quite low, and certainly not close to the demand. China, South Korea, and Hong Kong all have more demand for childcare than the number of available slots.

The childcare situation in Singapore has an unusual feature in that approximately 20 % of households have one or more domestic workers. These domestic workers are on fixed-term contracts and come primarily from Indonesia or the Philippines. If there are young children in the household, the domestic workers are likely providing childcare assistance.

Australia is now moving to help parents pay for childcare with means-tested financial support, but the conservative government of the late 1990s inadvertently reduced availability by stopping the grants made to community-based childcare centers and putting many of them out of business. In the United States, only about one-quarter of children less than age five are enrolled in a childcare center, and less than one-quarter of these are in a government-supported facility (Laughlin 2013).

Mothers in the Netherlands use childcare centers, but children tend to spend a limited number of hours in them. The short duration is related to the strong value position that mothers should care for their own children and the fact that many women are working part time.

Government-mandated paid maternity leave is not very generous in any of the countries covered in the present volume. The United States does not have a mandated paid maternity leave policy at all, although some employers do provide paid leave. In the Netherlands, maternity leave is only 16 weeks, but at 100 % pay. In Australia, universal paid maternity leave was introduced in 2012, but it is of short duration (18 weeks) and paid only at the minimum wage level. Singapore has only 16 weeks of paid maternity leave capped at S$20,000 (US$16,000) total for the first and second child, and S$40,000 (US$32,000) total for the third child. South Korea provides 90 days of maternity leave at 100 % of salary plus 1 year of childcare leave at 40 % of salary capped at KRW 1,000,000 (US$964) per month. Japan has the most generous policy with a 1-year paid leave at 50 % of salary. Neither Hong Kong nor China has universal paid maternity leave.

A number of the countries described here have mandated that employers take certain actions to ease the incompatibility between work and family responsibilities. For example, the South Korean government has attempted to expand employers' provision of childcare centers and has encouraged employers to allow more work flexibility. In the Netherlands, employers are supposed to pay one-third of childcare costs. Singapore has a "Work-Life Works" program where employers can apply for funding to support programs that would help their employees balance work and family responsibilities. In Japan, employers are required to offer parental leave, but compliance is not universal. Across these different countries, it appears that if employers are not forced to take steps to ease the incompatibility between work and family responsibilities, many do not.

Education Systems

Educational institutions and policies can have inadvertent, but strong, effects on fertility. Among the countries discussed in this volume, those with more flexible (and affordable) systems of education also have the highest fertility, and we suspect that these two observations are related. The effects of education on fertility can involve both the education of potential parents and the educational systems that their children will eventually face. Consider the education of potential parents first. In the Netherlands, with a few exceptions such as medicine, all students who graduate from an academically oriented secondary school can enroll in whatever university or field of study they choose, and, until recently, tertiary education was free. In the United States, the university system is open, in the sense that it is relatively easy to change fields of study, and students can drop out and reapply for re-entry later. In short, in these countries, women and men have the flexibility to have children and then finish their education and/or to change fields of study. It may not be easy to do so, but it is possible. Similarly in Sweden, Tesching (2012) shows that not only do some women go back to school after becoming mothers, but also that many who do return to school switch fields of study to train for occupations that are more compatible with motherhood.

In contrast, in Japan and South Korea, it is close to impossible to drop out of university and later return. Changing fields of study is also extremely difficult because entrance exams tend to be aimed at a specific field of study at a specific university rather than simply for university entrance. Also, in Japan and South Korea, the universities are ranked from top to bottom (with society-wide agreement on the rankings), and graduates of better universities have access to better entry-level jobs. As a result, competition is fierce to get into the best universities, which, in turn, affects competition to get into the best secondary schools and so forth. Expansion of the proportion of young men and women attending tertiary educational institutions[6] has not diminished the fierce competition to gain entry into the best possible schools. Hence in Japan and South Korea, decisions and efforts at a relatively young age set an individual on an educational (and career) trajectory that is all but impossible to change later in life. We suspect that the tertiary education systems in these Asian countries have led to lower fertility levels relative to the more flexible systems in the Netherlands and the United States.

Educational expectations for children also likely play a role in fertility decisions. In Hong Kong, Japan, Singapore, and South Korea, the primary and secondary education experience is extremely competitive, described by Jones and Hamid (Chap. 3, this volume) as an "educational arms race." There are exams, sometimes at quite young ages, which form the basis for tracking students into various educational programs or allowing entrance into the best schools. Parents enroll children in tutoring or after-school programs, often at considerable expense, to help them prepare for these important exams. Mothers frequently report that they go back to work specifically to pay for their children's after-school programs. When primary and secondary schools have catchment areas for students, there are anecdotal reports of parents renting a home within the catchment area of the best school in order to enroll their child there, although they do not actually live in the rental unit. In addition, mothers spend a great deal of time helping with homework and otherwise supporting their children's quest for educational success. Given Asian parents' onerous investment in their children's education, it is likely that the "educational arms race" tends to reduce fertility, albeit inadvertently.

At the workshop where the papers in this volume were originally presented and discussed, some from Western countries were taken aback upon learning the details of the contested nature of Asian educational systems, especially the competition at very young ages. While there is also obvious competition in the education systems of Australia, the Netherlands, and the United States, it is nowhere near the level found in these Asian countries. Indeed, given the very low levels of competition in the Netherlands, Mills (Chap. 9, this volume) comments that Dutch children are ranked as the world's happiest.

---

[6] In South Korea, approximately 80 % of secondary-school graduates now enroll in a post-secondary educational institution.

Availability of Housing for Young Families

An important component in the transition to adulthood as well as a consideration in forming a union is access to an appropriate dwelling unit. Where it is difficult to find or afford housing for a young family, people may delay or even avoid marriage and childbearing. Countries typically have various policies that affect the availability of housing, but such policies are generally set without regard to their effect on fertility. Singapore is an exception. Singapore's Housing and Development Board controls 85 % of the city-state's dwelling units and gives preference to married couples over single individuals. Given the tight Singapore housing market and the close marriage-fertility link, this could be a powerful policy lever. Yet Singapore still has a TFR in the range of 1.1–1.2 children per woman.

For the other countries, the effects of housing policies are inadvertent. The United States has a number of policies that serve to make home ownership more affordable than it would be otherwise, including government-backed mortgages, tax credits, and means-tested subsidized housing. The Netherlands has a large rental market of small apartments for students and young adults, but housing to accommodate a family is not so readily available and can be expensive. The system for rental housing in South Korea is unusual and may serve to postpone marriage and childbearing. Renters pay the landlord a down payment, the interest on the down payment serves as rent, and the tenants receive the down payment back when they leave. These down payments tend to be large, making them difficult for young people to afford, and this constraint likely leads some to postpone marriage and childbearing. Housing prices have increased substantially in China's cities, partly in response to massive migration from rural areas. Again, these costs could delay marriage, especially since housing prices in rural areas have plummeted, making it all but impossible to trade a rural dwelling unit for an urban one.

Besides expense, the size of a dwelling unit likely matters in the childbearing decision. It is clearly more difficult in myriad ways to raise children in cramped quarters than in more spacious ones. In Singapore, the average size of an apartment is 80 m^2 (861 ft^2), and in Hong Kong it is 45 m^2 (484 ft^2) (Basten, Chap. 4, this volume). By comparison, in the United States, the median size of a dwelling unit is 167 m^2 (1,800 ft^2) (United States Department of Housing and Urban Development 2014).

Government Subsidies for Raising Children

It can be dauntingly expensive to raise children to adulthood in economically advanced countries, although much of the expense tends to be back-loaded into the teen years, providing time for parents to accumulate the necessary resources. We have already noted how country-level variation in education systems can have a major impact on the cost of raising children. For the countries examined in this volume, there is also a wide range of government subsidies to help with childrearing costs. Subsidies include: government-provided schooling; baby bonuses; tax credits; school-provided meals; support for childcare, prenatal care, and birth expenses; and direct cash benefits. Singapore has the most generous subsidies, up to one-third of the cost of raising a child to age 18—yet Singapore's TFR is very low. While it is impossible to know the counterfactual, Singapore's generous government child-cost subsidies have not produced replacement-level fertility.

Limited Effects of Immigration

Both the Netherlands and the United States have had relatively high levels of immigration, and a common belief is that immigrants contribute significantly to the moderately high TFRs in both countries. Yet careful examination suggests that the new arrivals have a minor impact on total fertility levels and that their children have fertility levels comparable to the children of native-born parents. Part of the reason migrant fertility can appear high is that immigrants tend to be young (in their 20s or early 30s) and they tend to delay childbearing until they migrate. Their lifetime fertility, however, might not be particularly high. For one thing, fertility has been declining in many of the migrant-sending countries. Mexico, for example, is one of the main migrant-sending countries to the United States, and its TFR has declined to 2.2 (Population Reference Bureau 2014).

Frequent Policy Changes

One might presume that prospective parents would feel most comfortable if policies that affect having or rearing children remain constant so they can plan on those policies being in place when they need them. There are many examples in the following chapters, however, of policies being repeatedly changed. The Australia case is a good example of changes in policies as different political groups move in and out of office. Yet as can be seen in Fig. 1.1, the Australian TFR has been almost constant for 30 years. Perhaps the various policies do not matter, or perhaps the changes have not been drastic enough to have an effect.

China: Exceptional for Two Reasons

China, accounting for approximately one-fifth of the world's population, is distinctly different from the other countries covered in this volume in two ways. First, for three decades China has had a one-child policy that undoubtedly led to lower fertility levels, especially in its early years. More recently, there has been debate on whether this policy continues to have an effect because there are indications that fertility would remain low even in the absence of the one-child policy. For this and other reasons, demographers within and outside China have argued that the one-child policy should be relaxed or eliminated.

On 15 November 2013, China announced a step toward easing the restrictive policy. Now couples in which either spouse is an only child can apply for a permit to have a second child. It was estimated that approximately 11 million couples would be eligible to apply to have a second child under the new rule. During the first 6 months of 2014, however, only about 270,000 couples applied for a second-child permit—2.5 % of those estimated to be eligible. While much remains to be seen, this weak response suggests that completely eliminating the one-child policy would have a minor effect on China's total fertility rate.

The second unusual aspect of China's fertility situation has been the widespread uncertainty about the country's actual fertility level. Indeed, it is a compelling story of statistical mystery and intrigue. At about the time when the one-child policy was being rolled out in earnest, the statistical system, especially the system for birth registration, was deteriorating. There was debate among demographers, again both within and outside China, about the actual level of fertility, drawing on a wide variety of data sets. Then, even after there was agreement within the academic community about China's fertility level, Chinese government agencies consistently reported higher levels. Now there appears to be widespread, but not total, agreement that China's TFR is 1.5 or lower.

Discussion

An important lesson emerging from discussion of the fertility situation in these eight countries is that low or very low fertility levels can be reached by distinctively different pathways. Among the countries with fertility close to replacement level, the "Dutch fertility paradox" provides an excellent example. The Netherlands is a rich country with a highly educated population. Yet many Dutch people subscribe to the male-breadwinner model, and women are expected to stay at home with small children. Typically, childcare centers are only used on a part-time basis, housing can be expensive, and the duration of paid maternity leave is very short. The push for gender equality has been quite gentle. Yet the TFR is close to replacement level. Why? Of course we cannot say with certainty, but having the right to a part-time job without wage discrimination plus access to an educational system that is extremely flexible and, until very recently, entirely free likely plays a prominent role because these rights and access make it easier for parents to combine work with raising a family.

Mid-point in the second decade of the twenty-first century, it seems evident that employers want better-educated workers, women want to obtain as much education as their talents permit, most women want to be in the labor force either full or part time, parents want to be able to balance work and family obligations, young adults want suitable housing they can afford, and men and women want to have children and to be able to raise them in conformance with their preferences. If the institutions, history, culture, and policies of a country permit its citizens to achieve these goals, then the conflict between having children and achieving other goals is minimized and fertility is likely to be near replacement level. The greater the conflict among these competing goals, the lower fertility is likely to be. The countries represented in this volume illustrate diverse scenarios.

References

Bongaarts, J., & Feeney, G. (1998). On the quantum and tempo of fertility. *Population and Development Review, 24*, 271–291.

Carmichael, G. (2014). Non-marital pregnancy and the second demographic transition in Australia in historical perspective. *Demographic Research, 30*(21), 609–640.

Coale, A. J. (1972). *The growth and structure of human populations: A mathematical investigation.* Princeton: Princeton University Press.

Esping-Andersen, G. (2009). *The incomplete revolution: Adapting to women's new roles.* Cambridge: Polity Press.

Laughlin, L. (2013). *Who's minding the kids? Child care arrangements: Spring 2011* (Household economic studies). Washington, DC: United States Census Bureau.

McDonald, P. (2006). Low fertility and the state. *Population and Development Review, 32*(3), 485–510.

Monte, L. M., & Ellis, R. R. (2014). *Fertility of women in the United States: 2012.* Suitland: United States Census Bureau.

Piotrowski, M., Kalleberg, A. L., & Rindfuss, R. R. (2014, June). *Contingent work rising: Implications for the timing of marriage in Japan.* Paper presented at the meeting of the European association for population studies, Budapest.

Population Reference Bureau. (2014). *2014 world population data sheet.* http://www.prb.org/pdf14/2014-world-population-data-sheet_eng.pdf. Accessed 18 Sept 2014.

Preston, S. H., Heuveline, P., & Guillot, M. (2001). *Demography: Measuring and modeling population processes.* Oxford: Blackwell Publishers.

Steven, E. H. (2011). *Policy concerns of low fertility for military planning in South Korea* (Asia Pacific Issues No. 102). Honolulu: East–West Center.

Tesching, K. (2012). *Education and fertility: Dynamic interrelations between women's educational level, educational field and fertility in Sweden* (Dissertation Series, No 6). Stockholm: Stockholm University Demography Unit.

Toulemon, L. (2011). Should governments in Europe be more aggressive in pushing for gender equality to raise fertility? The first 'yes'. *Demographic Research, 24*, 179–200.

United States Department of Housing and Urban Development. (2014). *HUD releases 2009 American housing survey.* http://portal.hud.gov/hudportal/HUD?src=/press/press_releases_media_advisories/2010/HUDNo.10-138. Accessed 18 Sept 2014.

Wachter, K. W. (2014). *Essential demographic methods.* Cambridge: Harvard University Press.

World Bank. (2013). *Data: Indicators.* http://data.worldbank.org/indicator/SP.DYN.TFRT.IN. Accessed 21 Mar 2014.

Chapter 2
China's Long Road toward Recognition of Below-Replacement Fertility

Wang Feng

On 15th November 2013, following the close of the Third Plenum of the Communist Party's Eighteenth Party Congress, the Chinese government announced to the world that it would start to relax its three-decades-old one-child policy. The announcement itself came as a surprise, not so much the long-awaited policy change. Pressure for the policy change had been building up for a decade, and the promised relaxation is modest and partial. By allowing couples in which one spouse is an only child to have two children, the announced change is a cautious start at phasing out a uniquely strict and coercive birth-control policy.

The real surprise came from how the Chinese and international public reacted to this announcement. Among all the sweeping measures and grand promises for China's future announced at the time, this modest gesture grabbed headlines worldwide and overshadowed all others. For a casual observer, it seemed that all the Party Plenum was able to accomplish was to make this small change, along with abolishing the much-despised labor camp system.

Despite the enthusiastic popular response in the initial months of the policy relaxation, the behavioral response, as measured by the number of couples wanting to have a second child, has turned out to be extremely weak. As of June 2014, 6 months after the new policy was initiated, only about 270,000 couples nationwide had applied for approval to have a second birth. This represents about 2.5 % of the estimated 11 million eligible couples, far below all the projections made before the policy change (Xinhuanet News Service 2014). This low number is especially surprising because policymakers in Beijing had anticipated a rush to a second birth among couples who are nearing the end of their reproductive career. After decades of the one-child policy, the number of women waiting to have a second child has been accumulating, forming a large reservoir, so some kind of flooding was expected.

Wang Feng (✉)
Department of Sociology, University of California, Irvine, CA, USA

Fudan University, Shanghai, China
e-mail: fwang@uci.edu

In April 2011, there was another surprise in Beijing. At the press conference announcing results from China's 2010 census, the top official at the National Bureau of Statistics (NBS) admitted that they were caught by surprise by the decline in the population age 0–14 between 2000 and 2010, itself a direct result of declining birth numbers. And Chinese officials were surprised by the rapid speed of population aging, which is also in part an outcome of declining fertility in the preceding decades.

These should not be surprises. Since the early 1980s, when China emerged from the aftermath of the Cultural Revolution and 18 years after the 1964 census, the government has been collecting demographic data regularly and extensively. There were population censuses in 1990, 2000, and 2010 and large-scale inter-census surveys covering 1/100 of the population in 1995 and 2005. On top of these nationwide censuses and surveys, there have also been large-scale population surveys, such as the annual population surveys conducted by the National Bureau of Statistics and large-scale surveys conducted by the National Population and Family Planning Commission (NPFPC), which was in charge of population control until its merger with the Ministry of Health in March 2013. With these abundant data sources and the uniquely political importance that the Chinese government has placed on birth control, broad trends and patterns of population, such as growth rate and age structure, should be fairly well, if not perfectly, known. Yet it was not until well into the twenty-first century that a clear picture of China's fertility level began to emerge and the severity of China's population aging started to be appreciated.

How could this have happened? In this paper, I trace the process of China's route to below-replacement fertility and examine the underlying forces and likely future fertility trends. I also examine briefly the future trend of population aging and its economic and social implications. This examination is aimed at helping shed light on the surprising population trends in China, as well as the surprising reaction to China's recent modest relaxation of the one-child policy.

The Road to Below-Replacement Fertility: Three Decades, Three Stories

China's fertility decline to below-replacement level took three decades to accomplish, from the 1970s to the 1990s, and each decade had a very different story. Most of China's modern fertility decline was completed in one decade in the 1970s, more than 30 years ago (Wang 2011). In the 1970s, with a "later (marriage), longer (birth interval), and fewer (births)" policy nationwide, China's fertility level was reduced by more than one-half in 10 years, from a total fertility rate (TFR) of 5.8 births per woman in 1970 to 2.7 in 1979. Intensification of the birth-control campaign at the end of the 1970s, with the introduction of the draconian one-child policy in 1980, brought fertility further down to 2.3 in 1980, not much above the replacement level of 2.1.

It took a full decade of fertility fluctuation, during the 1980s, before fertility dropped to below replacement level. During that decade, fertility hovered slightly above replacement level, affected in part by several government policy shifts. There was first a change in the late-marriage policy at the start of the decade, implemented simultaneously as the one-child policy was rolled out. The new marriage law, passed in 1980, raised legal marriage ages from 18 to 20 for women and from 20 to 22 for men. The implementation of the new law effectively replaced the late-marriage policy of the 1970s, which set the age at marriage for women at 23 in rural areas and 25 in urban areas and for men at 25 and 27. The shift to earlier marriage that resulted from the new law pushed up fertility temporarily, from 2.3 in 1980 to 2.9 in 1982 (Coale and Chen 1987; Coale 1989; Feeney et al. 1989; Coale et al. 1991; Feeney and Wang 1993).

A forceful abortion and sterilization campaign quickly followed in 1982 and 1983, aimed at curtailing the increase in the number of births, which was caused largely by the shift toward early marriage. Abortion numbers shot up from 8.69 million in 1981 to 12.42 million in 1982 and 14.37 million in 1983. Female sterilization operations doubled in 1 year, from 1.59 million in 1981 to 3.9 million in 1982, then skyrocketed to 16.39 million in 1983 (Ministry of Health 2012, Table 7-6-1). The fertility level dipped temporarily, to 2.4 in 1983 and 2.2 in 1985.

The excesses and physical violence associated with the sterilization and abortion campaigns resulted in another cyclical change. Between 1984 and 1986, in response to the backlash caused by enforcing the one-child policy and the excesses of the sterilization and abortion campaigns, the Chinese government implemented a series of birth-control policy adjustments. The most important was to allow rural couples with a female first birth to have a second child (Greenhalgh 1986; Hardee-Cleveland and Banister 1988). That policy change apparently led to a "bunching" of births as couples rushed to take advantage of the new opportunity to have a second child. The fertility level went up to 2.6 in 1987. That year, 1987, was China's last fertility peak at above the replacement level.

In the early 1990s, fertility in China first dropped to below replacement level. Whereas this is now widely accepted, it took scholars almost a decade to realize and to confirm this fact, and it took the Chinese government another decade. Two important events during the 1990s marked the long process of fact-finding for scholars. The first event came when a national survey in 1992 reported that China's fertility level had dropped for the first time in history to below-replacement level (Fig. 2.1, 1992 Survey). That survey, conducted by the then State Family Planning Commission, had a national sample size of 380,000 and was modeled after successful 1982 and 1987 surveys. Both the 1982 one-per-thousand survey and the 1987 two-per-thousand survey had been well received, and they provided an important basis for demographic research in China (Coale 1984; Coale and Chen 1987; Coale et al. 1991). The 1992 survey, however, did not meet the same fate. With the lone exception of one published article by two distinguished demographic experts (Feeney and Yuan 1994), results from the 1992 survey were quickly dismissed and ignored by scholars. This finding, that fertility in China was below the replacement

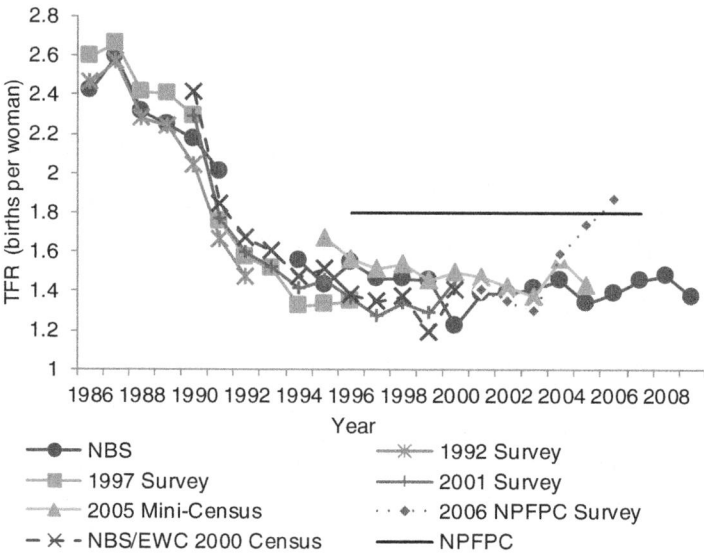

Fig. 2.1 China's route to low fertility: Eight estimates of the fertility trend, 1988–2008 (Guo 2011)

level, was deemed so incredible that after 1992 Chinese official statistical agencies stopped publishing total fertility rates for several years.

At least three reasons can be identified for the dismissal of the 1992 survey results: (1) the sudden and surprisingly low fertility level reported by the survey following a decade of fertility fluctuations; (2) the deterioration of data quality in general over the course of the 1980s as China's centrally planned economic system started to fall apart; and (3) perhaps most importantly, the beginning of the "one vote veto" birth-control-responsibility system for government officials at all levels down from the central government. Under this system, officials could be dismissed or denied promotion simply by failing to meet birth-control quotas. As a result, scholars reported widespread underreporting of birth numbers and questioned whether the fertility decline reported in the survey was real (Zeng 1996; Merli 1998; Merli and Raftery 2000).

A full decade passed before another event spurred Chinese scholars to revisit the question of fertility change. That event was a research conference on Chinese population change, organized in 2003 by Zhongwei Zhao at the Australian National University (Zhao and Guo 2007). Two papers, in particular, provided the basis for scholarly exchange and sparked renewed interest in examining fertility change in China. One, by Thomas Scharping (Scharping 2003a, b, 2007), convincingly laid out the complexity and confusion of Chinese fertility numbers and reminded people how impossible it was to get to the bottom of numbers in China. Another, by Zhang Guangyu (Zhang and Zhao 2006), provided strong evidence and a convincing argument that, despite problems in the collection system for Chinese birth statistics, fertility had really begun to decline again, starting in the early 1990s.

Galvanized by this scholarly exchange, and with the release of China's 2000 census data, researchers interested in population change in China took a renewed look at fertility and were able to see a new demographic trend. With multiple data sources available by then and with methods ranging from birth-history reconstruction to indirect estimation, a clear picture of China's new fertility regime quickly emerged (Guo 2004a, b; Retherford et al. 2005; Zhang and Zhao 2006; Guo and Chen 2007; Cai 2008; Gu 2009; Morgan et al. 2009). These studies all confirmed the onset of China's below-replacement fertility (Fig. 2.1, NBS/EWC 2000 Census). Even those who were skeptical of China's population data, after extensive and careful review of evidence, agreed that China indeed had entered the era of below-replacement fertility in the early 1990s (Goodkind 2004, 2011).

Chinese government agencies, however, especially the National Population and Family Planning Commission (NPFPC), preferred not to believe the results published by scholars and tried to prove a case otherwise. For two decades, including a full decade after scholars had confirmed China's below-replacement fertility, the Commission denied that fertility in China was well below replacement level. Official statements first insisted that China's fertility was "around the replacement level." This was the official position until the mid-2000s, when the Commission began insisting on a total fertility level, unchanged for years, of around 1.8.[1] Both estimates were well above the level reported by scholars. These official numbers were drawn from fertility estimates prepared by the Commission's handpicked experts for their National Strategic Study of Population and Development (Fig. 2.1, NPFPC).

The NPFPC favored studies showing higher fertility levels and even engineered a story of fertility rebound in the mid-2000s based on a flawed survey. Studies, sometimes co-authored by officials associated with the Commission, used school-enrollment data to adjust for alleged birth underreporting (Yu and Wang 2004; Zhai and Chen 2007). This source, as shown by others (e.g., Cai 2009), has its own limitations. In 2006, the NPFPC conducted another national fertility survey and concluded that China had experienced a fertility rebound in the mid-2000s. The total fertility level calculated from the 2006 survey increased from 1.59 in 2004 to 1.74 in 2005 and 1.87 in the 12 months leading up to the survey (Fig. 2.1, 2006 NPFPC Survey). A careful analysis by Guo Zhigang, whose results were first censored by the Commission, revealed that the survey design was seriously flawed. Discrepancies between the sex and age structure of this survey and that of the National Bureau of Statistics' 2005 1/100 population survey indicated that the NPFPC survey missed women of reproductive age who had changed residence, mostly rural-to-urban migrants. This serious deficiency in the survey design led to an inflated fertility level (Guo 2009).

---

[1]The official numbers released in 2006 were: 1.77–1.78 (1996), 1.73–1.77 (1997), 1.70–1.77 (1998), 1.69–1.77 (1999), 1.68–1.77 (2000), and "around 1.8" (2001–2004) (NPFPC 2006, 86). In subsequent years, 1.74 was given for the year 2005, presumably based on a flawed 2006 survey that showed a "rebound" in fertility (NPFPC 2009, 94).

To continue a story of high fertility and to reinforce the need to reduce fertility, the NPFPC tried to rein in other government organizations that collected demographic data, such as the National Bureau of Statistics. The Commission also used estimates from international organizations, including the United Nations Population Division (UNPD), to prove their case. Beginning in 2006, after the 2005 intercensus population survey, the National Bureau of Statistics broke ranks with the NPFPC and reported a fertility level of 1.6 or below (Fig. 2.1, NBS). The UNPD, after years of reporting China's fertility at 1.8, in part based on input from Chinese official sources, drastically revised estimates downward beginning with the 2010 world population projections (Gu and Cai 2011; Cai 2012). While UNPD's 2008 edition of *World Population Prospects* (United Nations 2009) projected that China's population would reach a maximum size of 1.463 billion in 2032, the 2010 edition (United Nations 2011), published in May 2011, projected a maximum size of 1.396 billion, to be reached in 2026. This is a difference of 6 years and 67 million people between projections published only 2 years apart.

It is by now beyond any doubt that fertility in China is well below replacement level and has been below replacement level for two decades, if not longer. Analyzing China's 2010 census, scholars have further confirmed these results (Guo 2011; Zhu 2012; Cai 2013). Even the NPFPC, before its merger into the Ministry of Health in March 2013, conceded that fertility in China was around 1.63, a level higher than what scholars had estimated but much lower than the level reported in its own earlier statements. After a two-decade delay, China has finally come to terms with its new demographic reality, a country with fertility substantially below the replacement level.

Causes and Implications of Low Fertility

Chinese officials and some observers in China and abroad tend to attribute China's fertility decline to the one-child policy. There is little doubt that China's birth-control policies—both the later-longer-fewer policy and the one-child policy—have played a significant role in reducing fertility. But while the less extreme later-longer-fewer policy may have played a significant role in China's early fertility decline, the importance of the one-child policy is often exaggerated, and its role is becoming smaller due to other forces at work.

The drop in fertility to below-replacement level occurred as Chinese society entered a new phase in its history. The onset of below-replacement fertility, in the early 1990s, took place at a time of substantial economic reforms and a historic economic boom. These developments triggered a fundamental shift in the context of childbearing (Wang and Mason 2008). For one thing, the two decades beginning in the early 1990s saw massive migration waves of young Chinese from rural to urban areas. These two decades saw the fastest pace of urbanization, expansion of higher education, and improvement in living standards in Chinese history (Table 2.1). Income level, measured at current purchasing power parity (PPP) in international dollars, increased by nearly tenfold in 20 years. Over a 20-year period, the gross secondary-school enrollment ratio more than doubled, from 38 % of children at secondary-school age in 1990 to 80 % in 2010. Over the same period, gross tertiary-school enrollment increased by eightfold, from 3 % of the appropriate age group in 1990 to 24 % in 2010. At the same time, the share of China's population residing in urban areas nearly doubled, from about one-quarter to one-half of the total, making this the largest urbanization process in world history (Table 2.1).

Two important forces linked to this rapid economic change contributed to China's renewed fertility decline—a complete shift of the cost of childrearing from the collective to the family and intensified pressure to "get ahead" generated by the opportunities and uncertainties associated with this period of hyper economic growth. Beginning first in the early 1980s in rural areas and in the late 1980s in urban areas, the socialist planned economic system that had previously supplied considerable support for childrearing started to disappear. The state and the collective were no longer responsible for food, housing, and employment. In rural areas in particular, public education and healthcare systems deteriorated rapidly, which shifted the cost of education and healthcare from the collective to individual families.

At the same time, the unprecedented economic opportunities attracted massive numbers of young people from the countryside to the cities and propelled urban youth to spend more time in school and to move around for better jobs and better pay. Urban housing reforms beginning in the late 1990s resulted in a construction

Table 2.1 Major demographic and socioeconomic indicators, China, 1990–2010 (mean age at marriage calculated from China censuses; other data from World Bank 2014)

Indicator	1990	1995	2000	2005	2010
Population (million)	1135.19	1204.86	1262.65	1303.72	1337.71
Annual birth rate (per 1,000 population)	1.4673	1.0865	0.7880	0.5881	0.4830
Life expectancy (years)	69.47	70.33	72.14	74.05	74.89
Total fertility rate (children per woman)	2.5	1.75	1.51	1.59	1.65
Female mean age at marriage (years)	22.0	22.9	23.2	23.5	23.9
Per capita Gross National Income (GNI), purchasing power parity (PPP) in current international dollars	800	1,480	2,340	4,090	7,510
Percent urban	26.4	31	35.9	42.5	49.2
Secondary-school enrollment ratio (% gross)	37.65	52.24	62.09	n.a.	80.05
Tertiary-school enrollment ratio (% gross)	3.04	3.67	6.75	17.74	24.34
Mobile phone subscribers (per 1,000 population)	0.0016	0.2989	6.72	30.09	65.04
Internet subscribers (per 1,000 population)	0	0.0049	1.78	8.52	34.3

boom and housing bubble and sent housing prices, especially in China's major cities, skyrocketing. The arrival of the Internet connected Chinese youth to other young people within China and beyond. Suddenly, young parents who grew up in China's post-Mao era realized that having children is truly expensive, both in terms of time and money.

Studies of China's low fertility in recent years confirm the role of socioeconomic changes, independent of government policy, in producing a new calculus of childbearing. Comparing aggregate fertility data from 151 counties in Jiangsu and Zhejiang Provinces with measures of birth-control policy and economic and social development, Cai (2010) reports that variations in fertility in 2000 were predominantly an outcome of variations in development, not policy. He concludes, "A key finding from this exercise is that these development factors are so powerful that, combined, they explain a much larger proportion of fertility variation in Jiangsu and Zhejiang than do the policy factors" (2010, p. 433).

Studies based on individual-level data report similar results. Another longitudinal study in Jiangsu Province, launched in 2006, found that the one-child family has become a new norm, with cost the top concern. Among more than 4,000 women who were eligible to have two children under the current birth-control policy, 55 % reported one child as their ideal family size. Among all the reasons given for their preference, "costs too much to raise a child" and "one child is enough" topped the list, with more than 70 % of respondents choosing one or the other of these explanations. By contrast, only 32 %, cited "following the government's call [for birth control]" as a reason for wanting only one child. The cost of raising children, in these respondents' minds, is not simply the immediate requirement to provide food and clothing, but the more general and long-term costs, as only 33 % reported "current economic status not good" as a reason for wanting only one child (Zheng et al. 2009). These concerns and constraints are very similar to those mentioned by young people in other low-fertility settings in Asia (Jones et al. 2009).

Shifts in other demographic behavior, not affected directly by China's birth-control policy, offer further evidence of the importance of economic and social change. Over the past three decades, there has been a clear trend toward later marriage and a related change in the age pattern of fertility. Both trends have accelerated in recent years and are beyond the requirement of the one-child policy. Women's mean age at first marriage, as shown in Table 2.1, rose by nearly 2 years in one decade—from 22 in 1990 and to 23.9 in 2010. The proportion of women never married at age 25–29 rose from 5 % in 1982 to 9 % in 2000 and 22 % in 2010, indicating the most pronounced change in the decade between 2000 and 2010 (Fig. 2.2). In urban China, the share of never-married women age 25–29 reached 30 % in 2010 (not shown in the figure).

Such numbers, while still low in comparison with current levels in Japan and South Korea, closely follow the same trajectory. In Japan, the share of never-married women age 25–29 reached urban China's current level in the mid-1980s and in South Korea, in the mid-1990s (Lee 2013; Tsuya 2013). Urban China, in other words, is about two decades behind Japan and one decade behind South Korea in the trend toward late marriage for women. As perhaps a prediction for China, in both

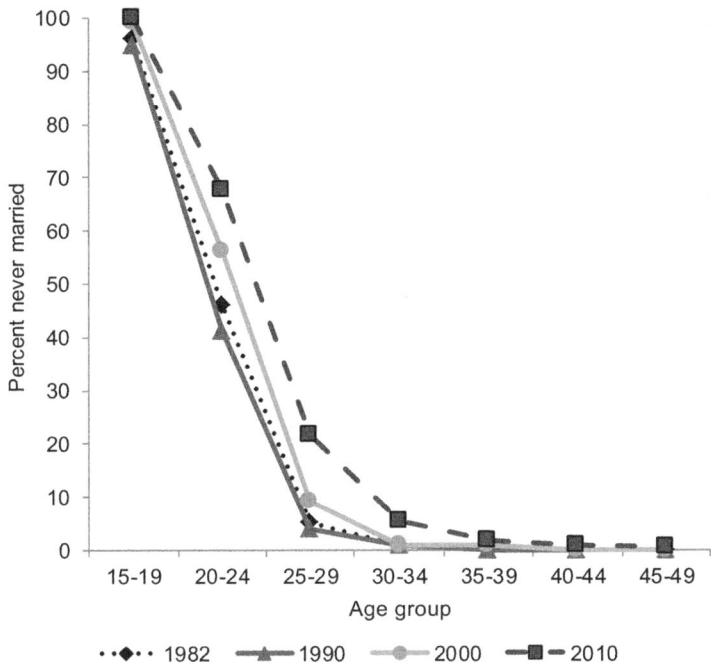

Fig. 2.2 Changing pattern of marriage in China: Percentage of women never married by age, 1982, 1990, 2000, 2010 (author's calculations from Chinese census data)

Japan and South Korea, women continue to marry later and later, if at all. Today, 20 % of Japanese women age 35–39 and 20 % of Korean women age 30–34 are still unmarried.

Comparisons of age-specific fertility rates show a similar trend. Following an initial shift toward earlier fertility after 1980, a direct and immediate result of the change in the marriage law, the peak age of childbearing has moved steadily later. The trend is especially striking after 1990 (Fig. 2.3). Delaying marriage and childbearing, as also shown by other studies (e.g., Morgan et al. 2009), have been major factors in China's move toward below-replacement fertility.

The prolonged period of below-replacement fertility during the past two decades is contributing to a dramatic acceleration of population aging. China's latest census reported that in 2010 the share of the population age 60 and above was nearly 14 % and the share age 65 and above was nearly 9 %. Assuming a fertility level of 1.47, which is very close to the current observed level, the proportion of Chinese age 60 and above will rise to 25 %, or 1 in 4 persons, by 2030. Over the same time frame, the number of Chinese age 60 and above will rise from about 180 million to more than 350 million (Fig. 2.4). Moreover, the number of the oldest old, age 80 and above, will rise from less than 20 million to more than 30 million. The population age 65 and above will increase from 9–25 % in less than 30 years. By comparison, the same process took and will take Western industrialized societies from 70 to

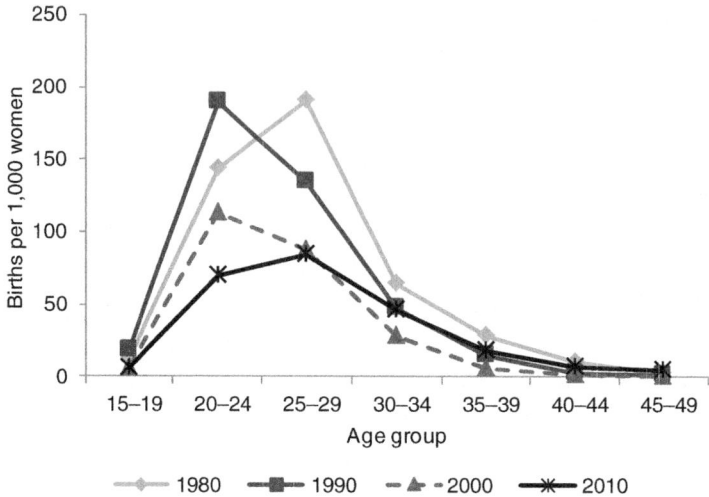

Fig. 2.3 Changing pattern of fertility in China: Births per 1,000 women by age, 1980, 1990, 2000, 2010 (from various Chinese censuses) *Note:* Numbers for 2000 and 2010 are not adjusted for underreporting

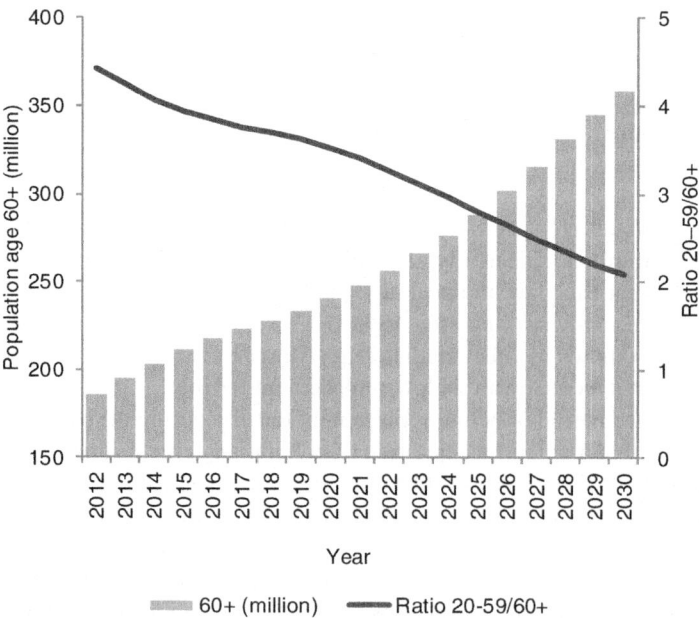

Fig. 2.4 Population aging in China: Size of population age 60 and above and ratio of population age 20–59 to population age 60 and above, 2012–2030 (projections calculated by Cai Yong and Wang Feng) *Note:* Based on an assumed total fertility rate of 1.47

more than 100 years. China, along with South Korea, Taiwan, and to some extent Japan, is among the fastest-aging societies in the world.

A rapid transition to low fertility and associated population aging pose significant challenges. For China, sustained low fertility over the past two decades has already set in motion a drastic change in the ratio between the working-age population and the population of elderly dependents. It is reasonable to use the age group 20–59 as the working and tax-paying population (China's current maximum retirement age is 60) and the age group 60 and above as the benefit-receiving population. The ratio between these two population groups will be more than halved in 20 years, from almost 5:1 in 2010 to 2:1 in 2030 (Fig. 2.4). Such a major change, driven by the continued decline in the young labor force, drastically increases the tax burden of the working-age population. The economic ramifications are many, ranging from labor-force supply, savings, investment, and tax burden to consumption patterns. As the demand to support the expanding elderly population grows, resources that could be devoted to childcare facilities and schools might be sacrificed, which will further depress fertility.

Apart from below-replacement fertility, China's three-decades-long enforcement of the one-child policy has resulted in a special feature, the large share of Chinese families with only one child. China now has more than 150 million families with only one child, or one in every three households. Among couples who have recently completed childbearing, the share is more than 40 %. In half of China's provinces, the share is more than 50 %, with the highest up to 80 %. And in China's urban areas, the share is even higher, with an average of more than 90 % of families with only one child (Wang et al. 2012). Many of the only children in these families will face the burden of providing economic support to their elderly parents, either through taxes, or within the family, or both. More importantly, they will face the demand on their time to provide irreplaceable physical and emotional support when their parents need them. The pressure faced by China's only-child generation may prompt them to want to have more than one child themselves, but it also presents them with a hard choice—between raising another child and supporting their aging parents.

The Long Road toward a Policy Response

China's policy response to below-replacement fertility and to rapid population aging has been extraordinarily slow. Countries in East and Southeast Asia that experienced rapid fertility decline all had a time lag between the point when fertility dipped to below-replacement level and the point when governments began to change their birth-control policies (Choe 2008; Jones 2008; Jones et al. 2009; Frejka et al. 2010). In South Korea, the time lag was one decade. In Singapore, it was 12 years, and in Taiwan, it was 15 years. In China, by contrast, the time interval between the onset of below-replacement fertility and the introduction of a pro-natalist policy (which has not happened yet) could be 25 years or longer.

China's unique demographic, social, and political context helps explain the government's unusually slow policy response to below-replacement fertility. In the late twentieth century, the country's large population and fast population growth cast a long Malthusian shadow of concern about overpopulation. In this context, the Chinese leadership's political mandate to increase per capita income tied birth control to its own legitimacy. The Chinese style of non-democratic, opaque, closed-door policymaking, backed by a statist view that treats people like numbers to be planned, has made policymakers indifferent to public criticism and, to some extent, unaccountable. These characteristics led to the launch of an extreme birth-control policy more than three decades ago, when much of China's fertility decline had already been accomplished (Wang et al. 2012).

The same political factors have continued to contribute to the leadership's slow pace of policy change against repeated advice and appeals from the public. After almost all academic population experts in China and many former government officials from the birth-control apparatus joined forces to call for relaxing the one-child policy, the Chinese government waited for almost a full decade to act (Gu and Li 2010). In fact, the government relied on its control over official media and other channels to silence the voices of scholars. False information on China's demographic situation promulgated by the birth-control agencies further confused the public and obstructed policy change. It was the confusion created by government-sponsored propaganda, the silencing of scholars' independent voices, and the obstruction to policy change that created the surprise when the 2010 census reported a decline in the share of the young population and a rapid increase in the relative size of the elderly population.

The extent to which Chinese policymakers are out of touch with the public explains the other surprise, namely the public's enthusiastic response to the modest relaxation of the one-child policy announced in mid-November 2013. The leadership perhaps did not expect that such a minor policy change, affecting only a very small proportion of Chinese couples, would receive such broad and overwhelming support and praise from the public.

With the recent announcement to begin phasing out the one-child policy, the government has made an historic shift in its response to below-replacement fertility and population aging. In addition to allowing couples in which one partner is an only child to have two children, the same document announced that the government would study and implement a gradual extension of the retirement age, which is now 55 for women and 60 for men. After years of resistance and denial, the Chinese government seems to have finally come to terms with a new reality and will revise its birth-control policy and introduce policies to mitigate the effects of population aging.

The next 1–3 years will be crucial to see how quickly and completely China can leave its one-child policy behind. The recent minor adjustment of the birth-control policy could represent a decisive moment that paves the way for a quick abandonment of the one-child policy altogether by allowing more couples to have two children. Or it could be part of a stalling strategy that allows bureaucrats to maintain the status quo in the face of public criticism. Given how unwilling and protracted the process of policy change has been so far, the second scenario, namely a further delay, cannot be ruled out.

Despite the policy announcement, the Chinese public has conveyed a clear message—it is too costly to have children. Online surveys and media interviews with young people have all converged on one set of numbers, that only about 60 % of couples with one child are considering having a second. Fudan University recently conducted a survey of more than 2,000 respondents in Shanghai who were born in the 1980s, and results were similar: about 60 % of respondents consider two or more children as an ideal family size, but only 45 % stated that they themselves wanted to have two children. The 873 respondents who already had one child wanted on average 1.46 children. The 1,364 respondents who were childless, and who presumably were also younger, wanted on average only 1.38 children. Studies of the preferred number of children among Chinese couples all portray a similar picture. The mean number of desired children is well below the replacement level, suggesting that even if the government's birth-control policy were completely dismantled, fertility would increase only modestly (Merli and Morgan 2011; Basten and Gu 2013; Hou and Huang 2014). If young Chinese act on their fertility preferences, then China will have below-replacement fertility for a long time to come.

These fertility preferences of young Chinese, as reported by recent studies, reflect the reality of childbearing and childrearing in China. With a per capita income of $9,000 (PPP in current international dollars) in 2012, quadrupling from only $2,350 in 2000 (World Bank 2014), China has joined the ranks of upper-middle-income countries. This rapid economic growth, while raising standards of living for most, has also greatly increased the cost of having children and the degree of uncertainty in people's lives.

In the two decades since China's fertility level dropped to below-replacement level, the share of the agricultural sector shrank from 25 % of gross domestic product (GDP) in the early 1990s to 10 % in 2012 (World Bank 2014). Over the same period, the share of the service sector rose from about one-third of total GDP in the early 1990s to 45 % in 2012. Such an economic transformation, still ongoing, brings with it higher requirements and competition for education and skills and more fluidity and uncertainty in the workplace. Young people are spending more time in school and longer hours at work. They continue to move in massive numbers from rural to urban areas and between jobs. In the first decade of the twenty-first century alone, the share of China's urban population rose from 36 to 50 %, translating into 210 million new urban residents. And the urbanization wave is still continuing.

Increasingly, in addition to cost, availability of childcare has emerged as a major constraint for young couples thinking of having children. Massive rural-to-urban migration has separated young people from the older generation, so that couples cannot count on grandparents for childcare as they used to. With only one or two children, young Chinese parents also want their children to receive the best care and education, and from the youngest age. Competition for places in educational institutions has moved down from universities to high schools, middle schools, primary schools, and now to kindergartens. Although the number of births has dropped by nearly one-quarter since the late 1990s (from close to 20 million annual births to a little more than 15 million), demand for pre-school-age care and education has risen rapidly. The number of children in nursery schools and kindergartens rose from 20 million in 2001 to 27 million in 2009. In the 2 years between 2010 and 2012, nearly 30,000 new pre-school facilities were opened, and the number of kindergarten pupils increased further to 37 million (Ministry of Education 2014). This increase of 10 million kindergarten pupils between 2010 and 2012 is almost twice the total increase between 2001 and 2009.

Pre-school education increases the direct out-of-pocket cost of childrearing considerably. Yet complaints about lack of pre-school facilities are widespread. The childrearing environment in China, in a nutshell, is similar to the situation in China's neighboring East Asian societies, with one major difference—in China, everything is changing faster.

With sustained low fertility and the prospect of rapid population aging, China faces critical challenges in public policymaking over the next 3–5 years. Swiftly and completely eliminating the outdated one-child policy is only the first and easiest step. The more daunting tasks lie in the areas of social-security and healthcare reform and in creating a child-friendly and family-friend social and economic environment.

China's social-security system is currently highly inadequate and inequitable. In 2010, only about 30 % of the elderly relied on public transfers, such as pensions, as their major source of income, and almost all of those receiving pensions were urban residents. The same is true for China's healthcare system. While coverage has been extended in recent years—in principle, to the entire population—the level of coverage varies widely among different segments of society. With costs rising much faster than incomes, the current system is not only inadequate and unfair, but also unsustainable. In addition, the government will need to initiate policies to make Chinese society more "child friendly" and "family friendly," as the lack of childcare and difficulties in balancing work and family life are becoming major factors affecting fertility. All these reforms and policy changes will become more difficult to initiate and to implement than in the past because China's period of very rapid economic growth has come to an end. The growth rate of government revenue is slowing down just as the demand for old-age support is going up.

It did not take a long time for China to reach below-replacement fertility. It only took one decade to bring fertility down from more than five to close to two children per woman and only one more decade of fluctuation around the replacement level before fertility dipped even further. What took a long time was the official recognition of fertility decline and the beginning of a policy response. As a result of this unusually slow pace, China has lost precious time to prepare for population aging, both in the short and long term.

References

Basten, S., & Gu, B. (2013). *Childbearing preferences, reform of family planning restrictions, and the low fertility trap in China* (Working Paper 61). Oxford: Department of Social Policy and Intervention, Oxford Center for Population Research, University of Oxford.

Cai, Y. (2008). An assessment of China's fertility level using the variable-r method. *Demography, 45*(2), 271–281.

Cai, Y. (2009). Are enrollment statistics the gold standard for estimating fertility level in China? [in Chinese]. *Population Research, 2009*(4), 22–33.

Cai, Y. (2010). China's below-replacement fertility: Government policy or socioeconomic development? *Population and Development Review, 36*(3), 419–440.

Cai, Y. (2012). China's demographic prospects: A UN perspective [in Chinese]. *International Economic Review, 97*(1), 73–81.

Cai, Y. (2013). China's new demographic reality: Learning from the 2010 census. *Population and Development Review, 39*(3), 371–396.

Choe, M. K. (2008, 25–27 May). *Policy responses to very low fertility in selected East-Asian societies.* Paper presented at Shanghai Forum 2008: Economic globalization and the choice of Asia, Fudan University, Shanghai.

Coale, A. J. (1984). *Rapid population change in China, 1952–1982* (Committee on population and demography, Report 27). Washington, DC: National Academy Press.

Coale, A. J. (1989). Marriage and childbearing in China since 1940. *Social Forces, 67*(June), 833–850.

Coale, A. J., & Chen, S. L. (1987). *Basic data on fertility in the provinces of China, 1940–82* (Population Institute Paper). Honolulu: East–West Center.

Coale, A. J., Wang, F., Riley, N. E., & Lin, F. (1991). Recent trends in fertility and nuptiality in China. *Science, 251*, 389–393.

Feeney, G., & Wang, F. (1993). Parity progression and birth intervals in China: Policy initiatives and demographic responses. *Population and Development Review, 19*(1), 61–101.

Feeney, G., & Yuan, J. (1994). Below replacement fertility in China? A close look at recent evidence. *Population Studies–A Journal of Demography, 48*, 381–394.

Feeney, G., Wang, F., Zhou, M., & Xiao, B. (1989). Recent fertility dynamics in China: Results from the 1987 One Percent Population Survey. *Population and Development Review, 15*(2), 297–322.

Frejka, T., Jones, G., & Sardon, J. P. (2010). East Asian childbearing patterns and policy developments. *Population and Development Review, 36*(3), 579–606.

Goodkind, D. (2004). China's missing children: The 2000 census underreporting surprise. *Population Studies–A Journal of Demography, 58*(3), 281–295.

Goodkind, D. (2011). Child underreporting, fertility, and sex ratio imbalance in China. *Demography, 48*(1), 291–316.

Greenhalgh, S. (1986). Shifts in China's population policy, 1984–86: Views from the central, provincial, and local levels. *Population and Development Review, 12*, 491–515.

Gu, B. (2009). The arrival of low fertility in China. In P. Straughan, A. Chan, & G. Jones (Eds.), *Ultra-low fertility in Pacific Asia: Trends, causes and policy issues* (pp. 73–95). London: Routledge.

Gu, B., & Cai, Y. (2011). *Fertility prospects in China* (Expert Paper 2011/14). New York: Department of Economic and Social Affairs, Population Division, United Nations.

Gu, B., & Li, J. (Eds.) (2010). *The debate on China's population policy in the 21st century* [in Chinese]. Beijing: Social Sciences Academic Press.

Guo, Z. (2004a). On low fertility in China in the 1990s [in Chinese]. *Population Research, 2004*(4), 16–24.

Guo, Z. (2004b). Studies of China's fertility level in the 1990s [in Chinese]. *Population Research, 2004*(2), 10–19.

Guo, Z. (2009). Causes of recent fertility rebound [in Chinese]. *Chinese Journal of Population Science, 2009*(2), 2–15.

Guo, Z. (2011). 2010 Population census data indicate serious miscount in past population estimation and projection [in Chinese]. *Chinese Journal of Population Science, 2011*(6), 2–13.

Guo, Z., & Chen, W. (2007). Below replacement fertility in mainland China. In Z. Zhao & F. Guo (Eds.), *Transition and challenge: China's population at the turn of the twenty-first century* (pp. 54–70). Oxford: Oxford University Press.

Hardee-Cleaveland, K., & Banister, J. (1988). Fertility policy and implementation in China, 1986–88. *Population and Development Review, 14*(2), 245–286.

Hou, J., & Huang, S. (2014). Changes in the ideal number of children in China, a historical analysis [in Chinese]. *Social Sciences in China, 4*, 78–97.

Jones, G. (2008, 25–27 May). *Very low fertility in East Asian countries: Causes and policy responses*. Paper presented at Shanghai Forum 2008: Economic globalization and the choice of Asia, Fudan University, Shanghai.

Jones, G., Straughan, P. T., & Chan, A. (Eds.). (2009). *Ultra-low fertility in Pacific Asia: Trends, causes and policy issues*. London: Routledge.

Lee, S. Y. (2013, 12–13 December). *Low fertility, population aging, and policy response in South Korea*. Paper presented at the EWC-KIHASA conference on low fertility, population aging, and population policy, East–West Center, Honolulu.

Merli, G. M. (1998). Underreporting of births and deaths in rural China: Evidence from field research in one county of northern China. *China Quarterly, 155*, 637–655.

Merli, G. M., & Morgan, S. P. (2011). Below replacement fertility preferences in Shanghai. *Population, 66*(3–4), 519–542.

Merli, G. M., & Raftery, A. E. (2000). Are births underreported in rural China? Manipulation of statistical records in response to China's policies. *Demography, 37*(1), 109–126.

Ministry of Education. (2014). *China pre-school-age educational statistics* [in Chinese]. http://www.ahchys.cn/Article_Print.asp?ArticleID=2161. Accessed 27 Feb 2014.

Ministry of Health. (2012). *China's public health statistics yearbook 2012* [in Chinese]. Beijing: Peking Union Medical College Press.

Morgan, S. P., Guo, Z., & Hayford, S. R. (2009). China's below-replacement fertility: Recent trends and future prospects. *Population and Development Review, 35*(3), 605–629.

NPFPC (National Population and Family Planning Commission of China). (2006). *Booklet of frequently used population and family planning data, 2005* [in Chinese]. Beijing: China Population Press.

NPFPC (National Population and Family Planning Commission of China). (2009). *Booklet of frequently used population and family planning data, 2008* [in Chinese]. Beijing: China Population Press.

Retherford, R. D., Choe, M. K., Chen, J., Li, X., & Cui, H. (2005). How far has fertility in China really declined? *Population and Development Review, 31*(1), 57–84.

Scharping, T. (2003a). *Birth control in China, 1949–2000: Population policy and demographic development*. London: Routledge Curzon.

Scharping, T. (2003b, December). *The 2000 census and the decay of Chinese birth statistics: A review of figures, procedures, and policies*. Paper presented at the workshop on recent demographic changes in China, Canberra, Australia.

Scharping, T. (2007). The politics of numbers: Fertility data in recent decades. In Z. Zhao & F. Guo (Eds.), *Transition and challenge: China's population at the turn of the twenty-first century* (pp. 34–53). Oxford: Oxford University Press.

Tsuya, N. O. (2013, 12–13 December). *Below replacement fertility in Japan: Patterns, factors, and policy implications*. Paper presented at the EWC-KIHASA conference on low fertility, population aging, and population policy, East–West Center, Honolulu.

United Nations, Department of Economic and Social Affairs, Population Division. (2009). *World population prospects: The 2008 revision*. New York: United Nations.

United Nations, Department of Economic and Social Affairs, Population Division. (2011). *World population prospects: The 2010 revision*. New York: United Nations.

Wang, F. (2011). The future of a demographic overachiever: Long term implications of the demographic transition in China. *Population and Development Review, 37*(Suppl), 173–190.

Wang, F., & Mason, A. (2008). The demographic factor in China's transition. In L. Brant & T. Rawski (Eds.), *China's great economic transformations* (pp. 136–166). Cambridge: Cambridge University Press.

Wang, F., Cai, Y., & Gu, B. (2012). Population, policy, and politics: How will history judge China's one-child policy? *Population and Development Review, 38*(Suppl), 115–129.

World Bank. (2014). *Data: Indicators*. http://data.worldbank.org/indicator. Accessed 27 Feb 2014.

Xinhuanet News Service. (2014). *Population commission: 270,000 people applied* [in Chinese]. http://news.xinhuanet.com/health/2014-07/10/c_126737502.htm. Accessed 9 Sept 2014.

Yu, X., & Wang, G. (2004, April). *How low is China's fertility level?* Paper presented at the international conference for China's 2000 Census, Beijing.

Zeng, Y. (1996). Is fertility in China in 1991–1992 far below replacement level? *Population Studies, 50*, 27–34.

Zhai, Z., & Chen, W. (2007). China's fertility in the 1990s [in Chinese]. *Population Research, 2007*(1), 19–32.

Zhang, G., & Zhao, Z. (2006). Reexamining China's fertility puzzle: Data collection and quality over the last two decades. *Population and Development Review, 32*(2), 293–321.

Zheng, Z., Cai, Y., Wang, F., & Gu, B. (2009). Below replacement fertility and fertility intention in Jiangsu. *Asian Population Studies, 5*(3), 329–347.

Zhu, Q. (2012). Estimating China's fertility between 2000 and 2010 using the 2010 census data [in Chinese]. *Chinese Journal of Population Science, 2012*(4), 68–77.

Zhao, Z., & Guo, F. (2007). (Eds.). *Transition and challenge: China's population at the turn of the twenty-first century*. Oxford: Oxford University Press.

Chapter 3
Singapore's Pro-natalist Policies: To What Extent Have They Worked?

Gavin W. Jones and Wajihah Hamid

Singapore is a pioneer in the Asian region, in terms of both the timing of its fertility decline to ultra-low levels and the timing of introducing policies to counter the trend. While nobody would argue that Singapore has done all that could be done to counter very low fertility, it is unique in the Asian region in terms of the range and scope of its pro-natalist policies.

This chapter outlines the fertility trends in Singapore in comparison with those of other Asian countries currently facing ultra-low fertility, the evolution of pro-natalist polices over the past three decades, and the possible relationship between policies and fertility trends. The chapter attempts to compare the timing and scope of pro-natalist policies in Singapore with policies in other low-fertility Asian countries (in particular, South Korea and Taiwan) and to draw some tentative conclusions about the relationship of policy to fertility in Singapore.

Fertility Decline in Singapore, South Korea, and Taiwan

Like other developing countries, Singapore, South Korea, and Taiwan had very high levels of fertility in 1960, the highest of all being South Korea. Japan was in a different league. Its fertility had fallen to low levels far earlier, reaching replacement level in the mid-1950s (Frejka et al. 2010, p. 581). Although the total fertility rate (TFR) in Japan remained low, it was above the replacement level of 2.1 children per woman for a period and then fell below replacement level in 1973. Aside from

---

G.W. Jones (✉)
Australian Demographic and Social Research Institute, Australian National University, and Asia Research Centre, Murdoch University, Murdoch, WA, Australia
e-mail: gavinj881@gmail.com

W. Hamid
Asia Research Institute, National University of Singapore, Singapore, Singapore

Japan, Singapore reached below-replacement fertility soonest, in 1975. Singapore had a head start of a few years on Hong Kong and almost a decade's head start on South Korea and Taiwan in this respect. (Both Taiwan and South Korea reached replacement-level fertility in 1983.) From the mid-1980s, however, Hong Kong has been the clear leader in ultra-low fertility.

Figure 3.1 shows the more detailed trends over the past 15 years. If we smooth over the "blip" in TFRs in 2000 due to the dragon-year effect,[1] Singapore, South Korea, and Taiwan all experienced considerable fertility decline over the 1997–2003 period, reaching Japanese levels and even going below them. From this 2003 low point (2005 in the case of Japan and South Korea), most of these countries have shown little change, with fertility remaining through and beyond the first decade of the twenty-first century at levels referred to as "ultra-low" by Jones et al. (2009). These are the very lowest levels in the world, although showing a tendency for TFR to rise very slightly. The latest (2012) figures are of course influenced by the latest Year of the Dragon. Too much should not be made of slight year-to-year fluctuations in TFR at these levels, however. While these fluctuations affect annual births, they probably have no effect on a cohort's completed fertility.

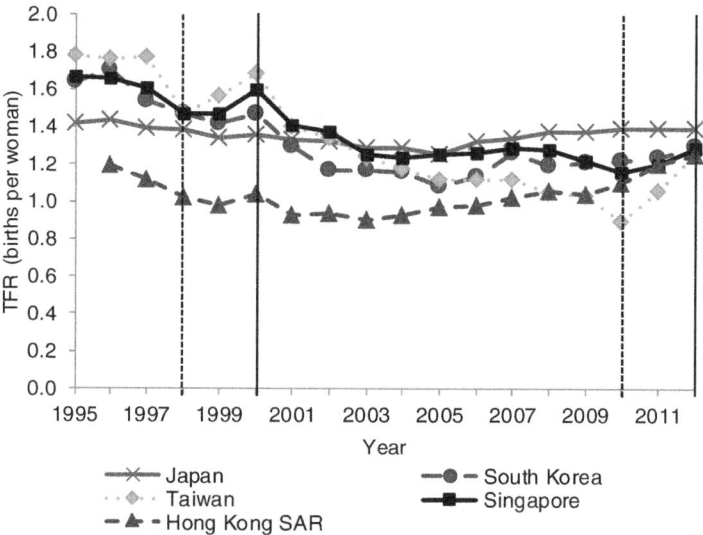

Fig. 3.1 Trends in total fertility rates (TFR) of selected East Asian countries, 1995–2012 (Jones 2007, Table 1) *Note:* Updated from official sources for each country; 1998 and 2010 were Years of the Tiger in the Chinese zodiac cycle, indicated by *dotted lines* in the figure; 2000 and 2012 were Years of the Dragon, indicated by *solid lines*

---

[1] The Year of the Dragon is considered to be the most auspicious sign of the Chinese twelve-animal zodiac cycle (Saw 1990). The Year of the Tiger (which comes 2 years before the dragon year) is considered inauspicious for births. Dragon years and tiger years are indicated by vertical lines in Fig. 3.1.

Trend in Singlehood

To understand low fertility in Asian countries we need to understand the changing economic and social conditions in these countries and the way they influence the perceived desirability and feasibility of building a family. The focus is typically on the pressures on married couples, with insufficient attention given to the factors influencing whether people marry in the first place. It is important to understand the reasons behind the marriage trends because marriage is essentially the gatekeeper to childbirth in these societies, with fewer than 2 % of children born outside marriage (Frejka et al. 2010, fn. 10).[2] And in all of these countries, singlehood has been sharply rising over the period of declining and low fertility. It has been estimated that in Singapore over the period 1990–2005, declines in proportions married were responsible for one-third of the decline to ultra-low levels of fertility (Koh 2011).

Figure 3.2 illustrates the rising trend of singlehood at ages 30–34. The trend in this age group is consistent with evidence for other age groups (e.g., 35–39) and with the singulate mean age at marriage (SMAM). Singapore stands out from the other countries in that while its proportion of singles has been increasing, the rise has been much more modest than in South Korea or Taiwan. In 2010, Singapore had the lowest proportion of singles among these countries, for both women and men—a notable reversal of the situation two decades earlier. At ages 30–34, the proportion of single women in Singapore was 25.1 % while the proportion of single men was 37.1 %. Hong Kong and Taiwan are leading the trend in rising singlehood for both men and women. Both South Korea and Taiwan experienced a rapid increase within the 10 years from 2000 to 2010.

What Is Driving Trends in Fertility?

In order to assess the likely impact of pro-natalist policies, it is necessary to understand the reasons why fertility has reached such a low level. There is a considerable literature on this,[3] which we will not attempt to summarize in detail here, but we will simply note what appear to be the key reasons in the countries under discussion. These countries are consumerist societies, stressing achievement and upward social mobility above all else (see Chang 2010 on South Korea). They are vastly wealthier than they were four or five decades ago, when parents routinely had four or five children. Nowadays, paradoxically, many feel a sense of relative deprivation, which

---

[2] The 2 % figure is in some ways misleading, however, as a considerably higher proportion of births are conceived outside marriage, and the pregnancy precipitates the marriage. These should not necessarily be understood as "shotgun marriages" according to the traditional understanding of this term, as there is evidence, at least from Japan, that many unmarried couples are fairly relaxed about the possibility of a pregnancy and are ready to marry should a pregnancy occur.

[3] For more detailed discussions, see Tsuya et al. 2009; Suzuki 2008, 2009; Eun 2007; Jones 2007; Frejka et al. 2010.

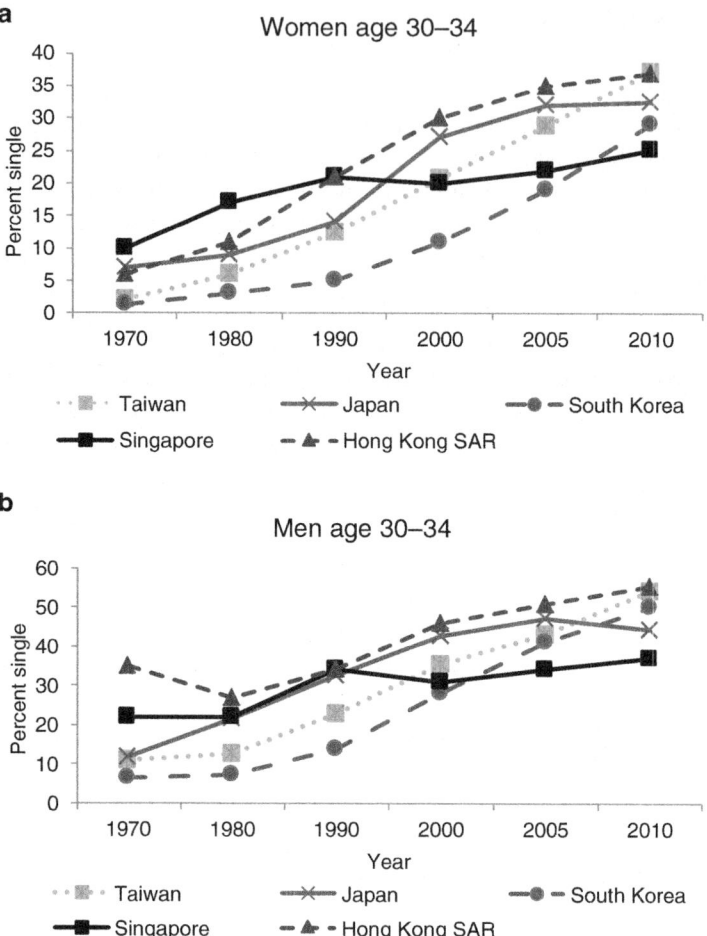

Fig. 3.2 Trends in proportion single among women and men age 30–34, 1970–2010 (*Sources:* For Japan, Statistics Japan 2014; for South Korea, KOSIS 2014; for Taiwan, National Statistics 2014; for Singapore, Department of Statistics 2014; for Hong Kong, Census and Statistics Department 2014)

means that aspirations can only be met by both parents working. The financial and opportunity costs of raising children are considerable, particularly as parents face enormous pressure for their children to succeed in education. In this competitive education "arms race," in the context of limited parental time and financial resources, the "quality/quantity trade-off" comes down heavily in favor of quality.

Strong familism and patriarchy characterize these societies. Economic development and social modernization clash with traditionalism in the household. As a result, women face conflicting roles in balancing work and family life. Access to childcare services is limited, and working women face the tradition of long working hours and a work environment often unfriendly to the need for flexible hours and childcare leave. These are highly urbanized societies, with long travel times to work coupled with limited and expensive housing to meet the needs of larger families.

Given the many dilemmas that are part and parcel of marrying in these societies (the notion of a "marriage package," as described by Bumpass and colleagues (2009) in Japan, is equally relevant here), it is small wonder that there is increasingly later and less marriage. Aside from volitional reasons, non-volitional factors are also operating, including the inadequate replacement of traditional matchmaking systems, and continued hypergamy and homogamy, leading to a marriage squeeze for certain groups. The combination of a rise in age at marriage, a situation where 15 % of women will be permanently removed from the reproductive population by non-marriage (probably within 10 years), and continuing high levels of divorce bodes ill for any substantial rise in fertility. Furthermore, there is little indication of a trend toward more cohabitation, and even less so of acceptance of childbearing in cohabiting relationships—trends that have propped up fertility rates in many Western countries.

Policy Development: Singapore's Switch from Anti-natalism to Pro-natalism

Singapore achieved self-government in 1957, entered the Federation of Malaysia in 1963, but left the Federation to become a separate, independent state in 1965. Facing very high fertility levels combined with uncertainties about the political and economic future of what was considered an over-populated island, the government introduced a national population-control program, passing the Singapore Family Planning and Population Act in 1965 and establishing the Singapore Family Planning and Population Board in 1966. A series of anti-natalist measures were introduced, including the Voluntary Sterilization Act in 1969, as well as a set of incentives and disincentives to encourage small families in 1972. Some of the measures introduced and implemented during the anti-natalist period included the reduction of income tax relief to cover only three children, lowering of priority for primary school admission for fourth-order and above children, elimination of the housing subsidy for large families, and limitation of paid maternity leave to first and second births (Sun 2012, p. 63).

The pace of fertility decline that followed was one of the most rapid in the world. It was widely attributed to the anti-natalist policies, although many other factors were clearly involved. Although Singapore's fertility reached replacement level in 1975, the anti-natalist policies were kept in place until 1983. Then in 1984, the state implemented selective pro-natalist policies, described as the "eugenic phase" of Singapore's population policy. Educated women were given incentives to reproduce under the "Graduate Mother Scheme," while sterilization cash incentives were offered to less educated women (Straughan et al. 2009, p. 184; Saw 2005, p. 212). These policies proved to be very unpopular with broad sections of the public. They were abandoned in 1985, followed by the closure of the Singapore Family Planning and Population Board in 1986. The following year (1987), the fertility policy in Singapore took on a broadly pro-natalist stance, with the introduction of both slogans and policies to support having three or more children based on affordability. This stance has shaped Singapore's fertility policy until the present, with various policies to increase fertility introduced and strengthened over the years.

There was an interval of 15 years between the time fertility first dipped below replacement level and the introduction of pro-natalist policies directed at the population as a whole. As the pioneer in fertility decline in the region, with a history of strong and effective anti-natalist policies, it is perhaps not surprising that there was hesitation to reverse these policies until it was clear that no resurgence in fertility was likely. The subsequent history of policy reversals in other Asian countries shows that Singapore was no exception in delaying its policy reversal (see Table 3.1).

Table 3.1 Delays in reversing anti-natalist policies, selected East Asian countries

Country	Year in which replacement fertility was reached	Year in which anti-natalist policy was reversed	Number of years elapsed	Percent below replacement when policy reversed	Comments
Singapore	1975	1984	9	25	Selective pro-natalist policies for highly educated
Singapore	1975	1987	12	25	More general pro-natalist measures
South Korea	1984	1996	12	20	Very mildly pro-natalist policies
South Korea	1984	2004	20	50	More serious pro-natalist measures
Taiwan	1984	1992	8	20	Pro-natalist statement but no measures
Taiwan	1984	2006	22	47	Specific pro-natalist measures introduced
Japan	1973[a]	1990	17	25	Mildly pro-natalist measures
Japan	1973	1994	21	32	Angel plan introduced in 1994, revised in 1999; more forceful pro-natalist measures
China	1992(?)	No reversal	21+	n.a.	25–30 % below replacement in 2013; policy modified to allow only child to have two children after marrying

[a]Japan's TFR was slightly below replacement level as early as the 1950s, but it hovered around that level for two decades and did not fall definitively below replacement level until 1973

The Development of Singapore's Pro-natalist Policies

Policies emphasizing larger families and early family formation were implemented during the late 1980s to the late 1990s. Some of the measures and incentives that were introduced included subsidized childcare, tax rebates for third children, and public housing schemes encouraging early family formation and larger families, such as the Fiancé/ Fiancée Scheme, the Parenthood Priority Scheme, and other schemes for first-time married couples.

Then, in 2000, the government introduced a number of new policies and revisions. Importantly, the Baby Bonus Scheme was introduced. This two-tiered system involved distribution of cash benefits on the birth of second and third children. It also included a co-savings arrangement set up by the government, which was payable over a 6-year period, with maximum contributions capped at S$6,000 for the second child and S$12,000 for the third child.[4] This co-saving could be used for all children. Tax rebates, which were offered only to the third child in 1987 and to the third and fourth child in 1989, were extended to include the second child. Singapore's total fertility rate (TFR) continued to decline from 2001 to 2003, however, despite the introduction of these and a variety of other incentives aimed at encouraging marriage and childbearing. The TFR fell from 1.61 children per woman in 1997 to 1.25 in 2003.[5]

In 2004, the Baby Bonus Scheme was extended to include the birth of first and fourth children, when S$3,000 and S$6,000 were given to parents. This cash gift was distributed in five instalments over an 18-month period as opposed to over 6 years previously. In 2008, the payout to first and second children was raised from S$3,000 to S$4,000.

Since 2003, Singapore's TFR has stayed in the 1.2 region, with minor changes until 2010, when it fell slightly lower to 1.16. This could be because 2010 was a Year of the Tiger, which is considered to be inauspicious for birth in the Chinese zodiac cycle. In the following year, the rate rose marginally to 1.20 and in 2012—a Year of the Dragon—it went up to 1.29 (see Fig. 3.1).

Policies were further boosted in January 2013 in the form of a Marriage and Parenthood Package, aimed at helping Singaporeans "to form families and raise children" (NPTD 2013a). This enhanced package includes giving priority in the assignment of a first-time public-housing apartment to couples who have children. It also includes enhancing Co-Funding for Assisted Reproduction Technology (ART) Treatment, waiving accouchement fees in public hospitals to all mothers irrespective of the birth order of the child, extending paid childcare leave, and introducing paid adoption leave, 1 week paid paternity leave, and shared parental leave (see Appendix for details of policy enhancements).

---

[4] All dollar figures in this paper are in Singapore dollars. In 2013, S$1 = US$0.80.
[5] There was a blip to 1.60 in the 2000 Year of the Dragon—up from 1.47 in 1998 and 1999.

Categories of Pro-natalist Policies in Singapore

McDonald (2002), citing Heitlinger (1991), categorized fertility policies under:

1. Financial incentives
2. Support for parents to combine work and family
3. Broad social change supportive of children and parenting

Policies to influence marriage are not specifically included here. Although marriage is affected by fertility desires,[6] thus being affected by all the above elements of fertility policy, there are other factors influencing whether people marry. One way to think of factors affecting marriage is to divide reasons for not marrying into volitional and non-volitional categories. Singapore has had specific policies to influence marriage, and the government clearly considers marriage policy important in its armory of policies to influence fertility. Marriage policies will therefore be included as a fourth type of pro-natalist policy.

Financial Incentives

Lump-sum payments or loans, tax rebates, subsidized or free services and goods for children, and housing subsidies fall under the category of financial incentives. Singapore has implemented all four of these types of policy. With the introduction of the two-tiered Baby Bonus Scheme in 2000, the Singapore government began offering cash payments to parents. In 2013, the amount offered was increased to S$6,000 (up from S$4,000 previously) for the birth of a first or second child and S$8,000 (up from S$6,000 previously) for the birth of a third or fourth child. The cash grant is given only through the birth of the fourth child. It is now fully disbursed earlier, within 12 months of the child's birth as compared to 18 months previously.

The scheme also involves setting up a Child Development Account (CDA), which is essentially a co-savings arrangement between parents and the Singapore government. When it started in 2000, only second and third children were eligible, and the duration of the CDA was 6 years. Since 2008, the government will match dollar-for-dollar the amount saved by parents for first- and second-born children, up to a maximum of S$6,000 each. For third- and fourth-born children, the government contribution is capped at S$12,000 each, and for fifth-born children and beyond, the contribution is capped at S$18,000 (Ministry of Social and Family Development 2013). In 2013, the duration of the CDA was extended for another 6 years, enabling parents to receive matching contributions until a child turns 12, but the maximum levels of government contributions remain unchanged.

---

[6] Indeed, Raymo (2003) has argued in the case of Japan that changes in the desire for children are more important in understanding marriage behavior than changes in the desirability of marriage itself.

Singapore also offers tax rebates for working mothers and various housing-subsidy schemes (see Appendix for details). The government does not offer much in the way of free or subsidized services or goods for children, however. Services include education, dental and medical care, while goods could include textbooks or leisure and sporting equipment (McDonald 2002, p. 437).

In early 2013, Singapore introduced a Medisave Grant for newborns. Medisave falls under the Central Provident Fund (CPF). Under this scheme, a CPF Medisave account is opened for each newborn citizen, and a Medisave grant of S$3,000 is deposited. The first S$1,500 is deposited after birth registration, and the remaining S$1,500 is deposited in the subsequent year, provided that the child remains enrolled in MediShield or a Medisave-approved Integrated Shield Plan.

Support for Combining Work and Family

Under the category of support for combining work and family, McDonald (2002, pp. 438–42) listed childcare, flexible working hours, anti-discrimination legislation, and gender equity in employment practices. Singapore increased paid maternity leave from 8 to 12 weeks in 2004 and from 12 to 16 weeks in 2008. In 2013, the government introduced a 1-week paternity leave and allowed the father to take an additional week out of his wife's 16-week maternity leave under a new "Shared Parental Leave" scheme. Paid adoption leave of 4 weeks was introduced in 2004 and made mandatory in 2013. In order to facilitate alternative childcare arrangements, the government offers grandparent caregiver relief, domestic worker levy relief, and childcare subsidies. A 5-day work week was introduced in 2004 for government-employed civil servants, although total working hours were held constant, thus requiring extended working hours on the five working days (see Appendix for details of policies).

Broad Social Change Supportive of Children and Parenting

Under broad social change supportive of children and parenting, McDonald (2002, pp. 440–42) listed employment initiatives, child-friendly environments, gender equity, marriage and relationship supports, followed by development of positive social attitudes toward children and parenting. Singapore introduced the "Work-Life Works" Fund in 2004, under which private-sector firms can apply for grants to defray the cost of introducing measures that would help employees achieve better work-life harmony. Although this was a good introductory move, the implementation is left largely to the employers' discretion. In light of other opportunity costs and market considerations, it might not necessarily be in the interest of competitive private companies (especially small and medium enterprises—SMEs) to implement this new program.

Marriage Policy

Rising singlehood has been one of the major direct causes of fertility decline in Japan, South Korea, Taiwan, and Singapore. Singlehood is particularly high in cities and for well-educated women. In the younger adult ages, there are now few women with primary-school education or less, so the key comparison is between the high-school and tertiary educated. In all four countries, delayed and non-marriage is considerably higher for tertiary-educated women.

As early as 1984, Singapore had identified rising singlehood, especially among its well-educated women, as an issue to be addressed and began setting up agencies to provide match-making services. The services and range of activities offered through the Social Development Network (SDN) are now varied, sophisticated, and Internet-based. Services include personalized matchmaking, overseas trips, and engagement with the private sector through accreditation of dating agencies.[7] It is difficult to assess whether the claims for success of the SDN are well justified, however. Statistics published to indicate that a substantial number of Singaporeans who were registered with the SDN eventually married cannot address the counterfactual—how many of these people would have married anyway in the absence of the government's programs (Jones 2012, p. 324)?

The two other key ways in which Singapore has influenced the incidence of marriage are through housing policy and the policy on granting Permanent Residence (PR) status. Singlehood is discouraged by eligibility rules for Housing and Development Board (HDB) apartments, in which about 85 % of Singaporeans live. Singles must be over 35 to be eligible to purchase this form of subsidized housing. Also, various housing inducements are offered to Singaporeans planning to marry, all of them directed toward shortening the waiting time for apartments or widening the scope for this group to buy or rent an apartment (for details, see Jones 2012, pp. 323–4). As for PR status, permanent residents in their 30s are twice as likely to be married as Singapore citizens, suggesting that the government's criteria for approval of permanent-residence applications may, in part, be aimed at raising the proportion married (Jones 2012, p. 325).[8]

One point should be made about policy developments in Singapore. The government has consulted the public widely, particularly in recent years, before introducing changes in family policy. The National Population and Talent Division, which is now responsible for population policy, had a program of wide community consultation before introducing the new measures in 2013. Sociologist Paulin Straughan, who also served a term as an appointed Member of Parliament, noted that the new measures gave a message to the Singapore population that the government prizes a pro-family and gender-equal environment as much as it does a competitive, business-

---

[7] Details of the range of services offered can be found at http://app.sdn.sg/DatingServices/OnlineorPersonalisedMatching.aspx.

[8] Citizens and permanent residents together make up the resident population, which is the denominator for the calculation of Singapore's demographic rates.

friendly climate. One intention of the policies, she said, "was to set the ideological tone, to say very boldly that the government stands behind family formation" (Chang 2013).

Timing and Nature of Policies: Comparison between Singapore, South Korea, and Taiwan

It is interesting to take a cross-sectional snapshot of fertility policies in the region as of 1995. Keep in mind that fertility rates in 1995 were well below replacement level in Singapore, South Korea, and Taiwan and at ultra-low levels (TFR below 1.5) in Japan. Singapore had begun promoting the formation of families in 1987, and by 1995 Singapore had more pro-natalist policies in place than the other countries. In fact, it had been 8 years since the Singapore government had introduced income-tax relief, tax rebates, childcare subsidies, and housing subsidies for larger families. By the early 1990s, housing incentives to encourage early family formation included HDB's Fiancé/Fiancée Scheme, under which couples intending to marry could register for an apartment together and marry within 3 months of taking possession. This scheme aimed to enable couples to have a ready home upon marriage. In 1990, the Domestic Worker Levy Relief was introduced to encourage working mothers to continue working while having someone to take care of their child. Despite all these pro-family and pro-fertility measures, however, fertility continued to decline.

Both Taiwan and South Korea reached replacement level fertility in 1984 but by 1995 had no pro-natalist policies in place. The Taiwanese government had made a pro-natalist statement but had not introduced any concrete measures. It was only in 2006 that both Taiwan and South Korea implemented their respective pro-natalist policies.

The South Korean government was very slow to reverse its anti-natalist policies. In 2002, the Noh Mu-Hyeon government took a step toward initiating pro-natalist policies, but it took a few more years for the policies to actually be implemented. At this time, South Korea's TFR was the lowest in the world, declining in 2005 to 1.08 (Lee 2009, p. 57). It was only in 2006, however, that the South Korean government announced an integrated package, the "Saeromaji Plan 2010," which comprised a variety of pro-natalist measures (Suzuki 2008, p. 37). These measures included tax rebates, expansion of maternity and childcare leave, and improvement of childcare services. South Korea was not able to offer a universal child allowance, however, due to budget constraints.

Taiwan's TFR started declining gradually from 1995, but in the 1998 Year of the Tiger, it declined drastically—to 1.47 from 1.77 in 1997. Beside the Year of Tiger being inauspicious for birth, the financial crisis of 1997 also contributed to this decline. In the following 2 years, the TFR rose slightly, then declined sharply again in 2001, to 1.40 from 1.68 in 2000. Following this decline, Taiwan's TFR has declined consistently, with the exception of the years 2005–2007 when it remained at 1.12. In the 2010 Year of the Tiger, Taiwan's TFR plunged to 0.89, probably the lowest level of fertility ever reached in any country with a population in excess of ten million. As in South Korea, Taiwan had no pro-natalist policies until 2006, when measures such as maternity and parental leave and a childcare subsidy system were introduced under the "Mega Warmth Social Welfare Program" (Freijka et al. 2010, p. 599). This was followed by the 2008 White Book of Population Policy. Since the introduction of these measures, the TFR has yet to increase significantly, although the increase to 1.26 in the 2012 Year of the Dragon raises hope that the inevitable subsequent decline will still leave fertility somewhat higher than it was before.

Clearly Singapore was a little faster than Taiwan or South Korea in reacting to a fertility decline and beginning to reverse its anti-natalist policies. But now that both South Korea and Taiwan have had pro-natalist measures in place for some years, it is worth comparing the similarities and differences between their policies, those of Japan, and those of Singapore. Singapore's policy of financial incentives has been expanded over time and now is clearly the most comprehensive among the four countries. On the birth of a child, Japan offers a cash payment of 10,000 yen (roughly US$100) monthly until the child turns three. The Japanese government does not offer large tax deductions for children, however (Frejka et al. 2010, p. 598). Neither Taiwan nor South Korea offers cash payments, the former due to feminist protests and the latter due to budgetary constraints, although South Korea has lower taxes for large families or families with young children.

In terms of support for combining work and family, Taiwan provides paid maternity leave up to 8 weeks, with 70 % of the cost payable by the employer (Frejka et al. 2010, p. 600), and 3 days of paternity leave. South Korea offers 12 weeks of paid maternity leave and 3 days of paternity leave. Paternity leave is not paid by the government, however, but is left to the discretion of employers. Again, Singapore's policy is more comprehensive, with longer paid maternity leave and (since early 2013) more paternity leave.

Both Taiwan and South Korea have enhanced their support for childrearing with improved childcare subsidies and provision of high-quality childcare. Singapore also subsidizes center-based infant care and childcare, differentially for working and non-working mothers. Its policy is complicated by the fact that "childcare" and "pre-school education" are related but have somewhat different goals. Singapore also offers grandparent caregiver relief and reduced maid levy to help working mothers who rely on grandparents or maids for infant and childcare.

Singaporean families with two or three children can now expect to receive significant financial incentives as a result of the overall package offered by the government. Indeed, the National Population and Talent Division gave an estimate in early 2013 that a family with two children can enjoy benefits of about S$100,000 in baby bonus payments, Medisave grants for newborns, infant care and childcare subsidies, and tax savings by the time both children turn 13. If the value of paid maternity and paternity leave and paid childcare leave is added in, the total benefits sum to about S$166,000. This estimate excludes housing subsidies and the equivalent of S$12,000 in additional tax savings beyond the children's first 13 years. While substantial, these figures need to be compared with rough estimates that the total financial cost of having a baby and raising it to age 18 is somewhere between S$250,000 and S$350,000, depending on choices on schooling and life style (Cheam 2013), or between S$500,000 and S$700,000 for two children. Beyond age 18, university fees add considerably to that cost (Tan 2010). Thus the common comment of young Singaporeans—that the government support is much appreciated but that it will probably not be a major factor in their decision on whether to have children—makes sense, although it may reflect a lack of appreciation of just how substantial government contributions are, in fact offsetting as much as one-third of the cost of raising a child to age 18.

When considering policies under broad social change supportive of children and parenting, Singapore, Taiwan, and South Korea could all go further by introducing more flexible working hours, anti-discrimination legislation, and gender equity in employment practices. Singapore has taken steps toward these goals with the introduction of paid paternity leave in 2013. Singapore also seems to be the only Asian country actively promoting marriage and early family formation through its subsidized match-making services and housing subsidies.

All the countries discussed here seem to be promoting the development of positive social attitudes toward children and parenting in various ways. The big question is how these societies will be able to overcome deeply entrenched societal pressures and expectations that work against family formation. One of these is the strong pressure on parents to raise quality children through intensive parenting, supplementing what the school can do by providing coaching, extra-curricular activities, and parental assistance with homework. Awareness of these pressures is leading some people to avoid having children or to have only one or two (e.g., see Anderson and Kohler 2013).

Singapore Realities: Childrearing Issues Facing Working Mothers

Government policy to influence fertility must deal with the reality that most married couples in Singapore expect both wife and husband to work. Many wives feel the need to return to work as soon as possible after the birth of a child. This is facilitated in many cases by foreign domestic workers (who are employed in about one in six Singapore households)[9] or grandparents assuming responsibility for childcare. Where these two possibilities are not available, however, paid childcare is the only option. Although subsidized for Singapore citizens, paid childcare still represents a financial burden, especially for low-income households. It also forces mothers to choose between not working and leaving their young children in childcare for long hours because there are very few workplace-based childcare facilities.

---

[9] These workers are on fixed-term contracts and are mainly drawn from the Philippines and Indonesia, with smaller numbers from Myanmar and Sri Lanka. Lower-income families cannot afford the cost of employing a domestic worker.

Working hours are typically long, and there are relatively few part-time work opportunities. In June 2012, among the resident population, fewer than 10 % of those employed worked less than 34 h a week. The average number of hours worked per week was 45.6 among all employees and 48.2 h among full-time employees (Ministry of Manpower 2012, Table 5). The average cost for a full-day infant-care program (up to age 18 months) has increased from S$1,206 a month in 2008 to S$1,376 in late 2013. The average cost for a childcare program has increased from about S$699 a month in 2008 to S$1,000 a month in early 2014. Working mothers with a monthly family income of less than S$7,500 can receive subsidies of S$600 per month toward the cost of infant care and S$300 per month towards the cost of childcare. This still leaves a substantial gap to be paid by the parents, which would be felt particularly by low-income families earning less than S$3,000 a month.

Working mothers face many issues even after their children enter primary school. The mismatch between working hours and school hours is obvious. Normal primary-school hours in Singapore are from 7.30 a.m. to 12.30 p.m. (although in some of the older schools there is a separate afternoon shift). Extra-curricular activities may keep the child at school for some additional time. After that, if there is nobody at home, the parents will have to make separate arrangements for their children's care, sometimes available in school-based student care centers (which cater for students age 7–14 and charge about S$260 per month) and sometimes in community centers.[10] Students can stay at these centres until 6:00 or 7:00 p.m.

A litany of stresses on a working mother can be cited: arranging infant care; waking before daylight to get children off to school; making arrangements for after-school care, coaching, and other after-school activities; helping with homework; arranging leave to care for sick children or to take them to the doctor; and dealing with expectations from other parents for intensive childrearing that leads to academic success.

Has Singapore Shown Any Signs of Doing Better in Fertility Recovery Than Other Countries?

Singapore's population reached replacement fertility in the mid-1970s, whereas fertility in Hong Kong, South Korea, and Taiwan declined to this level in the 1980s. Among these countries, Singapore led in the implementation of pro-natalist policies and has gone further than other countries in many policy areas. We might expect, then, to see more impact on fertility. There have been no more signs of fertility recovery in Singapore, however, that in the other countries. Indeed, Singapore has not matched Japan, Hong Kong, or South Korea in showing slight increases in TFR in recent years. This is partly because the fertility of the Malay population, who

---

[10] Low-income families can apply for financial support for this.

3 Singapore's Pro-natalist Policies: To What Extent Have They Worked?

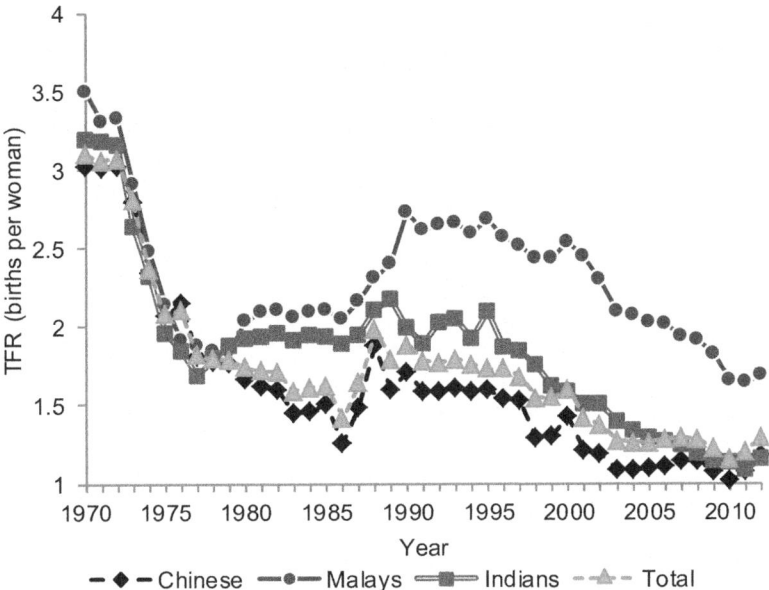

Fig. 3.3 Trends in total fertility rate (TFR) by ethnic group, Singapore, 1970–2012 (Department of Statistics 2009, 2013)

account for about 14 % of the total, fell quite sharply from relatively high levels over this period (see Fig. 3.3).

Given Singapore's physical size and bearing in mind that it is a city-state, comparisons with other cities in the region may be more appropriate than comparisons with other countries. When compared with other cities, Singapore does not fare badly. Singapore's TFR is roughly 10–25 % higher than that of Tokyo, Seoul, Busan, Taipei, Kaohsiung, or Hong Kong (Table 3.2; see also Jones 2012). The contrast with Beijing and Shanghai, where TFR is well below 1, is even greater. However, these city-to-city comparisons are also problematic in some ways. As a city-state, Singapore can control immigration in a way that the other cities cannot. Fertility in the other cities might be held down by selective in-migration of those who are less interested in having children or who intend to postpone childbearing until they have returned home.

It is difficult, if not impossible, to test the effects of various pro-natalist measures on Singapore's fertility, but two alternative assumptions might be used to set some kind of extreme limits on their likely impact. The first would be that, because there has been no clear increase in TFR since policy measures were strengthened in 2004 and 2008, the policies have had no impact. The second would be that in the absence of the policies, fertility would have declined even lower than it did. One hypothesis would be that without the policies, fertility would have been at much the same level as that of other major cities in East Asia—Tokyo, Seoul, Busan, Taipei, and Hong

Table 3.2 Singapore total fertility rates (TFRs) compared with those of other large cities in East Asia

City	Average TFR 2008–2012	Ratio of Singapore TFR to TFR in this city	Ratio of Chinese Singaporeans' TFR to TFR in this city
Singapore	1.23	–	–
Singapore (Chinese only)	1.10	1.12	–
Beijing[a]	0.71	1.73	1.55
Shanghai[a]	0.74	1.66	1.49
Tokyo[b]	1.10	1.12	1.00
Seoul	1.01	1.22	1.09
Busan	1.04	1.18	1.06
Taipei	1.08	1.14	1.02
Kaohsiung	0.93	1.32	1.18
Hong Kong	1.13	1.09	0.97

Sources: For Singapore, Department of Statistics 2014; for Beijing and Shanghai, National Bureau of Statistics of China 2014; for Tokyo, Statistics Japan 2014; for Seoul and Busan (2008–2012), KOSIS 2014; for Taipei and Kaohsiung, Ministry of the Interior, Republic of China (Taiwan) 2014; For Hong Kong, Census and Statistics Department 2014
[a]2010 estimate, from 1 % sample of the 2010 Population Census
[b]Tokyo Prefecture; for Central Tokyo (ku-bu), the TFR is 1.08

Kong (but not Beijing or Shanghai, since their fertility is strongly influenced by China's one-child policy). According to this hypothesis, Singapore's fertility may be 10–25 % higher than it would have been without the policies that have been introduced.

Both these assumptions are extremely crude, but at least they provide hypotheses that can guide thinking about demographic impacts. While there are clearly differences in the socio-cultural and economic situation of the different Asian countries, there are enough similarities to make the comparison at least plausible. As we have seen, however, the specificities in the Singapore case—for example, its multi-ethnic population and its policies toward accepting people for permanent residence—must be kept in mind in any attempt to assess the role that policy has played. For example, if only the ethnic Chinese population of Singapore is used (to control for the effect of other ethnicities, particularly the Malay, in propping up Singapore's overall fertility), the fertility differential between Singapore and other Asian cities narrows—to less than a 10 % difference, and indeed to no difference at all in the cases of Tokyo, Taipei, or Hong Kong (see Table 3.2). Clarity of interpretation is further muddied by the fact that differences in TFR between Hong Kong and the Chinese population of Singapore have shifted over the past decade. In 2001, fertility was 30 % higher among Chinese Singaporeans, around 2009 fertility was similar in both populations, and since then fertility has been higher in Hong Kong.

What Can Other Countries Learn from the Singapore Experience?

In attempting to deal with ultra-low fertility, Singapore faces the same key problems as do Japan, South Korea, and Taiwan. In the face of remarkable improvements in women's education, changing labor markets, and the economic pressures of a neoliberal, consumerist economy, cultural and social norms have not been adapting rapidly enough, especially as they bear on the situation of increasingly educated women. In general, the problems Singapore faces are as intractable as elsewhere. Despite ongoing attention to population policy issues and considerable modification and tinkering with policies over time, there is no clear evidence that Singapore's policies have had much impact on fertility rates.

Perhaps one message to emerge is that policies bearing on fertility need to be seen as part of family policy, as they are in most European countries. Whether or not they have much impact on fertility, they can be considered successful if they make life better for families. In this context, some of the proposals that the Association of Women for Action and Research (AWARE) prepared in advance of the 2013 policy changes deserve mention (AWARE 2012). One recommendation was to convert paid childcare leave into leave for the care of dependents, who may include older children or elderly parents. Another was to widen access to childcare subsidies, motherhood benefits, and housing benefits to cover all parents, whether married or single, working or stay-at-home (eliminating the current discrimination against unwed mothers). AWARE noted that "the current exclusion of unmarried parents from certain housing benefits, parental leave, subsidies and bonuses are [sic] not only unfair but they hurt the families who most need the support."

Extended (and increasingly, permanent) singlehood is a key contributing factor to "ultra-low fertility" in East Asian societies, given that very few children are born outside marriage. For this reason, Singapore's experience with pro-marriage policies might usefully be examined by other countries.

Feedback from research in Singapore (Sun 2012) has shown that there has been a lack of communication and discussion of policies among the citizenry. Over time, however, consultation has increased, particularly in preparation for the 2013 policy changes.[11] Broadening current channels of communication and initiating new approaches to outreach will enhance policy formulation and implementation.

South Korea could explore policies beyond tax-rebates to offer some form of cash payment that would benefit children more directly. Singapore implemented the Baby Bonus in 2000, but South Korea has apparently been unable to implement a similar direct cash reward system due to budget constraints (Suzuki 2008, p. 38). Measures to ease re-entry into the labor force following periods of leave related to

---

[11] During a four-month consultation period prior to the announcement of the Enhanced Marriage and Parenthood Package in January 2013, the National Population and Talent Division received more than 800 items of feedback from community organizations, employers, and members of the public.

childcare (McDonald 2002, p. 440) should be considered by all the countries under discussion, and more research is needed on the provision of child-friendly environments.

In all these countries, insufficient attention has been paid to housing issues as a factor influencing marriage and family formation. While only in Singapore does housing policy actively and deliberately foster marriage by discriminating against singles, the housing situation in other large East Asian cities may *de facto* be encouraging marriage. In fact, singles are discriminated against in the housing market in other cities such as Tokyo. "Within the Japanese housing system, choices for the unmarried are both limited and limiting" (Ronald and Nakano 2012, p. 462), with many young singles living in capsule-like rental dwellings. But the poor housing choices facing singles has not prevented the continued rise of singlehood. Of course, in East Asia, singles are expected to live in the family home until marriage, but in the past marriage was universal and occurred at much younger ages than today. The notion that young adults will avoid marriage and continue to live with their parents was the basis for the term "parasite singles" in Japan (Masahiro 1999). The issue is complex. In a city such as Hong Kong, where the average size of apartments is very small for everyone, it is hard to say who is disadvantaged most by the housing situation—singles or families. Certainly, the shortage and high cost of housing that can adequately accommodate a family of, say, three children are evident in all East Asian cities.

Summary and Conclusions

Singapore was slow to move from anti-natalist to pro-natalist policies, but not as slow as Taiwan or South Korea. In fact, Singapore began adopting pro-natalist policies two decades before the other two countries (Singapore in 1987; South Korea and Taiwan in 2006). Despite this, Singapore experienced a sharp fertility decline from 1997 to 2003, and fertility has shown no clear sign of recovery since then. Growing government concern led to the revision and enhancement of various pro-natalist policies in 2004, 2008, and 2013. The fertility rate in Singapore has not risen appreciably, however, following these policy modifications and remains amongst the lowest in the world. The 2013 policies have not had time to have an effect, but most academic experts do not expect much. The Singapore government appears to have settled on a TFR of about 1.6 as its most optimistic target for fertility in the next few years.

Given that Singapore has adopted more comprehensive pro-natalist measures than other low-fertility countries in Asia, its experience provides little basis for expecting that pro-natalist measures will succeed elsewhere. Appropriate comparison in some ways is with large cities, however, rather than with countries as a whole. Compared with Hong Kong, Shanghai, Beijing, Tokyo, Seoul, Busan, and Taipei, Singapore definitely has higher fertility, although when only the Chinese Singaporean population is considered, Singapore's fertility has no edge at all over Tokyo, Taipei, or Hong Kong. Singapore does seem to have had a degree of success in limiting the trend toward ever-increasing levels of singlehood. The ways it has done this may not be relevant to other countries, however, and anyway, a levelling off of singlehood rates has not led to an increase in fertility.

Data from the Marriage and Parenthood Survey conducted in 2012 by the National Population and Talent Division (NPTD 2013a, b) suggest that financial costs of raising children and problems in combining work and family life are the key "crunch points" for fertility decisions. This suggests that two things may be essential if fertility levels in Singapore are to be substantially raised. The first is for the government to provide considerably higher financial incentives by raising baby-bonus payments and providing universal childcare along the French model. This would come at a substantial cost. The second requirement may be even harder to achieve, however. This would be to change the economic and social institutions, regulations affecting working conditions, and popular norms in directions that will enable work and childrearing to be more readily combined.

Appendix

A chronology of pro-natalist policies in Singapore

Policy area	Pro-natalist policies as of about 1987 "Have three or more if you can afford it"	Policy revisions 2000	Policy revisions 2004 "Singapore: A great place for families"	Policy revisions 2008	Policy revisions 2013
A Monetary incentives					
A.1 Income tax relief	Income Tax Relief: Introduced in 1988; S$750 per child for first two children, S$500 (later increased to S$750) for third child. From 1989, the maximum amount was changed to S$1,500 for the first four children	Unchanged	Unchanged	Qualifying Child Relief (QCR) and Handicapped Child Relief (HCR) replace Income Tax Relief: Working parents can claim S$4,000 per child for all children under QCR or S$5,500 per child under HCR	Unchanged
	Enhanced Child Relief: Working mothers could claim 5 % of earned income for first child, 10 % for second, 15 % each for third and fourth child. The maximum amount was S$10,000 per child, and the eligibility criterion was 5 GCE O-Level passes	Unchanged	Working Mother's Child Relief replaces Enhanced Child Relief: Working mothers could claim 5 % of earned income for first child, 15 % for second, 20 % for third, 25 % for fourth. The maximum amount was raised to S$25,000 per child	Working Mother's Child Relief: Working mothers could claim 15 % of earned income for first child, 20 % for second, 25 % for third and subsequent children. Maximum amount raised to S$50,000 per child	Unchanged

3 Singapore's Pro-natalist Policies: To What Extent Have They Worked?

	In 1989, the tax relief amount was raised to 15 % of earned income for second child, 20 % for third, 25 % for fourth. The maximum amount was raised to S$15,000 per child	Unchanged	Unchanged	Unchanged	Unchanged
A.2 Tax rebates	Tax rebate of S$20,000 for third child in 1987, extended to fourth child in 1989	Second-Child Tax Rebate: Offered for second child on a sliding scale from S$20,000 if child born before mother turned 28 to S$5,000 if born before mother turned 31	Parenthood Tax Rebate: S$10,000 for second child and S$20,000 for third and fourth child. The age requirement for second birth was removed	New Parenthood Tax Rebate: S$5,000 for first child, S$10,000 for second, and S$20,000 per child for all subsequent children	Unchanged
	Delivery and hospitalization expenses for fourth child offset against parents' earned income. Maximum amount capped at S$3,000	Unchanged	Unchanged	Unchanged	Unchanged
A.3 Child- and infant-care subsidies	Childcare Subsidy: For children of working mothers: A monthly subsidy was offered of S$100 for each of first three children under age 7 who attended full-day childcare. The subsidy was paid directly to childcare center rather than to parents	Childcare Subsidy for Non-Working Mothers: A monthly subsidy of S$75 was introduced for children of non-working mothers enrolled in childcare centers	Unchanged	Increased Childcare Subsidy (age 19 months–7 years): For working mothers, the subsidy offered was increased to a maximum of S$300/month. For non-working mothers, the amount was increased to S$150/month	Families with monthly household incomes of S$7,500 or below are eligible for an Additional Subsidy, and lower-income families could receive more. Larger families with many dependents can choose to have their Additional Subsidy computed on a per capita income (PCI) basis

(continued)

(continued)

Policy area	Pro-natalist policies as of about 1987 "Have three or more if you can afford it"	Policy revisions 2000	Policy revisions 2004 "Singapore: A great place for families"	Policy revisions 2008	Policy revisions 2013
	n.a.	Infant Care Subsidy: Given to working mothers with infants age 2–18 months enrolled in childcare centers. Subsidy ranged from S$150/month for full day to S$75/month for half day	Increased Infant Care Subsidy: Subsidy increased to S$400/month for full-day care	Increased Infant Care Subsidy: Subsidy increased to S$600/month for all children	Unchanged
A.4 Use of Medisave Accounts (medical savings accounts within Central Provident Fund (CPF))	Medisave for delivery and hospitalization charges: Payment of delivery and hospital charges for third child can be made from Medisave account; maximum is S$3,000	Unchanged	Use of Medisave for maternity extended to fourth child: Can be used for pre-delivery and delivery medical expenses for fifth child onwards, provided parents have combined Medisave balance of at least S$15,000 at the time of delivery	Medisave Maternity Package: Parents may withdraw up to S$450 from Medisave for pre-delivery medical expenses for the first four children	Introduction of Medisave Grant for Newborns: CPF Medisave account opened for each citizen newborn, with a Medisave grant of S$3,000; first S$1,500 deposited after birth registration, second S$1,500 deposited in the following year, provided the child remains enrolled in MediShield or a Medisave-approved Integrated Shield Plan

3 Singapore's Pro-natalist Policies: To What Extent Have They Worked?

	Accouchement fees for post-partum sterilization in government hospital: Waived after third or higher-order birth	Unchanged	Medisave can be used for expenses associated with assisted conception procedures. Withdrawal limit raised from S$4,000 to S$6,000 for first three cycles	Unchanged	Introduction of Medishield Coverage for Congenital and Neonatal Conditions: Newborns covered under MediShield from birth with no underwriting, including for congenital and neonatal conditions, so long as their parents do not opt them out
A.5 Maid Levy relief and reduction	Foreign-Maid Levy Relief for Working Mothers: In 1990, income-tax relief equal to two times annual foreign-maid levy was introduced. This was only for working mothers	Unchanged	Maid Levy Concession: Monthly maid levy reduced from S$345 to S$250 per foreign maid for families with children under 12 or elderly persons age 65 and above. This concession was capped at two foreign workers at any one time	Foreign Domestic Worker Levy Concession: Monthly maid levy reduced to S$170 per foreign maid for families with children under 12 or elderly persons age 65 and above. Then further reduced to S$95	Rebate given on foreign domestic worker levy increased from S$95 to S$145 for households with a child below 12, an elderly family member, or a family member with a disability
A.6 Cash benefits	n.a.	Baby Bonus: S$3,000 cash given to parents for second child and S$6,000 for third child. This was paid over 6 years	Baby Bonus: Extended to include first and fourth child. Parents receive S$3,000 cash for first and second child, S$6,000 for third and fourth child. Cash given in five instalments within 18 months of child's birth	Baby Bonus: Parents receive S$4,000 for first and second child	Enhanced Baby Bonus scheme: Parents receive S$6,000 cash for first and second child and S$8,000 for third and fourth child; cash given within 12 months of child's birth

(continued)

(continued)

Policy area	Pro-natalist policies as of about 1987 "Have three or more if you can afford it"	Policy revisions 2000	Policy revisions 2004 "Singapore: A great place for families"	Policy revisions 2008	Policy revisions 2013
	n.a.	Children Development Account (CDA): Co-savings arrangement to be used for childcare or child development; government matches savings up to S$6,000 for second child, S$12,000 for third; parents can save into CDA and use CDA funds until end of year when child turns 6. Savings may be used for all children	Children Development Account (CDA): Government matches savings up to S$12,000 for fourth child	Children Development Account (CDA): Government matches savings up to S$6,000 for first and second child, up to S$12,000 for third and fourth child, up to S$8,000 for fifth child and beyond	Children Development Account (CDA): Parents can save into CDA and use CDA funds until end of year when child turns 12
A.7 Grandparent caregiver relief	n.a.	n.a.	Working mothers can claim S$3,000 relief if their parents or parents-in-Law take care of their children below age 12	Unchanged	Unchanged

	Public Housing Upgrades for Three-Child Families: Rules altered to make it easier for families with a third child to sell their three-room or larger apartment and buy a bigger one	Public Housing for Newly-weds: Down payment for the purchase of a four-room apartment can be made in two stages, 10 % to be paid when signing the agreement and another 10 % when taking possession	CPF Housing Top-Up Grant for Singles Getting Married: When they decide to marry, singles who previously received government housing grant may receive top-up to match amount given to couples	Third Child Priority: 5 % of available apartments set aside for families with more than two children; included in HDB first balloting round[a]	Parenthood Priority: Proportion of apartments set aside for married couples with children (including those expecting a child) who have not previously applied or been given priority for HDB apartments
B Housing incentives through Housing and Development Board (HDB) and Central Provident Fund (CPF)	n.a.	n.a.	n.a.	n.a.	Parenthood Provisional Housing: First-time married couples may rent an apartment from HDB at an affordable rate while awaiting completion of their new apartment
C Education	Primary school registration: Previous disincentives against third and higher-order births removed	Unchanged	Unchanged	Unchanged	Unchanged
D Work-family balance					
D.1 Paid maternity leave	n.a.	Working mothers may take 8 weeks paid maternity leave for first three children (previously available for first two children only); paid by government (rather than employer); capped at S$20,000	Paid maternity leave extended up to fourth child; increased from 8 to 12 weeks for first four births	Paid maternity leave increased from 12 to 16 weeks. For first and second child, first 8 weeks paid by employer, second 8 weeks paid by government, capped at S$20,000. For third and higher-order births, full 16 weeks paid by government, capped at S$40,000	Working fathers may take 1 week of their wives' 16 weeks paid maternity leave, subject to agreement of the wife. Also known as Shared Parental Leave

(continued)

(continued)

Policy area	Pro-natalist policies as of about 1987 "Have three or more if you can afford it"	Policy revisions 2000	Policy revisions 2004 "Singapore: A great place for families"	Policy revisions 2008	Policy revisions 2013
D.2 Paid paternity leave	n.a.	n.a.	n.a.	n.a.	Paternity Leave: Working fathers may take 1 week of paid paternity leave
D.3 Paid childcare leave	n.a.	n.a.	Two days per year of employer-paid childcare leave for each working parent with a child under age 7	Increased to 6 days per year for each working parent	In addition, 2 days per year for each working parent with a child age 7–12
D.4 Adoption leave	n.a.	n.a.	Four weeks adoption leave paid by government on recommendation of employer	Unchanged	Offer of adoption leave made mandatory for mothers of adopted children below 12 months
D.5 Unpaid childcare leave	n.a.	n.a.	n.a.	Each parent may take 6 days a year of unpaid childcare leave for each child under age 2	Unchanged
D.6 Maternity protection	n.a.	n.a.	n.a.	Employer required to pay maternity-leave benefits if employee is dismissed without sufficient cause or retrenched within the last 6 months of pregnancy or retrenched within the last 3 months of pregnancy	Enhanced Maternity Protection for Pregnant Employees: Working mothers eligible for maternity leave benefits if they are dismissed without sufficient cause or retrenched within the full duration of their pregnancy

3 Singapore's Pro-natalist Policies: To What Extent Have They Worked?

D.7 Government-paid maternity benefit	n.a.	n.a.	n.a.	Working mothers who are not eligible for maternity leave may receive government-paid maternity benefit if they have been employed at least 90 days in the 12 months before childbirth
D.8 "Work-Life Works!" fund	n.a.	n.a.	S$10 million fund; private-sector employers may receive grants to defray cost of measures to help employees achieve better work-life harmony	Unchanged

Adapted from Sun (2012); Yap (2009); updated based on NPTD (2013a, b).
^aThis means that they may cast their vote in the first balloting round for an apartment. There are multiple rounds, and families without priority have to wait their turn

References

Anderson, T., & Kohler, H. P. (2013). Education fever and the east Asian fertility puzzle: A case study of low fertility in South Korea. *Asian Population Studies, 9*(2), 196–215.

AWARE (Association of Women for Action and Research). (2012, July). *Marriage and parenthood trends: Some suggestions from AWARE.* Singapore: A submission to the National Population and Talent Division (NPTD) Office.

Bumpass, L. L., Rindfuss, R. R., Choe, M. K., & Tsuya, N. O. (2009). The institutional context of low fertility: The case of Japan. *Asian Population Studies, 5*(3), 215–236.

Census and Statistics Department, Government of the Hong Kong Special Administrative Region. (2014). *Hong Kong statistics.* http://www.censtatd.gov.hk/hkstat/index.jsp. Accessed 10 Apr 2014.

Chang, K. S. (2010). *South Korea under compressed modernity: Familial political economy in transition.* London: Routledge.

Chang, R. (2013, 22 January). Package sends pro-family, gender-equal message: Experts. *Straits Times.*

Cheam, J. (2013, 18 August). Baby bonus won't solve our fertility problem. *Straits Times.*

Department of Statistics, Singapore. (2009). *Population trends 2009.* Singapore: Department of Statistics, Ministry of Trade and Industry.

Department of Statistics, Singapore. (2013). *Population trends 2013.* Singapore: Department of Statistics, Ministry of Trade and Industry.

Department of Statistics, Singapore. (2014). *Population: Births and deaths.* Singapore: Department of Statistics, Ministry of Trade and Industry. http://www.singstat.gov.sg/statistics/statistics.html. Accessed 11 Apr 2014.

Eun, K. S. (2007). Lowest-low fertility in the Republic of Korea: Causes, consequences and policy responses. *Asia-Pacific Population Journal, 22*(2), 51–72.

Frejka, T., Jones, G., & Sardon, J. P. (2010). East Asian childbearing patterns and policy developments. *Population and Development Review, 36*(3), 579–606.

Heitlinger, A. (1991). Pronatalism and women's equality policies. *European Journal of Population, 7*, 343–375.

Jones, G. W. (2007). Delayed marriage and very low fertility in Pacific Asia. *Population and Development Review, 33*(3), 453–478.

Jones, G. W. (2012). Population policy in a prosperous city-state: Dilemmas for Singapore. *Population and Development Review, 38*(2), 311–336.

Jones, G., Straughan, P. T., & Chan, A. (Eds.). (2009). *Ultra-low fertility in Pacific Asia: Trends, causes, and policy issues.* London: Routledge.

Koh, E. C. (2011). The state of marriage in Singapore. In G. Jones, T. Hull, & M. Mohamad (Eds.), *Changing marriage patterns in southeast Asia: Economic and socio-cultural dimensions.* London: Routledge.

KOSIS (Korean Statistical Information Service). (2014). *Statistical database.* http://kosis.kr/eng/statisticsList/statisticsList_01List.jsp?vwcd=MT_ETITLE&parentId=A. Accessed 12 Apr 2014.

Lee, S. S. (2009). Low fertility and policy responses in Korea. *Japanese Journal of Population, 7*(1), 57–70.

Masahiro, Y. (1999). *Parasaito shinguru no jidai* [The age of parasite singles]. Tokyo: Tokyo Gakugei University.

McDonald, P. (2002). Sustaining fertility through public policy: The range of options. *Population, 57*(3), 417–446.

Ministry of Manpower, Singapore. (2012). *Labor force in Singapore, 2012.* Singapore: Manpower Research and Statistics Department.

Ministry of Social and Family Development, Singapore. (2013). *Hey baby—Marriage and parenthood package enhancements at a glance.* http://www.heybaby.sg/havingchildren/baby_bonus.html. Accessed 3 Apr 2014.

Ministry of the Interior, Republic of China (Taiwan). (2014). *Statistical yearbook of interior: Fertility rates of childbearing age women.* http://sowf.moi.gov.tw/stat/year/elist.htm. Accessed 12 Apr 2014.

National Bureau of Statistics of China. (2014). *Tabulation on the 2010 population census of the People's Republic of China.* http://www.stats.gov.cn/english/Statisticaldata/CensusData/rkpc2010/indexch.htm. Accessed 12 Apr 2014.

National Population and Talent Division (NPTD) Singapore. (2013a). *Marriage and parenthood package 2013.* Singapore: NPTD, Prime Minister's Office, Department of Statistics, Ministry of Home Affairs, and Immigration and Checkpoints Authority.

National Population and Talent Division (NPTD) Singapore. (2013b). *Press release: Marriage and parenthood study.* Singapore: NPTD, Prime Minister's Office, Department of Statistics, Ministry of Home Affairs, and Immigration and Checkpoints Authority.

National Statistics, Republic of China (Taiwan). (2014). *Population and housing.* http://eng.stat.gov.tw/np.asp?ctNode=2168&mp=5. Accessed 12 Apr 2014.

Raymo, J. (2003). Educational attainment and the transition to first marriage among Japanese women. *Demography, 40*, 83–103.

Ronald, R., & Nakano, L. (2012). Single women and housing choices in urban Japan. *Gender, Place, and Culture, 20*(4), 451–469.

Saw, S. H. (1990). *Changes in the fertility policy of Singapore.* Singapore: Institute of Policy Studies and Times Academic Press.

Saw, S. H. (2005). *Population policies and programmes in Singapore.* Singapore: Institute of Southeast Asian Studies.

Statistics Japan. (2014). *Social indicators by prefecture 2014.* http://www.stat.go.jp/english/data/shihyou/index.htm. Accessed 10 Apr 2014.

Straughan, P. T., Chan, A., & Jones, G. (2009). From population control to fertility promotion: A case study of family policies and fertility trends in Singapore. In G. Jones, P. T. Straughan, & A. Chan (Eds.), *Ultra-low fertility in Pacific Asia: Trends, causes and policy issues.* London: Routledge.

Sun, S. H. L. (2012). *Population policy and reproduction in Singapore: Making future citizens.* London: Routledge.

Suzuki, T. (2008). Korea's strong familism and lowest-low fertility. *International Journal of Japanese Sociology, 17*(1), 30–41.

Suzuki, T. (2009). Fertility decline and governmental interventions in eastern Asian advanced countries. *Japanese Journal of Population, 7*(1), 47–56.

Tan, L. (2010, 4 July). The dollars and sense of parenthood. *Straits Times.*

Tsuya, N. O., Choe, M. K., Wang, F. (2009, 2 October). *Below-replacement fertility in East Asia: Patterns, factors, and policy implications.* Paper presented at the 26th IUSSP International Population Conference, Marrakech.

Yap, M. T. (2009). Ultra-low fertility in Singapore: Some observations. In G. Jones, P. T. Straughan, & A. Chan (Eds.), *Ultra-low fertility in Pacific Asia: Trends, causes and policy issues.* London: Routledge.

Chapter 4
Understanding Ultra-Low Fertility in Hong Kong

Stuart Basten

In 2013, the Special Administrative Region of Hong Kong (hereafter Hong Kong) had a total population of more than 7.2 million and a gross domestic product of US$263 billion (UNPD 2013; World Bank 2014)—both roughly the same size as Singapore. Yet, while low fertility and population policy in Singapore have been the subject of a large number of books, chapters, and journal articles, the situation in Hong Kong is relatively under-studied.[1] In terms of conventional boundaries of age distribution, Hong Kong is "aging rapidly." In 1980, just one in 15 of the population was above age 65. In 2006, this ratio increased to one in eight. By 2040, over a quarter of the population—26 %—will be age 65 and above; more than double the current level of 12 %.

Conventional thinking would therefore suggest that the working population of the future will have a much larger number of retirees to support—as measured by the Old Age Dependency Ratio (OADR) (see Fig. 4.1). These dramatic increases in the OADR have caused great alarm among local policymakers (see Basten 2013b). Despite the fact that some studies have presented a rather more optimistic view of aging in Hong Kong by recalculating the OADR to take into account improved life expectancy and the general absence of large-scale state-defined pension obligations (Basten et al. 2013),[2] there is no doubt that Hong Kong will see a rapid increase in

---

[1] See Basten and Verropoulou 2013; Yip et al. 2001, 2002, 2006; Yip and Lee 2002.

[2] As Basten (2013b) observes, the social-policy system prevalent in East Asia means that the "watershed age" of 65 is of less primary importance than in Europe, where many state pension systems begin to pay out at 65. Sanderson and Scherbov (e.g., 2007, 2010) propose an alternative set of measurements that take account of projected improvements in life expectancy and health. Rather than being based on the number of years that a "dependent" person has lived, these measurements are instead based upon the likely additional number of years that such a person will live—a more dynamic measurement. Basten and colleagues (2013) have calculated these Prospective Old Age Dependency Ratios (POADR) for Hong Kong based upon the assumption

S. Basten (✉)
Department of Social Policy and Intervention, University of Oxford, Oxford, UK
e-mail: stuart.basten@spi.ox.ac.uk

© Springer International Publishing Switzerland 2015
R.R. Rindfuss, M.K. Choe (eds.), *Low and Lower Fertility*,
DOI 10.1007/978-3-319-21482-5_4

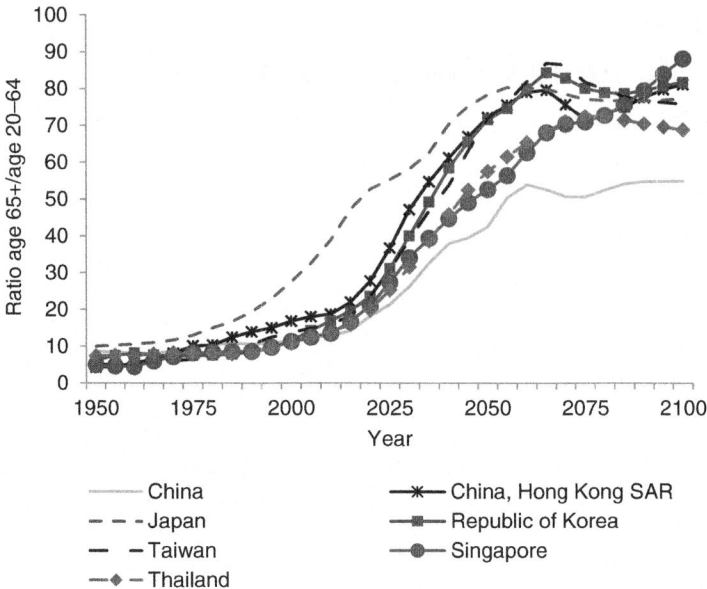

Fig. 4.1 Old-age dependency ratio of selected advanced Asian economies, population age 65+/age 20–64 (Based on UNPD 2013 data, medium estimate). *Note:* Taiwan denoted as "Other non-specified areas" in UNPD (2013)

the size of its older population over the coming decades. This will, in turn, bring with it a wide array of policy challenges.

Of course, this degree of aging has been driven from both "above" and "below." Life expectancy at birth increased by more than 10 years between 1971 and 2006, reaching 79.5 years for men and 85.6 for women—values that are among the highest in the world (HKCSD 2013). But, the primary factor shaping the rapid pace of aging is low fertility. In this chapter, we examine recent fertility trends in Hong Kong and try to identify some of the reasons why the territory has one of the lowest total fertility rates (TFR) in Asia. Using this information on the "causes" of ultra-

---

that the majority of chronic ill health—when an individual is truly dependent on others and unable to work at all—is concentrated in the last 15 years of life. This assumption has been expressed by Sanderson and Scherbov (2007, 2010) as well as other scholars (e.g., Fuchs 1984). The new "dependent" population is defined as one with a remaining life expectancy (RLE) of 15 years. Improvements in mortality in Hong Kong have been dramatic, such that the age at which the population has a remaining life expectancy of 15 years (RLE_{15}) for men was 60.6 in 1971, rose to 70.4 in 2011, and is projected to rise to 73.2 by 2041. For women, the age at RLE_{15} has risen from 67.2 in 1971 to 75.6 in 2011 and is projected to rise to 78.6 by 2041 (HKCSD 2012a). Under these conditions of "prospective measurement," the POADR remains almost constant at around 10.0–12.0 up to 2030 (compared to the OADR, which more than doubles to more than 45.0). Of course, this should really only be interpreted as a highly optimistic outside boundary. In other words, Hong Kong's population will age rapidly in the sense that the age structure will become increasingly "top heavy," but there is a degree of flexibility in the extent to which this can be mitigated.

low fertility[3] in Hong Kong, we will then consider possible future trajectories of fertility and how, in relation to other factors such as immigration, this might shape the future population age structure. Finally, we conclude with a discussion of recent trends in policy relating to fertility and Hong Kong's aging society. While the boundaries between the two are quite porous, we consider both explicitly macro-level population policies and the role of family-friendly policies.

Since 1997, Hong Kong has been a Special Administrative Region (SAR) of the People's Republic of China (PRC).[4] Under the "One Country, Two Systems" rule, Hong Kong has had—and continues to have—a high degree of autonomy from the Beijing government as enshrined in the so-called "Basic Law." But examining Hong Kong as an independent unit apart from China would be a fundamental error. Demographically, the border with Guangdong Province has shaped marriage patterns and the number of births in recent years and is hugely important for both long-term migration and commuting. Furthermore, in terms of aging, large numbers of elderly Hong Kong residents are choosing to retire in the cheaper mainland, thus potentially "outsourcing" an element of elder care. In addition, the territory is becoming ever more closely linked to the Chinese mainland economically, institutionally, and in terms of infrastructure. Finally, while the Hong Kong government does have a high degree of autonomy, it would be a mistake to ignore the mainland is political and economic influence in policy formation.

Despite this caveat, Hong Kong SAR (hereafter "Hong Kong") is clearly an important unit to consider in understanding policy responses to rapidly aging populations. This is because Hong Kong is a Special Administrative Region of the People's Republic of China, and also because Hong Kong has a particular historical legacy that places an unusually strong emphasis on a capitalist ethos characterized by a limited acceptance of social welfare and the role of social policy.

Fertility Change in Hong Kong

Trends in Period and Quantum Fertility

As with most settings in Asia, mid-twentieth-century Hong Kong was characterized by high fertility rates, with TFRs of above 4.0 births per woman and crude birth rates of around 35–39 per 1,000 until the late-1950s (Tu et al. 2007). As Fig. 4.2 shows, Hong Kong has seen a dramatic decline in its total fertility rate (TFR) since

---

[3] The term "ultra-low fertility" has been applied to Asian settings such as Hong Kong in a wide variety of papers, not least in Jones and colleagues' book on childbearing in the region (Jones et al. 2009). "Ultra low" or "lowest low" fertility usually refers to a TFR of less than 1.3.

[4] In this chapter, we refer to the People's Republic of China (PRC) as a separate governmental body under the "One Country, Two Systems" mode of government in Hong Kong. "The mainland" is used interchangeably with the PRC; it is the term usually used in Hong Kong to refer to the "rest of China."

the 1960s, reaching a low point of 0.9 children per woman in 2003. Hong Kong currently vies with the Republic of Korea and Taiwan for having the lowest TFR in East Asia (UNPD 2013).

As can be seen in the inset in Fig. 4.2, there has been a notable increase in TFR since 2003, most likely related to an increase in fertility among older women. Like many settings across East Asia and Europe, there has been a significant rise in the postponement of childbearing in Hong Kong. The mean age of women at first birth increased from 25.5 in 1976 to 28.7 in 2001, and at second birth from 27.8 to 31.4 over the same period (Tu et al. 2007). Crucially, the marital fertility rates for women aged 30–49 increased from 28.3 per 1,000 in 2001 to 43.8 in 2011 (HKCSD 2012d). This has clearly played an important role in shaping the recent upturn in period total fertility rates.

At the same time, there has been a clear shift away from the absolute primacy of the two-child family in Hong Kong. From the cohorts born in the mid-1950s through to those born in the mid- to late-1960s, the share of two-child families has declined from 45 to 35 % (Frejka et al. 2010). As Fig. 4.3 demonstrates, a concomitant result of this has been the rise of childlessness and of the one-child family. High-parity births have all but disappeared; of the 865,224 births registered in Hong Kong between 1995 and 2009, 7.7 % were parity 3, 1.4 % were parity 4, and 0.4 % were parity 5 or above.

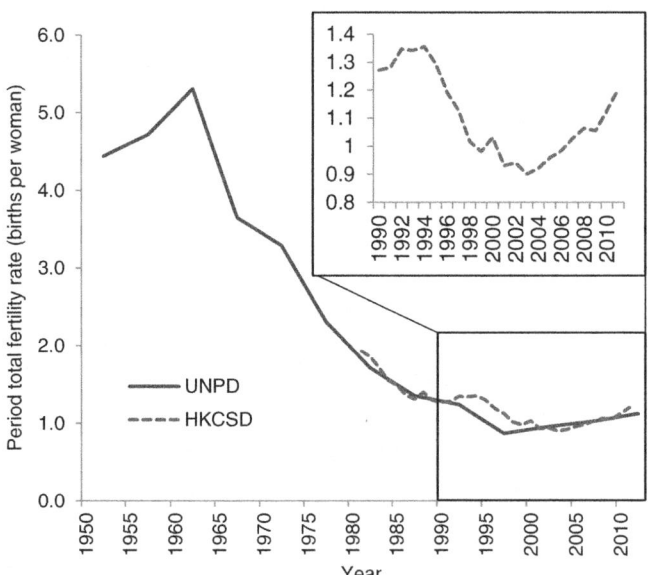

Fig. 4.2 Trends in period total fertility rate (TFR), Hong Kong SAR, 1950–2012 (HKCSD 2012d; UNPD 2013). *Note:* Estimates derived from the United Nations *World Population Prospects* from 1950 were used to supplement the officially recorded Hong Kong government's TFR data in order to provide a longer time series

4 Understanding Ultra-Low Fertility in Hong Kong

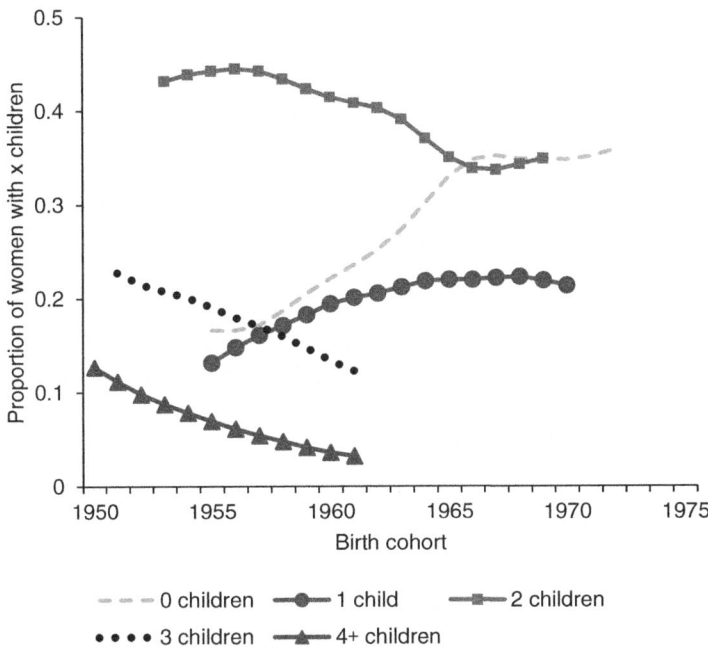

Fig. 4.3 Proportion of women with specific number of children by birth cohort, Hong Kong SAR (Adapted from Frejka et al. 2010)

A direct consequence of the decline in the first-parity fertility rate is a significant increase in the number of people age 50 or above without any children at all. For women born in 1946, the childless rate was just 2.6 %. This rose to 9.3 % and 16.6 % for the 1951 and 1956 cohort respectively. Tu and colleagues (2007) estimate that the childless rate for the 1961 birth cohort may reach 20 %, while Frejka et al. (2010) estimate childlessness among the cohorts born in the mid- to late-1960s to be as high as 35 %. As Fig. 4.4 demonstrates, these numbers are substantially higher than elsewhere in East Asia (Frejka et al. 2010). Within a familial reductionist social-policy context, where filial obligation still underpins notions of care for the elderly, unless these childless cohorts are able to set aside considerable personal savings, they could run into difficulties in securing support in later life. Furthermore, a number of recent studies have identified a series of negative outcomes for childless Hong Kong populations, such as an increased tendency to depression and loneliness (Cheng et al. 2014; Chou and Chi 2004).

We should, however, pause to consider the implications of a shift toward a growing number of (voluntarily chosen) one-child families. Firstly, it is possible to learn from the Chinese so-called "4-2-1 issue," where a couple made up of only children have to bear the responsibility for both of their sets of parents (in the absence of any kin support) as well as their child. Of course, the burden of care would likely fall disproportionately on the woman. This has been cited as a reason for possible long-term low levels of fertility in mainland China (Basten and Gu 2013). Given the rise

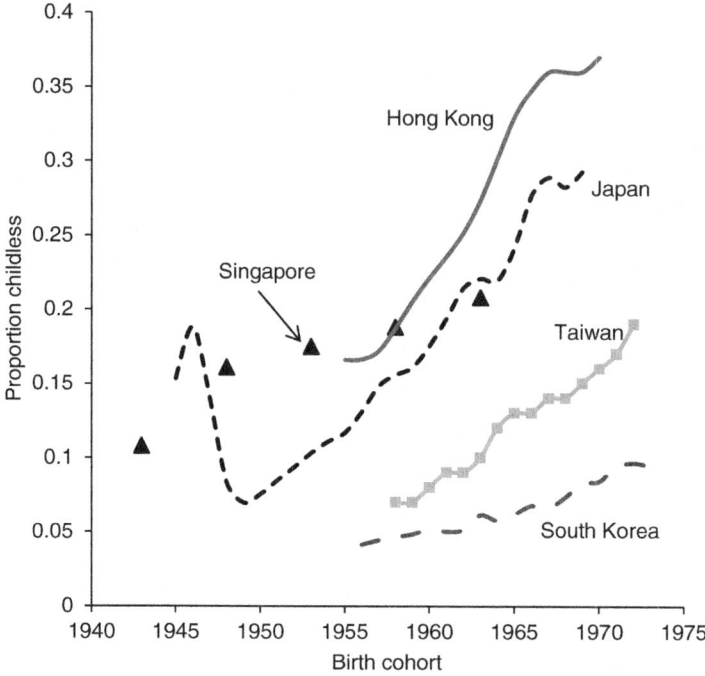

Fig. 4.4 Proportion of childless women, selected territories, birth cohorts 1943–1973 (Adapted from Frejka et al. 2010)

in the number of only children in the current marriage market, as well as an increasing preference for only having one child among current young people in Hong Kong (Basten 2013c), this burden of care has the potential to be a drag on future fertility—especially in the absence of significant improvements in the availability of (affordable) public private assistance for the elderly.

Recent Rise in Number of Live Births

The relationship between Hong Kong and mainland China is instrumental in shaping the population dynamics of the territory. During the period 1981–2001—an era of very low fertility rates in Hong Kong—the territory's population increased from 5.18 million to 6.27 million, primarily driven by the high number of entrants from mainland China rather than by natural increase (HKCSD 2001). Indeed, it is this dynamic which has largely shaped the recent trend in live births in the territory (see Figs. 4.5 and 4.6). As Basten and Verropoulou (2012, 2013) have observed, this increase in live births has been largely caused by an increase in what they term "maternity migration." In July 2001, the Court of Final Appeal ruled that babies born in Hong Kong to Chinese nationals had the right of abode in Hong Kong. In 2001, just 620 babies were born to mainland women whose spouses were not

4 Understanding Ultra-Low Fertility in Hong Kong

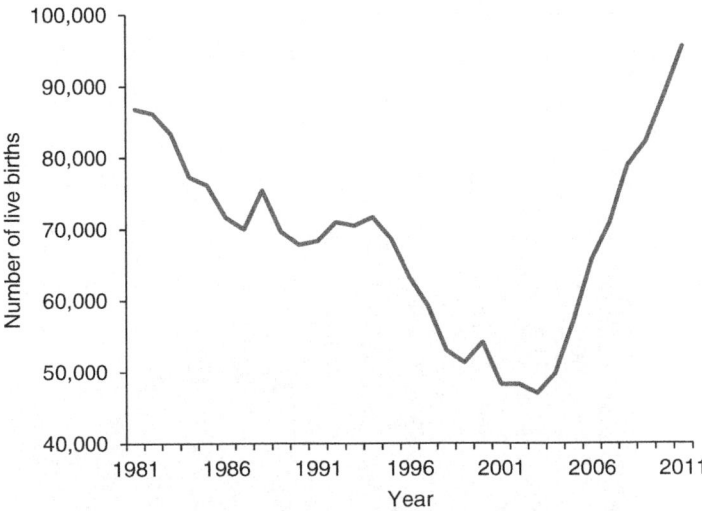

Fig. 4.5 Recent trends in live births, Hong Kong SAR (HKCSD 2012d)

Hong Kong permanent residents. By 2011, this figure had mushroomed to 35,736 (HKCSD 2012d).

Figure 4.6, which depicts the proportion of births by mother's residency, shows the increasing proportion of births ascribed to what the registers term "transient" mothers from the mainland. Basten and Verropoulou (2012, 2013) observe that there are a number of "push and pull" factors associated with this increase. For one thing, the right of abode brings certain key privileges, such as enhanced access to the territory's educational system and visa-free travel to many more countries than granted for mainland PRC citizens. Basten and Verropoulou (2013) have also demonstrated that Hong Kong has served as an outlet allowing mainland couples to evade the PRC's family-planning restrictions. Upon close inspection of the Hong Kong microdata, the vast majority of "transient" mothers, were giving birth to their *second* child in the territory. Furthermore, these second (and third) children were disproportionately male. This resulted in a highly skewed sex ratio at birth—something which, historically, was generally absent in Hong Kong. Finally, the average educational attainment level of such "transient" mothers was generally high, indicating a higher level of income.

Only births to mainland women whose partners are Hong Kong permanent residents (so-called "Type I" babies) are included in the calculation of the TFR by the Hong Kong Census and Statistics Department (HKCSD). Compared to "Type II" babies (born to mainland women whose partners are not Hong Kong permanent residents), such births increased only from 7,190 in 2001 to 9,879 in 2005 before falling back to 6,110 in 2011 (HKCSD 2012d). While the growth of maternity migration has been critical in shaping the *number of births* in Hong Kong, it has had relatively little effect on the recent increase in the officially reported *total fertility rate* because "Type II" babies are not included in the calculation of TFR. As noted above, changes in the TFR have predominantly been driven by the tempo effect of postponement of

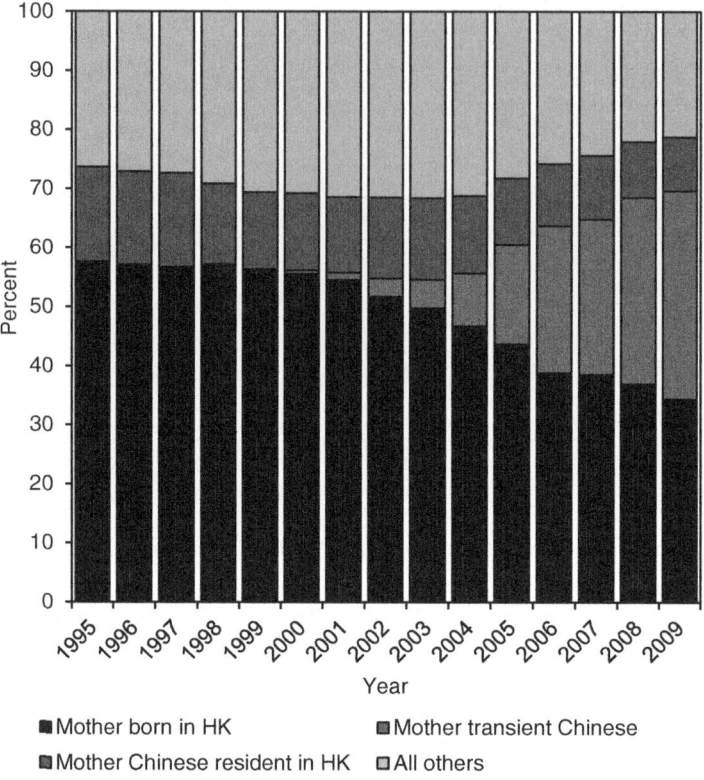

Fig. 4.6 Percentage distribution of births by immigrant status of mother, Hong Kong SAR, 1995–2009 (Basten and Verropoulou 2013)

births. That is not to say that maternity migration is irrelevant to a policy discussion of population in Hong Kong: As Basten and Verropoulou (2013) observe, while almost all "Type II" babies return to the mainland with their mothers immediately after birth, it is almost impossible to identify the point at which they may return to Hong Kong—if at all. This means that planning for future provision of public services and housing and, indeed, forecasts of the size of the labor force, must take into account the temporal uncertainty of "return" migration. This situation forms part of the broader difficulty in forecasting population dynamics for Hong Kong due to its border with the mainland.

Causes for Fertility Decline

In order to understand the reasons for fertility decline in Hong Kong, it is perhaps useful to differentiate between what might be termed the *proximate*, or demographic reasons, and the *cultural-social* reasons.

Later and Less Marriage Much of what might be termed a "retreat from motherhood" might better be linked to a notion of a "retreat from marriage"—not least because of the tight link between marriage and fertility. Although Basten (2012) has identified a growing trend towards pre-nuptial pregnancy in Hong Kong as well as relative increases in births outside of marriage, the proportion of extra-marital births is still low, at around 5 %—similar to the situation in other settings across East Asia. Demographically, later marriages combined with higher divorce rates generally serve to shorten the childbearing exposure period for women. Both are evident in Hong Kong. The median age of women's first marriage rose from 23.9 in 1981 to 28.9 in 2011, and the corresponding proportion ever-married among women aged 25–29 declined from 69 to 27 % (HKCSD 2012d). Finally, a growing number of women have eschewed marriage altogether. The percentage of never-married women in the age group 40–44 increased from 3 % in 1981 to 17 % in 2011. Clearly, in the context of low birth rates outside of marriage, there is a strong link between the increased prevalence of spinsterhood and childlessness.

According to various studies, the underlying reasons for this "retreat from marriage and motherhood" are two-fold: incompatibility between women's economic and domestic roles, and a squeeze in the marriage market (see, among many examples, Basten 2013c; Chang 2003; Frejka et al. 2010; Song et al. 2013; Jones et al. 2009; Sun 2012). The *public* roles of women have been revolutionized in advanced Asian economies to the extent that in many areas younger women are better educated than men, thus increasing—and enhancing the quality of—female labor-force participation (Esping-Andersen 2009; MacDonald 2000). Developments in the *private* sphere, meanwhile, have been much slower and more resistant to change. Entry into a married relationship where the onus is still frequently firmly placed upon the woman to care for children, parents, and parents-in-law, as well as look after the household, is often unappetizing given the extraordinarily high opportunity costs.[5] This so-called "Incomplete Gender Revolution" is held to be a key element in the avoidance of the "marriage package" of home and children (Esping-Andersen 2009).

Related to this is a squeeze in the marriage market. Although female public roles have changed dramatically, systems characterized by women marrying older and/or better-educated men (possibly of a higher social status) are arguably breaking down much more slowly (Jones and Gubhaju 2009). As such, increasingly educated women find themselves squeezed out of a marriage market privileged males "marrying downwards." The corollary of this, of course, is that many less-educated males also struggle to find partners. This pattern has been cited as a major cause of the increase in cross-border marriages elsewhere in East Asia (Jones and Shen 2008; So 2003).

Weak Provision of Services As in other East Asian settings, the social welfare system in Hong Kong is characterized by a "developmentalist" approach, with

---

[5] Wong and colleagues (2011) usefully frame these extremely high opportunity costs of marriage and childbearing in Hong Kong within Ulrich Beck's "Risk Society" framework.

social support seen as a supplement to economic growth and a reliance upon the family as the core element of support (Shik and Wong 2012; Song et al. 2013; Hong 2008).[6] Both in colonial times and after reunification with the PRC, the Hong Kong government has sought to minimize taxation and, as such, can be described as having a minimal state-driven social-security system. This means that current family policy provision is negligible, and filial obligation regarding care for the elderly has become, *de facto*, institutionalized (Wong et al. 2011). In other words, the space for policies that may have a direct or indirect impact upon fertility is relatively narrow. A further element that potentially limits this policy space is the overwhelming dominance of small and medium enterprises (SMEs) in the economy of the territory. This has the double effect of generally increasing resistance to business taxes (which often double as personal taxes in single-person or family-run SMEs) and preventing wide-scale, private sector-driven social policy initiatives, such as the corporate childcare provisions seen in Japan (Magoshi and Chang 2009). Even among many large employers, corporate family-friendly policies are still relatively limited (HKEOC 2010).

High Direct Costs of Raising a Child Raising a child is "expensive" in almost all societies. In East Asia, the high cost of childcare relative to income, combined with the high cost of housing, means the costs are often deemed prohibitive—especially if offset against a growing world of other consumption opportunities and where the burden of care for aged relatives is often placed on the shoulders of an increasingly small set of adult children. For one thing, the educational expectations in advanced Asian economies are exceptionally high and could be a key force in pushing down the number of children that people realistically assume they can raise (Lee 2005; Chang 2011; Choe and Retherford 2009; Ogawa et al. 2009). Private tutoring and "cram schools" are a very familiar phenomenon in Hong Kong. These appear to operate primarily as a result of a mismatch between the extremely high parental expectations placed upon children to achieve educationally and the prevailing view of an underperforming public-education sector. In Hong Kong in 2004, 47 % of children of school age received private tutoring at home or at educational institutions outside school hours, each for an average time of around 4.8 h per week. In 2007, it was estimated that households with students taking private tuition spent on average HK$1,150 (US$148)[7] per month on tuition fees (Chan 2010). It is common for Hong Kong parents applying for a place for their child in kindergarten to prepare a "portfolio" of their toddler's "skills."

Housing in Hong Kong is extremely expensive and has, in a recent economic analysis, been suggested to have a causal effect on Hong Kong's low fertility (Yi and Zhang 2010). A recent survey of 360 cities found that, with average home prices at 14.9 times the gross annual median household income, Hong Kong was the most unaffordable city in the world to buy property (Holliday 2014). The same

---

[6]The social-welfare system in Hong Kong has been covered in depth by Chan (2011).
[7]Throughout this paper we employ the Hong Kong dollar (HK$) as the unit of currency. As of November 2013, US$1 = HK$7.75, €1 = HK$10.54, and GB£1 = HK$12.65.

survey found that Singapore's house prices were 5.1 times the gross annual median household income. A commercial survey of 30- to 40-year-old middle-class individuals found that the high cost of property had an effect on personal decisions, with 53 % of the single respondents saying they would delay their marriage to have more time for saving. Nearly half of those who were married also chose to delay having children, or to have no children, so they could boost their savings. Tellingly, the survey found that "property purchase remained the top reason for savings, followed by travel, having children, and further education" (reported in Chen 2013a). This is despite the fact that almost one-half of all housing in the SAR is either "Public Rental Housing" or "Subsidized Home Ownership Housing" (HKHA 2013).

Other Structural Issues As well as some of the most expensive housing in the world, Hong Kong also has some of the smallest. According to a recent comparative analysis, average new home sizes in Hong Kong are just 45 m^2. Compared to higher-fertility (though still densely populated) settings such as the United Kingdom, at 76 m^2, this is certainly small. The average home size in Hong Kong is even considerably smaller than in urban China (60 m^2) or Japan (95 m^2). This roughly equates to around 15 m^2 of average residential space per capita in new housing in Hong Kong, compared with 20 m^2 in China, 33 m^2 in the UK, 22 m^2 in Russia, and 77 m^2 in the United States (Wilson 2013).

Finally, on a macro-level, it is worth remembering that Hong Kong has one of the highest population densities in the world, at more than 6,500 people/km^2. After taking into account that more than one-half of the SAR is extremely sparsely inhabited because of its mountainous terrain, the figures for population density in the other districts are even more striking. For example, in the Kowloon area, with more than two million people, the population density is 44,917 people/km^2, while for Hong Kong Island as a whole the total is 15,924 people/km^2 (even though, again, much of the southern part is very sparsely populated due to its topography) (HKCSD 2012c). For comparison, the population density of Manhattan is 10,194 people/km^2, while in Tokyo Prefecture it is 6,029 people/km^2 (Tokyo Metropolitan Government 2014).

Long working hours and the negative impact upon work-life balance have been widely cited as a drag on fertility in East Asia (McDonald 2006). The average *contracted* working hours in Hong Kong are 45.2 h per week, ranging from 40.6 h for the lower quartile (LQ) to 49.7 h for the upper quartile (UQ). Clearly, however, overtime forms a critical part of the structural labor system in Hong Kong. On top of contracted working hours, lower-skilled workers tend to work an average of 7.0 h (LQ: 2.0; UQ: 9.7) paid overtime, while in more professional sectors between one-fifth and one-third of workers work an average of 8.0 h (LQ: 5.0, UQ: 10.0) unpaid overtime. Overall, a survey conducted in 2011 by the Hong Kong Labour Department found that the average number of hours worked by full-time employees was 49.0 (HKLD 2012, p. 129)—compared to a range of 39.1–43.7 h among member countries in the European Union. Around 10.3 % of people work 60–70 h per week, while around 3.0 %—mostly double-shift security guards—work more than 70 h per week (HKLD 2012, p. 130). It should not, however, be assumed that this only relates to employees working in corporate offices until late in the evening, as the East Asian stereotype might suggest (see Fig. 4.7). Closely related is the notion of a "24-hour city" with very long opening hours for shops, restaurants, and services. In this context, the rapid growth since 2001 in consumption-related employment among highly skilled workers (+28 %) and service and shop sales workers (+24 %) is also important (HKLD 2012, p. 110). The average contracted hours for those employed in hotels and restaurants is above 50 h per week, while in elderly homes it is 54.8 h (LQ: 45.0; UQ: 66.0), and in estate management and security it is 57.5 (LQ: 48.0; UQ: 69.2).

Finally, at just 7 %, Hong Kong has a very small proportion of the population in part-time employment (compared to an average of 14 % for developed countries that are members of the Organisation for Economic Cooperation and Development—OECD) because of the demand for full-time workers in a liberal labor market without working time regulations. While part-time employment has very different meanings in different parts of the world, even within low-fertility settings in East Asia such employment is more prevalent in Taiwan (8 %), Singapore (10 %), Korea (11 %), and Japan (20 %) than in Hong Kong (HKLD 2012, pp. 113–14). Such an emphasis on full-time employment and long working hours can create tremendous pressure, particularly on women, and works strongly against combining work and childrearing.

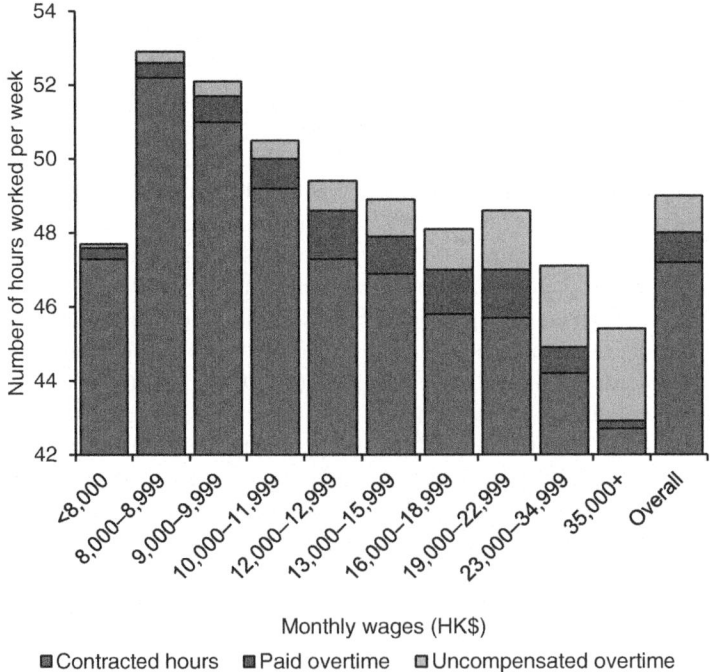

Fig. 4.7 Average estimated total working hours of full-time employees by monthly wage, Hong Kong SAR, 2011 (Adapted from HKLD 2012, 133). *Note:* Data are from 2011 Hong Kong Annual Earnings and Hours Survey and August–October 2011 General Household Survey. Extra hours worked to gain "time off in lieu of payment" (TOIL) are excluded

Even the Hong Kong government is pessimistic about a medium-term increase in period total fertility rates in the territory.[8] In their latest round of population projections, the HKCSD assumes that TFR will decrease from 1.204 in 2011 to 1.177 by 2016, then fluctuate at around 1.190 until 2031, before falling to 1.164 by 2036 and 1.151 by 2041 (HKCSD 2012b). Such tiny changes in fertility are, fundamentally, irrelevant, but the key message is one of assumed stagnation.[9] Unlike many other local statistical offices, the process of formulating the Hong Kong Census and Statistics Department's fertility assumptions "is not strictly a mechanical one that follows the extrapolated trends" (HKCSD 2012b). The overall pattern of marital fertility is projected to stay relatively constant to the end of the projection period (2041).[10] Most significantly, however, the department assumes a continuing pattern of later and fewer marriages. The Hong Kong government projects that by 2041 around one-third of all women will remain never married at the end of their childbearing period, compared with around one-eighth in 2012. If the link between marriage and childbearing stays strong, this will have a negative impact upon both the tempo and quantum of childbearing.

A second way to consider short- to medium- term prospects for fertility in Hong Kong is to examine reported fertility preferences—both as a micro-indicator of family formation and as a macro-indicator, or "barometer," of general attitudes towards childbearing at the societal level. Using evidence from a number of rounds of the Hong Kong Knowledge, Attitude, and Practice (KAP) Surveys, we can examine lifetime fertility ideals through the question "If you could start all over again, how many children would you like to have in your lifetime?" As Table 4.1 demonstrates, a majority of women questioned in 2007 desired two or fewer children (88.4 %), with around one-half (49.7 %) stating a preference for two children (HKFPA 2007). Regression analysis performed by the Hong Kong Family Planning Association on data from six rounds of the survey over 25 years demonstrates that an ever-increasing number of women state a preference for zero or only one child, while the proportion desiring three or four children is significantly decreasing. This evidence of aggregate fertility *ideals* well below two represents a paradigm shift compared with the results of similar surveys in Europe.

Of course, these stated ideals are themselves highly likely to be an over-estimate for two reasons. Firstly, they include the preferences of women who already have (or have already had) two or more children, and who are unlikely to state a preference below the total number of children they have borne. Secondly, fertility ideals are precisely that—the number of children that an individual would like to have. Under the given economic, social, and cultural constraints of a particular setting,

---

[8] Critically, this is in stark contrast to the medium fertility assumptions generated by the model employed in the UN's 2010 and 2012 *World Population Prospects* (Basten 2013a; UNPD 2011, 2013).

[9] See Basten (2013a) for a further discussion of locally defined future fertility assumptions in low-fertility Asian settings.

[10] An exception to this is a short-term rise in the marital fertility of women in their late twenties as a consequence of postponement.

Table 4.1 Women's ideal number of children, Hong Kong, 1982–2007 (HKFPA 2007)

Ideal number of children	Percent responding						Linear trend
	1982	1987	1992	1997	2002	2007	
0	2.1	4.8	5.1	10.9	15.2	12.5	↑↑
1	7.5	10.1	10.8	13.7	16.6	26.2	↑↑
2	53.7	58.4	59.0	52.9	51.2	49.7	NS
3	18.9	16.1	11.4	8.1	5.0	6.1	↓↓
4	11.2	7.3	4.5	3.4	2.1	1.3	↓↓
5 or more	1.9	0.8	0.3	0.2	0.3	0.9	NS
Number immaterial, depends on God's will	1.5	1.3	0.9	2.4	2.4	—	NS
Don't know/Never thought about it	2.9	0.9	3.7	5.0	3.9	3.3	NS
No response	0.4	0.1	2.3	1.4	0.0	—	NS
Not applicable	0.0	0.3	2.0	1.9	0.2	—	NS
Mean ideal parity	2.4	2.1	2.0	1.8	1.6	1.6	↓↓
Total percent	100.0	100.0	100.0	100.0	100.0	100.0	
Total respondents	1,403	1,511	1,681	1,511	1,607	1,437	

Note: 1982–2002, all female respondents; 2007, those female respondents who were fertile (including pregnant women)
↑↑: Significant increasing trend for the period 1982–2007; p<.01
↓↓: Significant decreasing trend for the period 1982–2007; p<.01
NS: Insignificant increasing or decreasing trend for the period 1982–2007

there may be a notable difference between the number of children that a woman would like to have and the number that she realistically intends to have. Among women of reproductive age in 2007 who already had one child, only a tiny fraction (2.4 %) stated an intention to have an additional child. The vast majority of these women stated an intention to have no further children.

This evidence can be validated by turning to a different survey showing that reported ideal family sizes among young people in Hong Kong are, indeed, well below replacement levels. Basten (2013c), using the Hong Kong Youth Sexuality Survey, found that "ideal parity for women age 18–27 has declined from 1.8 in 1991 to just 1.5 in 2011." Such fertility preferences are important indicators of overall trends in how many more children we can expect current incomplete cohorts to bear. The increasing preference for small families among young women no doubt reflects the disparity in gender roles within the family mentioned earlier as well as other, structural constraints on childbearing such as the cost of living, high levels of investment in education, lack of adequate state support, long working hours, and so on.

A third aspect of fertility projections for Hong Kong relates to the number of births. These numbers have been significantly affected in recent years by "maternity migration" from mainland China and the prevalence of babies born in Hong Kong to mainland women whose spouses are not Hong Kong permanent residents (so-called "Type II" babies) (Basten and Verropoulou 2013). Recently, a series of "administrative and operational measures" has been implemented in order to enforce a new "zero quota" for such babies.[11] This implies that the number of births in Hong Kong could decline dramatically as a consequence of the government's stated desire to see the number of "Type II" babies drop to zero. The potential success of these measures will depend on achieving a consensus between the private and public sectors, as well as implicit support from mainland authorities.

The final point concerning possible future trajectories of fertility in Hong Kong relates to a rather more holistic understanding of "positive feedback effects," perhaps best formulated in the "Low Fertility Trap" hypothesis (Lutz et al. 2006). The theory suggests that feedback effects that tend to lower fertility could operate through three mechanisms. The first, a demographic one, is related to negative population growth leading to fewer women of reproductive age and, hence, fewer births. The second mechanism concerns economic reasoning and, in particular, the impact of aging societies on pessimism among the young regarding their own economic opportunities and chances to receive limited state funds. This, combined with overall improvements in the standard of living and widening consumption opportunities, can lead to an ever greater gap between aspirations and income—a gap that childbearing would only exacerbate, apart from emotional gains. In the context of extremely high inputs to the development of personal human capital, it is possible that such aspirations could be difficult to meet in an increasingly crowded labor market. The third mechanism concerns social norms relating to ideal family size and fertility intentions. This assumes that, through socialization and social learning, family size ideals are influenced by people's experiences. Hence in an environment of small families (e.g., few or no siblings), children will figure less prominently in a young person's image of a desirable life.

Given all of the evidence presented above—of below-replacement fertility preferences, projected population decline, rapid aging, cramped housing, and little policy to support the young—it is tempting to suggest that Hong Kong may, indeed, have fallen into the "Low Fertility Trap."

---

[11] These include banning public hospitals from accepting bookings for delivery by non-local pregnant women and preventing the Department of Health from issuing "Confirmation of Delivery Booking" documents to mainland women. In addition to this, the Hospital Authority has raised the fees for emergency delivery to HK$90,000 (US$11,613) in order to deter "Type II" mothers from circumventing the booking system and arriving to deliver at a hospital's accident and emergency department. The Hong Kong Private Hospital Association has also indicated that a consensus has been reached not to accept any further deliveries of "Type II" babies. Furthermore, specific immigration measures have been introduced to prevent such pregnant women from arriving into Hong Kong. These include increased surveillance and removal actions and stepping up prosecution against individuals and "corporate intermediaries" who are found guilty of violating the regulations. Finally, "the Home Affairs Department has stepped up inspection and enforcement efforts against unlicensed guesthouses" in order to catch women who arrive early to avoid surveillance at the border (HKCSD 2012b, pp. 27–28).

Recent Developments in Population and Family Policy

Population Policy? Family Policy?

In many settings—not least in East Asia—distinguishing the boundaries between population policy and family policy can be a challenge. We might consider that the former is a macro-policy that typically addresses population growth (or decline)—including through tools such as migration—while the latter would concern micro-oriented policies that help individual couples and families to balance work and family life. This could be by providing direct assistance, such as childcare services, parental leave schemes, or child allowances, or by indirect assistance, such as by making the workplace more family friendly. It is clear, however, that addressing these latter issues is a core element of the "population policy" macro-response to population decline and low fertility in many parts of East Asia (see Chen 2012; Song et al. 2013; Sun 2012; Thévenon 2011; Gauthier 2007).

Part of this debate has often revolved around a difficult distinction between explicitly pro-natalist policies that directly "reward" childbearing and broader "family-friendly" policies that seek to help parents have the number of children they would like to have or cope more easily with the children they have already. In reality, these two suites of policies often form two sides of the same coin. In this section we examine the development of population policy in Hong Kong, with a special focus on policies that can be defined as "family friendly/pro-natalist" and policies that focus on social investment and have an impact upon family expenditure.

A Recent History of Fertility-Related Policy in Hong Kong

In September 2002, the Hong Kong government set up a Taskforce on Population Policy, which reported back in February 2003. The taskforce's report set out some basic principles to develop Hong Kong as a "knowledge-based economy" and, as such, was primarily based around "education, manpower development, training for new arrivals, and attracting talents and quality immigrants to Hong Kong" (Hong Kong Legislative Council 2013). In 2007, the Chief Executive (Hong Kong's *de facto* executive leader) set up a Steering Committee on Population Policy. This was comprised of officials from relevant government departments including the Financial Secretary, Secretary for Education, and Secretary for Home Affairs (Hong Kong Legislative Council 2013). A number of policies were introduced or extended in 2007–2008 that could be described as family friendly or having an impact on family expenditure.

In terms of an explicitly pro-natalist policy, the "child allowance under salaries tax"—in effect an annual tax deduction—was increased from HK$40,000 to HK$50,000 (US$5,161 to US$6,451) per child per year. This allowance was only applicable for the third to the ninth child, however, and, as such, was primarily designed to increase higher-order births. Given that the number of women of reproductive age with three or more children is extremely low, the impact of this policy would presumably be limited. More recently, this allowance has been extended to first- and second-born children and, from the 2013/14 tax year, was increased to HK$70,000 (US$9,032) per child per year. This is a tax allowance or deduction, however, in a system already characterized by very low rates of personal income tax, and not a baby bonus. Calculating the precise monetary saving for different income groups is not straightforward because of the various other allowances and progressive tax rate system. We estimate that around 31 % of all married couples would not be eligible for the benefit because their combined taxable income is below the ceiling to qualify for the married couple's tax allowance. A very rough estimate for those eligible would translate into a real cash saving of around HK$349 (US$45) per child per month—roughly the cost of 1.5 kg of baby formula or around 2 days of cram-school fees.

During this period, a number of small, piecemeal family policy initiatives were implemented (see Appendix). The government began providing direct school-fee subsidies for pre-primary education in eligible kindergartens from 2007 to 2008 and, from the following year, senior secondary education was made free of charge for all students in public-sector schools (Hong Kong Government 2009). In November 2012, 11 non-official members from the academic, human-resources management, business, social services, healthcare, and education sectors were appointed to the Steering Committee on Population Policy (SCPP) for 2-year terms (Hong Kong Legislative Council 2013). In addition to examining perennial issues such as manpower, skills, training, and how to attract high-talent migrants, the so-called "revamped" SCPP concentrated on two core issues—namely, the ramifications of the large number of children born to mainland women travelling to Hong Kong (see Basten and Verropoulou 2013) and the consequences of rapid aging (see Cheng et al. 2013; Chan 2003, 2011; Siu 2002). Relatively little attention was focussed on fertility and family issues beyond the issue of cross-border births.

When the 2012 SCPP Progress Report was issued, some members claimed that it was "not comprehensive enough and lack[ed] initiatives to boost up the fertility rate," and some stated that many of the population policy initiatives to date had been "piecemeal and lacked long-term vision." The government was strongly urged to "adopt a holistic approach, set clear directions and goals for the population policy and map out appropriate measures in the Policy Address and the Budget to achieve the goals" (Hong Kong Legislative Council 2013, p. 7).

In partial response to this, on 24 October 2013, the government launched its largest ever public consultation exercise on defining a future, holistic population policy (Hong Kong Government 2013). The consultation period ran until 23 February 2014 and was based around eliciting responses to an extensive consultation document (SCPP 2013b). As part of this process, citizens could attend public forums to discuss population issues, as well as send in suggestions and responses via a dedicated website replete with many resources (SCPP 2013a).

As well as previous emphases on skills development, migration, and support for the elderly, the consultation document covered some topics that had been relatively unexplored in the previous discourse. These included developing an environment that fosters active aging (Cheng et al. 2013; Basten et al. 2013), increasing labor-force participation by focusing on "female homemakers, early retirees, and the disabled," and enhancing and improving education, training, vocational skills, and continued learning. Crucially though, an entire section of the consultation document was devoted to "fostering a supportive environment for our people to form and raise families" (SCPP 2013b). Apart from statements regarding family values, this section gave a useful overview of the challenges of childbearing in Hong Kong and, in particular, the issues relating to cost of living and other burdens. The consultation paper poses and then responds to the question, "Should Governments do more to raise birth rates? If so, what?" The response is worth quoting at length, because it is as close as one can get to a statement on the issue by the Steering Committee on Population Policy:

> ...To some people, the question of childbirth is a family matter that should not involve government intervention. Some also consider that child caring is a family responsibility and the burden should not be shifted to taxpayers or employers. Others doubt the effectiveness of pro-birth policies or family support measures in raising fertility, in view of the mixed results achieved elsewhere. There are also questions on the relevance of overseas measures in Hong Kong's context. Public views are bound to be diverse as to whether we should spend substantial resources on measures to raise fertility in light of other competing policy and livelihood issues.
> ...The SCPP agrees that the Government should not interfere with the childbearing decisions of individuals. Noting from the KAP Survey 2012 that significantly more respondents than before considered that financial incentives and family-friendly measures would increase their desire to have children, the SCPP considers that a more supportive environment for forming and raising families should be explored. But this should be balanced against the additional financial burden on taxpayers and employers, the Government's other more pressing spending priorities due to aging population, and the need to maintain a low tax regime (SCPP 2013b).

This statement clearly emphasizes the long-term nature of problems associated with very low fertility, which are considered secondary to "other more pressing spending priorities...and the need to maintain a low tax regime." While we must wait for the outcome of the consultation process, it is hard to conclude that radical family-friendly policies will be likely in the light of this statement.

What Is the Potential for Policy?

Family-friendly policies, particularly where they have been evoked as a way to increase fertility, have been seen as a means—particularly in Europe—of "bridging the gap" between intentions and reality (Philipov et al. 2009). In Europe, there has generally been a tendency for couples to state an overall preference for two or more children (see Goldstein et al. 2003)—even in the face of the recent economic crisis (Testa and Basten 2012)—although actual fertility levels fall well below this number. This sizeable gap between fertility intentions (higher) and reality (lower) has been interpreted as presenting a policy space for initiatives to help couples realize their stated preferences (Testa 2007; Philipov 2009). In contrast, fertility preferences in Hong Kong, measured through ideal family sizes and intended future fertility at low parities, fall well below those generally reported for Europe (Basten 2013c). This provides evidence for a narrow gap between fertility preferences and reality, implying quite a limited scope for policy initiatives—especially small-scale, piecemeal policies as have been introduced recently in the SAR.

It is necessary to consider the parameters of any possible pro-natalist, family-friendly policy initiatives in Hong Kong in order to gauge their possible chances of success. Firstly, as already described, the territory has long been committed to low rates of both individual and corporate taxation. The lack of tax receipts necessarily limits the scope for the government to implement generous pro-natalist or family-friendly policies—for example, of the type seen in Singapore (Sun 2012; Chuan 2010; Jones 2012). Secondly, and related to the first, in the absence of wide-reaching, state-driven pro-natalist or family-friendly policies, it might be thought that the private sector could "step in" and act as provider in lieu of the public sector. However, as noted earlier, despite the visual spectacle of skyscrapers in the central district, business in the territory is more generally characterized by small- and medium-sized enterprises (SMEs) that are, by their very nature, limited in their ability to offer generous packages to support their workers' familial needs. This combination of a (deliberately) weak social policy capability and an economy dominated by SMEs suggests that the policy space for successful "top-down" pro-natalist or family-friendly policy initiatives is relatively small.

Finally, it is important to return to the relationship between Hong Kong and the rest of the PRC. To a certain degree, labor shortages can be met simply by further relaxing the migration policy that allows workers to cross over from the mainland. Similarly, under recent programs such as the "Guangdong Scheme," the Hong Kong government is making it easier for its elderly population to live on the mainland and still draw their state benefits.[12] Given the difficulties seen in implementing policies to directly, or indirectly, increase fertility across East Asia, and in conjunction with a highly liberal labor market and a low-tax commitment, it is surely tempting for the Hong Kong government to take advantage of its status as a Special Administrative Region within the PRC and implement these rather easier "solutions" to population aging—namely through immigration and outsourcing elder care.

---

[12] The "Guangdong Scheme" represents an innovative means of dealing with the territory's aging population—namely to effectively "outsource" the problem to the neighbouring area. This means that elderly Hong Kong residents are able to take their Old Age Allowance (OAA) and reside in Guangdong. In essence, this policy was an extension of the 1997 Portable Comprehensive Social Security Assistance (PCSSA) scheme that allows Hong Kong citizens age 60 and above to continue to receive their CSSA if they take up permanent residence in Guangdong Province (Hong Kong Social Welfare Department 2013). In 2005 this was extended to cover citizens who take up residence in Fujian Province. Reforms in 2011–12 allow citizens entitled to the OAA—i.e., aged 70 or above—to draw this allowance while resident in Guangdong (with a further eligibility criterion of residency in either Hong Kong or Guangdong for at least 60 days per year).

Conclusion

In order to reverse the very low fertility seen in Hong Kong, it would appear that there should to be "broad social change supportive of children and parenting" (Frejka et al. 2010). This would need to be mediated through explicit family-friendly policy as well as a comprehensive change in the cultural approach to gender roles, working hours, and educational performance, plus new strategies to tackle pressures caused by the cost of living. The extent to which these policies can be driven by the state or the corporate sector is, in the context of Hong Kong, highly questionable. The Steering Committee on Population Policy's 2013 statement on prioritizing more "pressing needs" and a "low tax regime" hardly gives much hope (SCPP 2013b). Rather, for these changes to occur, it may be necessary to have a "bottom-up" revolution in the way that citizens of Hong Kong see the relationship between family and work. While there is certainly evidence that some views are changing—for example, views of gender roles among the younger generation—it would be difficult to imagine that such a seismic change in fertility will happen any time soon. It is even possible to conclude that it may never happen at all.

Appendix: Piecemeal Family Policy Initiatives of the Late 2000s

- The Labour Department began to organize promotional activities (such as "roving exhibitions" and through its network of Human Resources Managers' Clubs) designed to "disseminate information on good family-friendly employment practices"
- The Civil Service Training and Development Institute continued the promotion of better work-life balance among civil servants through seminars, workshops, and online resources
- The Women's Commission co-organized a seminar in 2007 on family-friendly employment practices and issued a promotional leaflet that was widely distributed to business
- The Social Welfare Department stepped up efforts to promote more responsive neighborhood mutual-help childcare services and, from October 2007, to subsidize foster homes to provide non-residential daycare services
- The Community Investment and Inclusion Fund (CIIF) encouraged neighborhood support projects that have a childcare element
- "Family Council" was set up to advise the government on "the formulation of policies and strategies for supporting and strengthening the family and development of related programmes/activities"
- A number of initiatives designed to enhance active aging (for example, through enhanced civic participation and the foundation of 32 "Elder Academies") and improve elder health education and home visits began, and the commission of three studies on the adequacy of present arrangements for finances in retirement (*Source*: Hong Kong Government 2009)

References

Basten, S. (2012, May 3–5). *Changing sexual attitudes in urban East Asia: Extramarital births and premarital conception in Hong Kong SAR.* Paper presented at the annual meeting of the Population Association of America, San Francisco.
Basten, S. (2013a). Comparing projection assumptions of fertility in six advanced Asian economies; Or "thinking beyond the medium variant". *Asian Population Studies, 9*(3), 322–331.
Basten, S. (2013b). Redefining "old age" and "dependency" in East Asia: Is "prospective aging" a more helpful concept? *Asian Social Work and Policy Review, 7*(3), 242–248. doi:10.1111/aswp.12015.
Basten, S. (2013c). *Re-examining the fertility assumptions for Pacific Asia in the UN's 2010 World Population Prospects* (Barnett Papers in Social Research 2013/1). Oxford: Department of Social Policy and Intervention, Oxford Centre for Population Research, University of Oxford.
Basten, S., & Gu, B. (2013). *Childbearing preferences, reform of family planning restrictions, and the low fertility trap in China* (Working Paper 61). Oxford: Department of Social Policy and Intervention, Oxford Centre for Population Research, University of Oxford.
Basten, S., & Verropoulou, G. (2012). *A new look at sex ratios at birth in Hong Kong SAR* (Working Paper 8). Oxford: Department of Social Policy and Intervention, Oxford Centre for Population Research, University of Oxford.
Basten, S., & Verropoulou, G. (2013). "Maternity migration" and the increased sex ratio at birth in Hong Kong SAR. *Population Studies, 67*(3), 323–334.
Basten, S., Yip, P., & Chui, E. (2013). Remeasuring ageing in Hong Kong SAR; Or "keeping the demographic window open". *Journal of Population Research, 30*(3), 249–264. doi:10.1007/s12546-013-9113-1.
Chan, C. K. (2003). Protecting the ageing poor or strengthening the market economy: The case of the Hong Kong Mandatory Provident Fund. *International Journal of Social Welfare, 12*(2), 123–131. doi:10.1111/1468-2397.00250.
Chan, K. K. W. (2010). *Youth and consumption.* Kowloon: University of Hong Kong Press.
Chan, C. K. (2011). *Social security policy in Hong Kong: From British colony to China's Special Administrative Region.* Lanham: Lexington Books.
Chang, K. S. (2003). The state and families in South Korea's compressed fertility transition: A time for policy reversal? *Journal of Population and Social Security, 6*(21), 596–610.
Chang, K. S. (2011). *South Korea under compressed modernity.* Abingdon: Routledge.
Chen, Y. H. (2012). Trends in low fertility and policy responses in Taiwan. *The Japanese Journal of Population, 10*(1), 78–88.
Chen, A. (2013, August 9). Hong Kong's middle class most burdened by high housing costs. *South China Morning Post.*
Cheng, S. T., Lum, T., Lam, L. C. W., & Fung, H. H. (2013). Hong Kong: Embracing a fast aging society with limited welfare. *The Gerontologist, 53*(4), 527–533. doi:10.1093/geront/gnt017.
Cheng, S. T., Chan, T. W. S., Li, G. H. K., & Leung, E. M. F. (2014). Childlessness and subjective well-being in Chinese widowed persons. *The Journals of Gerontology Series B: Psychological Sciences and Social Sciences, 69B*(1), 48–52. doi:10.1093/geronb/gbt049.
Choe, M. K., & Retherford, R. D. (2009). The contribution of education to South Korea's fertility decline to "lowest-low" level. *Asian Population Studies, 5*(3), 267–288. doi:10.1080/17441730903351503.
Chou, K. L., & Chi, I. (2004). Childlessness and psychological well-being in Chinese older adults. *International Journal of Geriatric Psychiatry, 19*(5), 449–457. doi:10.1002/gps.1111.
Chuan, K. E. (2010). Will Singapore's fertility rise in the near future? *Asian Population Studies, 6*(1), 69–82. doi:10.1080/17441731003603462.
Esping-Andersen, G. (2009). *The incomplete revolution: Adapting to women's new roles.* Cambridge: Polity Press.
Frejka, T., Jones, G., & Sardon, J. P. (2010). East Asian childbearing patterns and policy developments. *Population and Development Review, 36*(3), 579–606.
Fuchs, V. R. (1984). Though much is taken: Reflections on aging, health, and medical care. *Milbank Memorial Fund Quarterly, 62*(2), 142–166.

Gauthier, A. H. (2007). The impact of family policies on fertility in industrialized countries: A review of the literature. *Population Research and Policy Review, 26*(3), 323–346. doi:10.1007/s11113-007-9033-x.

Goldstein, J., Lutz, W., & Testa, M. R. (2003). The emergence of sub-replacement family size ideals in Europe. *Population Research and Policy Review, 22*, 479–496.

HKCSD (Hong Kong Census and Statistics Department). (2001). *Population census 2001: Main report*. Hong Kong SAR: HKCSD.

HKCSD (Hong Kong Census and Statistics Department). (2012a). *Hong Kong life tables: 2006–2041*. Hong Kong SAR: HKCSD.

HKCSD (Hong Kong Census and Statistics Department). (2012b). *Hong Kong population projections 2012–2041*. Hong Kong SAR: HKCSD.

HKCSD (Hong Kong Census and Statistics Department). (2012c). Population density by District Council District, 2001, 2006 and 2011 (A202). In: *2011 population census*. http://www.census2011.gov.hk/en/main-table/A202.html. Accessed 28 Mar 2014.

HKCSD (Hong Kong Census and Statistics Department). (2012d). *The fertility trend in Hong Kong, 1981 to 2011*. Hong Kong SAR: HKCSD.

HKCSD (Hong Kong Census and Statistics Department). (2013). *Table E484: Hong Kong life tables, 1971–2012*. http://www.censtatd.gov.hk/hkstat/sub/sp190.jsp?productCode=D5320184. Accessed 28 Mar 2014.

HKEOC (Hong Kong Equal Opportunity Commission). (2010). *Research on family-friendly employment policies and practices in Hong Kong*. http://www.eoc.org.hk/EOC/Upload/UserFiles/File/news/ffep_annex_e.pdf. Accessed 28 Mar 2014.

HKFPA (Family Planning Association of Hong Kong). (2007). *Report on the survey of family planning knowledge, attitude, and practice in Hong Kong, 2007*. Hong Kong SAR: HKFPA.

HKHA (Hong Kong Housing Authority). (2013). *Housing in figures—2013*. Hong Kong SAR: HKHA.

HKLD (Hong Kong Labour Department). (2012). *Report on the policy study on standard working hours*. Hong Kong SAR: HKLD.

Holliday, K. (2014). *Hong Kong's housing market is "least affordable": Survey*. http://www.cnbc.com/id/101349774. Accessed 25 Mar 2014.

Hong, K. Z. (2008). Neither hybrid nor unique: A reinterpretation of the East Asian welfare regime. *Asian Social Work and Policy Review, 2*(3), 159–180. doi:10.1111/j.1753-1411.2008.00017.x.

Hong Kong Government. (2009). *Council for sustainable development's report on the public engagement process on population policy: Government response*. Hong Kong SAR: Hong Kong Government.

Hong Kong Government. (2013). *Transcript of remarks at press conference on population policy public engagement exercise*. http://www.info.gov.hk/gia/general/201310/24/P201310240695.htm. Accessed 28 Mar 2014.

Hong Kong Legislative Council. (2013). *Information note: Hong Kong's population policy (as at 20 March 2013) (IN04/12-12)*. Hong Kong SAR: Hong Kong Legislative Council.

Hong Kong Social Welfare Department. (2013). *Portable Comprehensive Social Security Assistance (PCSSA) scheme*. http://www.swd.gov.hk/en/index/site_pubsvc/page_socsecu/sub_portableco/. Accessed 28 Mar 2014.

Jones, G. W. (2012). Late marriage and low fertility in Singapore: The limits of policy. *Japanese Journal of Population, 10*(1), 89–101.

Jones, G. W., & Gubhaju, B. (2009). Factors influencing changes in mean age at first marriage and never marrying in the low-fertility countries of East and Southeast Asia. *Asian Population Studies, 5*(3), 237–265. doi:10.1080/17441730903351487.

Jones, G. W., & Shen, H. (2008). International marriage in East and Southeast Asia: Trends and research emphases. *Citizenship Studies, 12*(1), 9–25. doi:10.1080/13621020701794091.

Jones, G., Straughan, P. T., & Chan, A. (Eds.). (2009). *Ultra-low fertility in Pacific Asia: Trends, causes, and policy issues*. London: Routledge.

Lee, C. J. (2005). Korean education fever and private tutoring. *KEDI Journal of Educational Policy, 2*(1), 99–107.

Lutz, W., Skirbekk, V., & Testa, M. R. (2006). The low-fertility trap hypothesis: Forces that may lead to further postponement and fewer births in Europe. *Vienna Yearbook of Population Research, 2006*, 167–92. doi:10.1553/populationyearbook2006s167.

Magoshi, E., & Chang, E. (2009). Diversity management and the effects on employees' organizational commitment: Evidence from Japan and Korea. *Journal of World Business, 44*(1), 31–40. doi:10.1016/j.jwb.2008.03.018.

McDonald, P. (2000). Gender equity, social institutions, and the future of fertility. *Journal of Population Research, 17*(1), 1–16.

McDonald, P. (2006). Low fertility and the state: The efficacy of policy. *Population and Development Review, 32*(3), 485–510. doi:10.1111/j.1728-4457.2006.00134.x.

Ogawa, N., Mason, A., Chawla, A., Matsukura, R., & Tung, A. C. (2009). Declining fertility and the rising cost of children. *Asian Population Studies, 5*(3), 289–307. doi:10.1080/17441730903351586.

Philipov, D. (2009). Fertility intentions and outcomes: The role of policies to close the gap. *European Journal of Population, 25*(4), 355–361. doi:10.1007/s10680-009-9202-1.

Philipov, D., Thévenon, O., Klobas, J., Bernardi, L., & Liefbroer, A. (2009). *Reproductive decision-making in a macro–micro perspective (REPRO): State-of-the-art review* (European Demographic Research Papers 1). Vienna: Vienna Institute of Demography, Austrian Academy of Sciences.

Sanderson, W. C., & Scherbov, S. (2007). A new perspective on population aging. *Demographic Research, 16*(2), 27–58.

Sanderson, W. C., & Scherbov, S. (2010). Remeasuring aging. *Science, 329*, 1287–1288.

SCPP (Steering Committee on Population Policy). (2013a). *Thoughts for Hong Kong.* http://www.hkpopulation.gov.hk/public_engagement/en/index.html. Accessed 28 Mar 2014.

SCPP (Steering Committee on Population Policy). (2013b). *Thoughts for Hong Kong: Public engagement exercise on population policy.* Hong Kong SAR: SCPP.

Shik, A. W. Y., & Wong, C. (2012). Demise of the developmental state? Implications for social policy development in Hong Kong. *Asian Social Work and Policy Review, 6*(2), 95–110. doi:10.1111/j.1753-1411.2012.00065.x.

Siu, A. (2002). Hong Kong's mandatory provident fund. *Cato Journal, 22*(2), 317–343.

So, A. Y. (2003). Cross-border families in Hong Kong: The role of social class and politics. *Critical Asian Studies, 35*(4), 515–534. doi:10.1080/1467271032000147014.

Song, Y. J., Chang, K. S., & Sylvian, G. (2013). Why are developmental citizens reluctant to procreate? Analytical insights from Shirley Sun's *Population policy and reproduction in Singapore* and Takeda Hiroko's *The political economy of reproduction in Japan. Inter-Asian Cultural Studies, 14*(3), 481–492. doi:10.1080/14649373.2013.801624.

Sun, S. H. L. (2012). *Population policy and reproduction in Singapore: Making future citizens.* Abington: Routledge.

Testa, M. R. (2007). Childbearing preferences and family issues in Europe: Evidence from the Eurobarometer 2006 Survey. In *Vienna yearbook of population research, 2007* (pp. 357–379). Vienna: Vienna Institute of Demography, Austrian Academy of Sciences. doi:10.1553/populationyearbook2007s357.

Testa, M. R., & Basten, S. (2012). *Have lifetime fertility intentions declined during the "great recession?"* (Working Paper 1209). Vienna: Vienna Institute of Demography, Austrian Academy of Sciences.

Thévenon, O. (2011). Family policies in OECD countries: A comparative analysis. *Population and Development Review, 37*(1), 57–87. doi:10.1111/j.1728-4457.2011.00390.x.

Tokyo Metropolitan Government. (2014). *Population of Tokyo.* http://www.metro.tokyo.jp/ENGLISH/PROFILE/overview03.htm. Accessed 25 Mar 2014.

Tu, E. J. C., Xin, Y., & Xia, Z. (2007). Fertility transition in Hong Kong and Taiwan. In Z. Zhao & F. Guo (Eds.), *Transition and challenge: China's population at the turn of the twenty-first century* (pp. 71–85). Oxford: Oxford University Press.

UNPD (United Nations Population Division). (2011). *Assumptions underlying the 2010 revision*. New York: Population Division, Department of Economic and Social Affairs, United Nations.

UNPD (United Nations Population Division). (2013). *World population prospects: The 2012 revision*. http://esa.un.org/wpp/. Accessed 25 Mar 2014.

Wilson, L. (2013). *How big is a house? Average house size by country.* http://shrinkthatfootprint.com/how-big-is-a-house#Ds7iSzcEP56bFfSw.99. Accessed 25 Mar 2014.

Wong, C. K., Tang, K., & Ye, S. (2011). The perceived importance of family-friendly policies to childbirth decision among Hong Kong women. *International Journal of Social Welfare, 20*(4), 381–392. doi:10.1111/j.1468-2397.2010.00757.x.

World Bank. (2014). *World development indicators*. http://data.worldbank.org/data-catalog/world-development-indicators. Accessed 25 Mar 2014.

Yi, J., & Zhang, J. (2010). The effect of house price on fertility: Evidence from Hong Kong. *Economic Inquiry, 48*(3), 635–650. doi:10.1111/j.1465-7295.2009.00213.x.

Yip, P. S. F., & Lee, J. (2002). The impact of the changing marital structure on fertility of Hong Kong SAR (Special Administrative Region). *Social Science and Medicine, 55*(12), 2159–2169. doi:10.1016/S0277-9536(01)00359-8.

Yip, P. S. F., Lee, J., Chan, B., & Au, J. (2001). A study of demographic changes under sustained below-replacement fertility in Hong Kong SAR. *Social Science and Medicine, 53*(8), 1003–1009. doi:10.1016/S0277-9536(00)00395-6.

Yip, P. S. F., Lee, J., & Cheung, Y. B. (2002). The influence of the Chinese zodiac on fertility in Hong Kong SAR. *Social Science and Medicine, 55*(10), 1803–1812. doi:10.1016/S0277-9536(01)00312-4.

Yip, P. S. F., Li, B. Y. G., Xie, K. S. Y., & Lam, E. (2006). *An analysis of the lowest total fertility rate in Hong Kong SAR* (Discussion Paper). Tokyo: Center for Intergenerational Studies, Institute of Economic Research, Hitotsubashi University.

Chapter 5
Below-Replacement Fertility in Japan: Patterns, Factors, and Policy Implications

Noriko O. Tsuya

This chapter examines the patterns and factors behind Japan's fertility decline to below the replacement level of about 2.1 children per woman, reaching levels so low that its population started to shrink in the late 2000s. Like many other postindustrial societies, Japan has experienced two fertility transitions, the first a decline from historically high to replacement level, which occurred shortly after World War II, and the second a decline since the mid-1970s from replacement to a very low level of childbearing. While the first transition was due primarily to declining rates of childbearing among married couples, the second transition has been related almost entirely to decreasing rates of marriage among young Japanese. In recent years marital fertility has also started to show signs of decline. Combined with decreasing marriages, this reduction of marital fertility has brought Japan's fertility down to very low levels indeed.

The implications of ongoing very low fertility for Japan's labor needs and the challenges associated with rapid population aging and population shrinkage are formidable. But why are young Japanese women and men not marrying? And why are Japanese couples having so few children? This chapter first examines the trends and patterns of changes in fertility and nuptiality in postwar Japan. We next look at the social and economic factors associated with these changes in marriage and childbearing behaviors. To explore possible reasons behind the decline in the rates of marriage and childbearing, we then look at trends and patterns in the gender division of household labor among Japanese couples at reproductive age. The chapter concludes with a discussion of policy responses to these demographic changes and their implications.

N.O. Tsuya (✉)
Department of Economics, Keio University, Minato-ku, Tokyo, Japan
e-mail: tsuya@econ.keio.ac.jp

Trends and Patterns of Marriage and Childbearing

From shortly after World War II to the late 1950s, Japan experienced a sharp downturn in fertility. In a little more than one decade, the birth rate went down by more than one-half, from a total fertility rate (TFR) of 4.5 children per woman in 1947 to 2.0 in 1957 (see Fig. 5.1). After this dramatic decline, Japan's fertility stabilized at 2.0–2.2 children per woman until 1974, when it began to decline again.[1] Since the mid-1970s, fertility has declined to well below the replacement level of 2.1 children per woman, dipping to about 1.5 children per woman in the early 1990s. Since then, the TFR has gone down further, to 1.3–1.4 children per woman since 1995—the "lowest-low" level according to Kohler and colleagues (2002). Although this more recent decline to below-replacement fertility was less dramatic and slower than the earlier postwar decline, its demographic and socioeconomic consequences are much more serious because it has resulted in extreme population aging and population decline.

The two fertility transitions in postwar Japan are different in character and are associated with different demographic factors. The earlier fertility decline occurred not only among women in their prime reproductive years (age 20–34), but also among those age 35 and above (National Institute of Population and Social Security Research 2014, pp. 57–58), thereby suggesting a shift from a pattern of prolonged childbearing to one of deliberately stopping childbearing well before the onset of

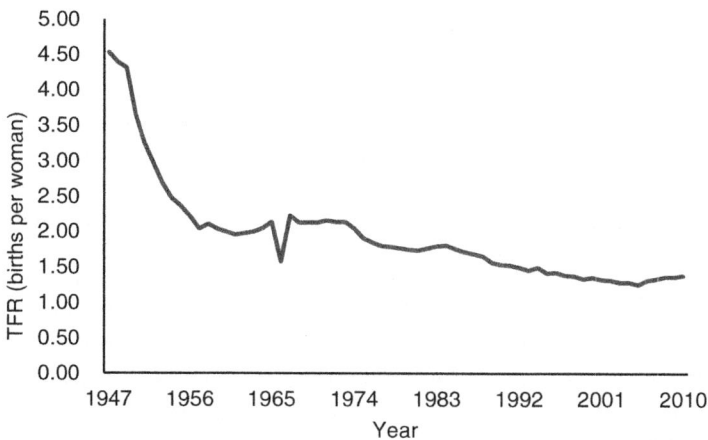

Fig. 5.1 Total fertility rate (TFR), Japan 1947–2010 (National Institute of Population and Social Security Research 2014, pp. 50–51)

---

[1] An exception was 1966, a year of *hinoe-uma* (fire horse) when TFR declined temporarily to 1.6 per woman. A year of *hinoe-uma* occurs every 60 years according to the Chinese zodiacal calendar. Fire-horse years were traditionally regarded as an unlucky years to give birth to a girl because girls born in such a year were believed to be stubborn and thus would find it difficult to attract a husband.

natural sterility. In contrast, the fertility decline to below-replacement levels involved a marked decrease in fertility among women in their 20s, but among women in their 30s fertility actually increased, reflecting delays of marriage and childbearing.

An examination of changes in the age pattern of women's marriage suggests that decreasing marriage has played a major role in Japan's fertility decline to below-replacement levels. After modest decreases during the earlier postwar fertility transition, the proportions never-married among women in their 20s and 30s were relatively stable until the mid-1970s when they started to rise precipitously. Among women age 25–29, the proportion never-married jumped from 18 % in 1975 to 60 % in 2010. Over the same 35-year period, the proportion never-married among women age 30–34 rose from 8 to 35 %, while among women age 35–39, the proportion never-married rose from 5 to 23 %. Among Japanese women, the celibacy rate, or proportion never-married at age 50, rose from 5 % in 1995 to 11 % in 2010.

The tendency toward delayed marriage or non-marriage is even more evident among Japanese men. Among men age 25–29, the proportion never-married rose from 48 % in 1975 to 72 % in 2010. Over the same period, the proportion never-married among men age 30–34 rose from 14 to 47 %, and among men age 35–39, the proportion never-married rose from 6 to 36 %. The celibacy rate for men increased from 2 % in 1975 to 20 % in 2010. This extremely rapid expansion of the population of single, middle-aged men (and, to a lesser extent, women) has profound implications not only for Japan's population, but also for its economy and society as a whole. Given a very low level of out-of-wedlock childbearing—around 1–2 % of all live births since 1960 (National Institute of Population and Social Security Research 2014, p. 67)—these unmarried men and women are likely to have no children to depend on in their old age. As Japan's social security and welfare schemes have been designed with family as the primary safety net, a proliferation of single, childless elderly people will certainly pose serious challenges for the country's social systems.

The declining marriage rate is confirmed by sharp increases in the singulate mean age at marriage (SMAM) for both sexes.[2] According to Japanese census data, the SMAM was relatively stable until 1975, when it started to increase, rising for women from 24.5 years in 1975 to 29.7 years in 2010 and for men from 28.7 years to 31.2 years over the same period.[3] Although several European countries, such as Sweden, Germany, and Spain, had comparable or even higher SMAMs in 2010 (UNECE 2013), the mean ages at first marriage for Japanese women and men are among the highest in the world today.

---

[2] The SMAM is an estimate of the average number of years lived by a cohort of persons before their first marriage. For specifics on this indicator of the timing of first marriage, see Hajnal (1953).

[3] Mean ages at first marriage can also be calculated directly from the registration of marriages, available for Japan since 1899. Based on this data source, the average age at first marriage rose between 1975 and 2010 from 24.7 to 28.8 for women and from 27.0 to 30.5 for men (National Institute of Population and Social Security Research 2014, p. 103).

Altogether, these numbers clearly indicate the rise of late marriage and non-marriage among Japanese women and men at reproductive ages since the mid-1970s. In the Asian context, where marriage has traditionally been universal and most women have typically married by their mid- to late twenties (Smith 1980), the increasing postponement or avoidance of marriage among young Japanese is indeed remarkable and has profound demographic and socioeconomic impacts.[4] With little childbearing outside marriage, delayed marriage and increasing non-marriage lead to delayed and less childbearing. As shown above, dramatic fertility declines to very low levels among women at prime childbearing years occurred at the same time as the sharp increase in proportions never-married among women in their 20s and 30s. This implies that decisions regarding marriage and childbearing are likely to be interdependent for young Japanese women and men. Put differently, they may be delaying or forgoing marriage because they do not (yet) want to have a child.

Turning to marital fertility, the mean completed family size of Japanese wives at reproductive ages has shown signs of decline in recent years. Based on time-series data drawn from Japan's national fertility surveys conducted from 1977 to 2010 (National Institute of Population and Social Security Research 2012b, pp. 28–37), the average number of children ever-born declined moderately but steadily from the early 1990s to 2010. Nevertheless, among wives married for 15 or more years (i.e., couples considered to have finished their family building), the average family size generally corresponds to the average *intended* number of children (around 2.0–2.3 children per couple). This suggests that although the completed family size of Japanese couples has been decreasing, couples in general are having as many children as they plan to have.

By contrast, the average *ideal* number of children (that wives report as ideal for themselves and their husbands) is considerably larger than the average number of children that couples actually have, although the number tends to be somewhat smaller among recently married couples. Among all married couples, the ideal number of children averaged 2.7 in 1987 and 2.4 in 2010. The corresponding number decreased from 2.5 to 2.3 among those who have been married for less than 5 years (National Institute of Population and Social Security Research 2012b, pp. 28–30). Altogether, it appears that a considerable proportion of Japanese couples do not have as many children as they want (see Tsuya et al. 2013b).

In summary, the findings presented in this section suggest that we have to examine the social and economic correlates of declining marriage to explain Japan's below-replacement fertility since the mid-1970s. In the following sections we will look at changes in educational attainment and employment—socioeconomic factors thought responsible for changing marriage behaviors of young Japanese women and men. To explore a possible factor associated with declining marital fertility, we will also compare men's and women's contributions to housework with hours employed outside the home in order to show the changing relationship, or lack thereof, between work and family life among Japanese couples.

---

[4] Delayed marriage has also occurred widely in other East and Southeast Asian countries in recent years. See Jones (1997, 2004).

Trends in Women's and Men's Economic Opportunities

To explore the socioeconomic factors underlying decreasing marriages, we first look at changes in educational attainment of young Japanese women as compared to their male counterparts. According to existing studies (Raymo 1998, 2003; Tsuya 2009, 2012; Tsuya and Mason 1995), young women's increasing educational attainment is a major factor that has caused delayed and fewer marriages in Japan since the mid-1970s. Table 5.1 shows changes, by sex, in the percentage of graduates advancing from junior high school to high school and on to junior college or 4-year college or university. Because Japan's formal education system is highly competitive, with strong age barriers, people rarely have the luxury of alternating their commitments between education and other activities, such as employment. Economic and social disadvantages accrue for those who do not succeed in a series of structured "contests" at specific time points in their educational careers or at their entrance into the labor market (Brinton 1988; Tsuya and Choe 2004; Turner 1960). As a result, in Japan advancement to higher education and entry into the labor market tend to occur mostly within a narrow time frame, from the late teens to the early twenties.

We can see from Table 5.1 that the rate of educational advancement beyond high school increased sharply for women between 1970 and 1975, which is just before the onset of fertility decline to below-replacement levels. In the same period, high-school education became virtually universal.[5] While a similar leap in the advancement rate from high school to university is seen for men in the same period, the male advancement rate shows moderate declines and stagnation from 1975 to the mid-1990s. Furthermore, whereas the female advancement rate to junior college peaked at around 25 % in the mid-1990s, the rate of females advancing on to university has continued to increase rapidly and steadily, reaching 45 % in 2010.

Given the rising advancement rates to higher education, the proportion of young women who are enrolled in or have completed junior college or 4-year college or university has increased sharply, with especially dramatic gains in the 1970s and 1980s. The proportion of women age 20–24 with higher education rose from 6 % in 1960, to 17 % in 1970, 40 % in 1980, and 60 % in 2010 (Sorifu Tokeikyoku 1964, 1973, 1984; National Institute of Population and Social Security Research 2014, p. 175). The proportion of women age 25–29 with higher education increased from 4 % in 1960 to 26 % in 1980, and 52 % in 2010.

These findings suggest that educational opportunities for women have expanded dramatically since 1970. Although the proportion of young men with higher education also increased after 1990 (and is still somewhat higher than that of young women), the increases among women have been steeper and more consistent.

How are these gains in educational attainment among young Japanese women related to their employment patterns? Table 5.2 shows the percentages of female

---

[5] Education through junior high school (9 years of schooling) is compulsory in Japan. Junior-high-school enrollment has been almost universal since World War II (Monbu-kagaku-sho 2012).

Table 5.1 Percentages of graduates advancing from junior high school to high school and from high school on to junior college or four-year college/university, by sex: Japan 1950–2010

Year	Percent advancing from junior high school to high school and from high school on to higher-level education					
	Females			Males		
	High school[a]	Junior college[b]	Four-year college/university[b]	High school[a]	Junior college[b]	Four-year college/university[b]
1950	37	–	–	48	–	–
1955	47	3	2	56	2	13
1960	56	3	3	60	1	14
1965	70	7	5	72	2	21
1970	83	11	7	82	2	27
1975	93	20	13	91	3	40
1980	95	21	12	93	2	39
1985	95	21	14	93	2	39
1990	96	22	15	93	2	33
1995	97	25	23	95	2	41
2000	97	17	32	96	2	48
2005	98	13	37	97	2	51
2010	98	11	45	98	1	56

Monbu-kagaku-sho (2012)
[a]Junior high school graduates who advanced to high school within 1 year after graduation. Figures include those who were working while enrolled in high school but exclude those who were *ronin* (literally, masterless *samurai*; this term refers to graduates who have failed to matriculate and are waiting for another chance to enter a higher-level school)
[b]Percentages are computed by dividing the number of persons who entered junior college or four-year college/university in a given year by the number of junior high school graduates 3 years before

and male graduates obtaining regular employment (full-time employment with job security and fringe benefits) within 1 year of graduation by educational level. The changing percentages from 1950 to 2010 reveal strikingly different trends for the two lower and two higher levels of education. For junior-high-school and high-school graduates, the rate of obtaining regular employment upon graduation declined precipitously in the 1970s and reached low levels in the 1980s and 1990s, presumably due to the rapid spread of higher education. In contrast, the rate of obtaining regular employment among female junior college and university graduates increased steadily from 1970 to 1990, with the gender gap among university graduates disappearing completely by 1990.

During the 1990s, the rate of obtaining regular employment upon graduation decreased dramatically for both sexes and at all educational levels. This was presumably triggered by the burst of Japan's "bubble economy" at the end of the 1980s, which set the stage for fundamental changes in the nature of the Japanese economy and the types of jobs available to young people. In the early 1990s, in an attempt to increase their competitiveness and profitability in the face of economic globalization, employers began to move away from offering lifetime employment, a long-prevalent feature of the postwar Japanese labor market (Cargill et al. 1997, pp. 91–116). This resulted in rapid increases of temporary employment such as

Table 5.2 Percentages of graduates obtaining regular employment upon graduation at different educational levels, by sex: Japan, 1950–2010

Sex and year	Percent obtaining regular employment by level of education completed			
	Junior high school	High school	Junior college	Four-year college/university
Females				
1950	44	36	–	45
1955	41	39	43	68
1960	38	59	50	64
1965	26	63	57	67
1970	16	61	69	60
1975	6	48	73	63
1980	3	46	76	66
1985	3	43	81	72
1990	2	36	88	81
1995	1	23	66	64
2000	1	16	57	57
2005	0	15	67	64
2010	0	13	67	67
Males				
1950	46	48	–	64
1955	43	54	67	75
1960	40	64	80	86
1965	27	58	84	87
1970	17	55	81	83
1975	6	41	76	78
1980	5	40	72	79
1985	5	39	73	79
1990	4	34	73	81
1995	2	28	57	69
2000	2	21	41	55
2005	1	20	51	57
2010	1	18	48	56

Monbu-kagaku-sho (2012)
Note: Figures are percentages of graduates who obtained regular employment (full-time employment with job security and fringe benefits) within 1 year of graduation

keiyaku (employment under a fixed-term contract with limited provision of social insurance) or *haken* (contract work whereby an agency sends workers to an organization for a specified period) (Igarashi 2009).

Workers with these temporary jobs tend to be young: 61 % of those employed as *keiyaku* or *haken* in 2005 were age 15–34 (Somusho Tokeikyoku 2005). Another notable phenomenon in the Japanese labor market is an increase of so-called "*freeta*," young people who do not hold a stable job but rather hop from one temporary job to another (Somusho Tokeikyoku 2005). This deterioration of employment prospects for young people has also occurred in newly industrializing economies in

Asia and in many industrialized countries in the West (Imai 1999; ILO 2011; Lee 2010; OECD 2002, pp. 129–69). As in other industrialized societies (Oppenheimer 1994; Oppenheimer et al. 1997), the proliferation of temporary employment has likely had a negative impact on marriage and the family in Japan (Igarashi 2009; Kohara 2010), particularly affecting the marriage prospects of young men with temporary jobs (Tsuya 2012).

To assess how young women and men fare once they enter the labor force, not just immediately after graduating from school, we next look at changes in age-specific labor-force participation rates by sex from 1960 to 2010. As shown in the upper panel of Table 5.3, the labor-force participation rate for women age 25–34 increased rapidly after the mid-1970s. Labor-force participation for women in their 30s still dips somewhat, compared with younger and older women, confirming the well-known M-shaped age pattern of Japanese women's employment (Brinton 1988), but the drop in labor-force participation among women at peak childrearing ages has become much less notable in recent years. Although there is still a tendency for Japanese women to exit the labor force upon the birth of their first child

Table 5.3 Labor-force participation rates (percent) by age and sex: Japan, 1960–2010

Sex and year	Percent participating in labor force by age and sex						
	15–19	20–24	25–29	30–34	35–39	40–44	45–49
Females							
1960	50	69	50	51	55	57	57
1965	38	70	47	48	58	62	63
1970	36	71	45	47	56	64	65
1975	23	67	44	43	53	60	62
1980	19	71	49	47	56	62	62
1985	17	73	54	49	58	66	66
1990	17	76	61	51	59	67	68
1995	16	74	66	53	59	67	69
2000	15	71	70	57	60	68	70
2005	16	69	73	62	62	69	73
2010	14	66	72	65	64	68	72
Males							
1960	52	88	97	98	98	98	97
1965	39	87	98	99	98	98	98
1970	37	84	98	99	99	98	98
1975	23	79	98	99	99	98	98
1980	20	75	98	99	99	98	98
1985	19	75	97	98	98	98	98
1990	20	75	97	98	98	98	98
1995	19	76	96	98	98	98	98
2000	17	70	92	95	96	96	96
2005	17	69	90	93	94	94	95
2010	15	66	86	89	91	91	92

National Institute of Population and Social Security Research (2014, p. 137)

and re-enter it once their last child enters school, it appears that this pattern now has less influence on labor-force participation rates, largely because of declining marriage rates among this age group. The labor-force participation rates for women in their late 30s and in their 40s has also risen substantially, implying that women at these higher reproductive ages are less likely to be married than in the past and, even if they are married, are more likely to be employed.

Men's labor-force participation rates have been declining slowly but steadily at all ages since the late 1990s, with an especially notable decrease among men age 20–34 (see the lower panel of Table 5.3). Given that almost all (98 % or above) married men age 20–49 are employed and a large proportion of them employed full-time (Tsuya et al. 2013a), this suggests that labor-force participation has gone down particularly steeply among unmarried men. Viewed from the other direction, this finding implies that men without a job (especially a regular job) are more likely to be unmarried than men who are employed full-time.

These findings show that women's employment has been rising since the mid-1970s, including among women of peak childbearing age. Because there is an obvious interdependence between women's employment and family formation, it is difficult to estimate the effects on marriage and childbearing of these changes in women's labor-force participation. Nonetheless, improved education and labor-market opportunities for young women—in the face of deteriorating employment prospects for men—may well lie behind the increasing postponement or avoidance of marriage (Tsuya 2009, 2012).

Gender Relations at Home

As shown in the previous section, women's educational attainment has reached levels comparable to men's, making possible an array of previously unavailable life options and, at the same time, providing exposure to values that compete with women's domestic roles. Views supporting traditional gender roles have been eroding in Japan, especially among young women (Bumpass and Choe 2004; Choe et al. 2014; Lee et al. 2010; Retherford et al. 1996), resulting in a widening gap between young women and men in their expectations about marriage.

A central factor in the context of these socioeconomic and attitudinal changes is the persistence of the traditional gender division of labor in Japanese marriages, which places heavy obligations on women for household maintenance and childcare and leaves men largely free of such domestic responsibilities. According to data drawn from a series of Japan's national time-use surveys, men's average share in total time devoted to housework and childcare in 1986 was only 5 % (Tsuya 2010). By 2006, Japanese men's share in time devoted to domestic tasks had increased to 15 %.[6] In contrast, significant increases in men's contributions to domestic chores

---

[6] South Korea also has a low level of men's domestic contribution, similar to Japan's. The average contribution of Korean men to time spent on housework and childcare rose modestly from 11 % in 1990 to 17 % in 2004. For details, see Tsuya (2010).

have been widely documented in many Western countries and, as a consequence, the gender gap in household task allocation has narrowed substantially (Bianchi et al. 2000; Fuwa 2004; Gershuny 2000). For example, men's average share in housework and childcare time increased in Norway from 16 % in 1972 to 40 % in 2000–2001. Likewise, it rose in the United Kingdom from 12 % in 1961 to 35 % in 2000–2001. In the United States, it increased from 21 % in 1965 to 38 % in 2006 (Tsuya 2010; United Nations 1991, pp. 101–102; 1995, pp. 132–33, 2010, pp. 211–12). Overall, compared with their Western counterparts, Japanese women shoulder a much larger share of domestic tasks, while Japanese men's contribution has remained notably low.

Furthermore, parenting tends to be much more intensive in Japan than in the West, and it is overwhelmingly the mother who is responsible for looking after children's daily needs and making sure they succeed in their education (Brinton 1990; Hirao 2001; Tsuya and Choe 2004). Under Japan's competitive education system, there are strong pressures for parents to enroll their children in academic after-school programs such as cram schools (called "*juku*") or private tutoring (called "*katei-kyoshi*"), and these programs can be costly both financially and in terms of the mother's time. Paying for children's education, especially after-school programs, has been the most frequently cited reason for mothers' employment in recent decades (Tsuya and Choe 2004). Using data drawn from the 1994, 2000, and 2009 national family surveys in Japan, we examine more closely recent changes in the household division of labor among currently married women and men age 20–49.[7] Looking at the average time that these couples spend each week on core housework tasks (the upper panel of Table 5.4), we can see, as expected, very large gender differences in all three survey years. While wives spent roughly 30 h per week on household tasks, husbands spent only 2–3 h per week. Women in other countries also spend more time on housework than men (Fuwa 2004; Gershuny 2000), but the differences in Japan are extreme.

Yet we also see some signs of change in the gender allocation of housework. Wives' average time spent on housework declined from about 33 h per week in 1994 to 27 h in 2009, while the corresponding hours for husbands increased modestly, from 2.3 to 3.4 h. Consequently, husbands' share in couples' time spent on housework rose from 7 to 12 %. These changes are all in the direction of more gender balance at home, although husbands' time devoted to housework is still very small. Another notable change is a sizable decline in the proportion of husbands who do not do any housework at all. This has gone down from approximately 42 % in 1994 to 22 % in 2009. Japanese husbands seem to be increasingly drawn into the domestic arena traditionally considered as female, crossing the symbolic gender barrier associated with doing any housework at all.

Turning to couples' employment time, we can see from the lower panel of Table 5.4 that in all 3 years almost all husbands were employed and their average

---

[7] For specifics of the 1994, 2000, and 2009 surveys, see Tsuya and Bumpass (2004), Rindfuss et al. (2004), and Tsuya et al. (2013a), respectively.

Table 5.4 Mean housework hours per week, percent employed, and mean employment hours per week: Currently married women and men age 20–49 and their spouses: Japan, 1994, 2000, and 2009

	Hours worked per week					
	1994		2000		2009	
	Mean	(N)	Mean	(N)	Mean	(N)
Housework[a]						
Wives' hours	33.4	(1,210)	28.8	(2,417)	27.4	(1,648)
Husbands' hours	2.3	(1,224)	2.7	(2,384)	3.4	(1,643)
Husbands' share (percent)	7.0	(1,202)	9.4	(2,366)	11.8	(1,634)
Percent of husbands who do no housework	41.9	(1,210)	30.4	(2,384)	22.0	(1,643)
Employment[b]						
Percent of husbands employed	99.5	(1,236)	98.6	(2,417)	98.5	(1,652)
Work hours of employed husbands	51.0	(1,230)	49.9	(2,383)	50.2	(1,627)
Percent of wives employed	58.3	(1,236)	62.1	(2,376)	61.5	(1,641)
Work hours of employed wives	35.8	(721)	33.1	(1,475)	32.0	(1,652)

Upper panel is from Tsuya et al. (2013a)
Note: Mean hours and percentages are weighted for 2000 and 2009, but unweighted for 1994; the number of cases is unweighted for all 3 years
[a]Computed by summing the time devoted to cleaning house, doing laundry, cooking, cleaning after meals, and grocery shopping. Housework hours do not include time spent on childcare
[b]Usual hours spent on employment per week, excluding commuting time

work hours, excluding commuting time, remained stable at around 50–51 h per week. Wives' employment patterns changed somewhat during the late 1990s, but there was little further change after 2000. Wives' employment rates rose from 58 % in 1994 to 62 % in 2000 and remained at that level thereafter. The average work hours of employed wives declined from 36 h per week in 1994 to 33 h in 2000 and 32 h in 2009. This decrease in employed wives' average work hours was due to decreases in the proportion of wives employed full time (working 35 or more hours per week) and increases in the proportion of those employed part time (working less than 35 h per week).

In summary, while the rate of employment among young, unmarried Japanese men has declined, virtually all married men at peak working ages are employed. Many of these husbands work for long hours—about 50 h per week excluding commuting time, i.e., 10 h per day assuming a 5-day work week. If commuting time is added to time spent at the workplace, husbands' time away from home becomes even longer, and this likely has a negative impact on their involvement in family life and their contribution to domestic tasks. On the other hand, roughly 60 % of Japanese wives at reproductive ages are employed, and about one-half of those who are employed work 35 h or more per week. Given that many of these employed wives are also mothers of preschool- or school-age children, they likely face difficulties in balancing their work and family responsibilities.

How does time spent on housework relate to time spent on the job? As shown in Fig. 5.2, wives' housework time declines as their own employment time increases, especially when they work full time (35 h or more per week), but husbands' housework time remains very low regardless of their wives' employment time. Husbands' housework hours do increase a bit when their wives work full time, and the increase is statistically significant. Nevertheless, the overall picture that we see from the figure is that Japanese wives are juggling their domestic and labor-market roles without much help from their husbands.

Finally, we explore how men's persistently low contribution to housework and the resulting unequal gender relations at home may be affecting marriage rates. We do this by comparing housework time of never-married Japanese men and women age 20–49 with that of their currently married counterparts. Based on data drawn from the same national family surveys in 1994, 2000, and 2009 used above, a large majority (roughly two-thirds) of never-married women spent fewer than 10 h per week on household tasks. In contrast, a sizable proportion (roughly 40–60 %) of their currently married counterparts spent 30 h or more per week on housework.[8] The small number of hours that unmarried women spend on housework is as expected, given that more than 80 % of them live with their parents, and their mothers are likely to be responsible for most of the housework. In contrast, whether they are married or not, men contribute, on average, only 2–4 h per week of housework. Although the percentage of men who do not perform any housework is declining, a large majority (roughly 70–80 %) continue to spend less than 5 h per week on household tasks.

These numbers clearly illustrate a dramatic change in women's lives after marriage—large increases in the time they spend on housework and caring for the family. By marrying, Japanese women change their position from a receiver to a primary provider of care. By contrast, Japanese men remain largely at the receiving end, with the main provider of domestic services switching from their mothers to their wives.

What does the future hold? Since many Japanese husbands currently spend little time on domestic tasks, if there is a change in their domestic contributions, the direction is likely to be upward. For this to occur, however, we need to see a movement toward husbands spending a great deal more time at home. Such a change seems unlikely, however, given the persistence of Japan's traditional workplace culture that places a high value on long work hours. Since their husbands are not helping much at home, wives often have no choice but to combine heavy domestic responsibilities with long hours of paid employment outside the home.

The unequal gender division of household labor is central to the traditional marriage "package" in Japan (Rindfuss 2004), and it has been slow to change. The persistence of an unequal gender division of labor at home, combined with increasing economic opportunities and rapidly changing gender roles in the workplace, make the traditional marriage package particularly unattractive to many young Japanese women. This situation likely discourages young women from marrying

---

[8] For more detailed information, see Tsuya et al. (2013a).

5 Below-Replacement Fertility in Japan: Patterns, Factors, and Policy Implications

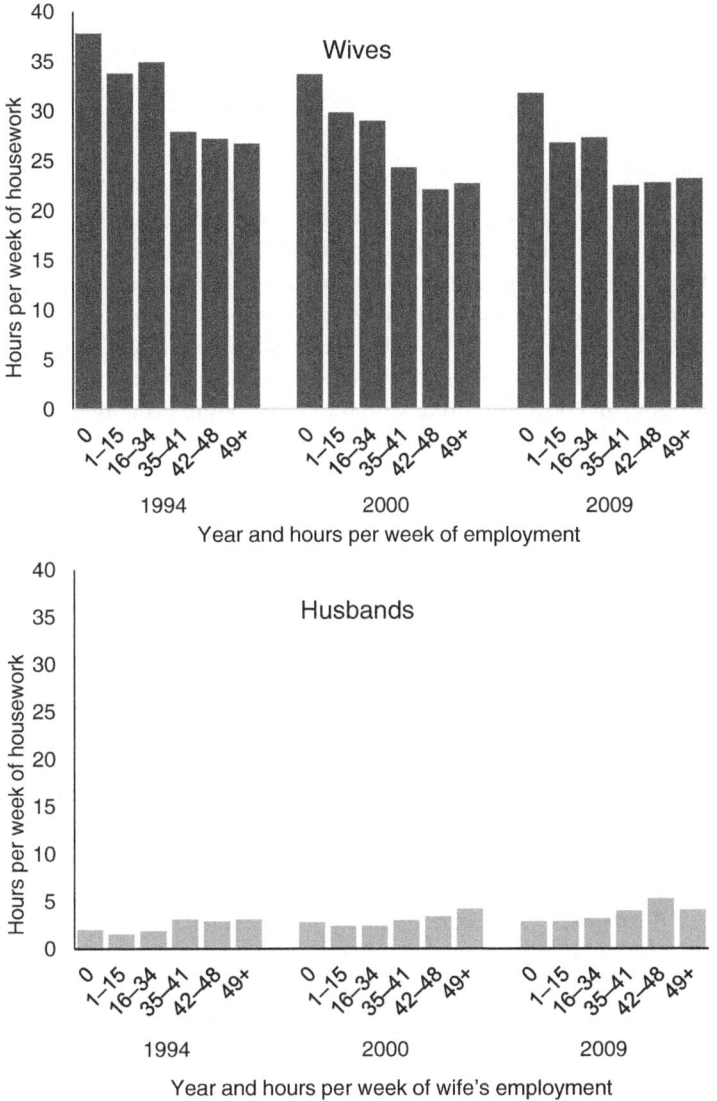

Fig. 5.2 Wives' and husbands' average housework hours per week by wives' weekly employment hours, Japan, 1994, 2000, and 2009 (Tsuya et al. 2013a)

and discourages wives from having more children. Men, too, may find the discrepancy between their expectations and those of potential spouses a cause for apprehension about marrying. Hence, making gender relations at home more equal may well be critical, not only to Japanese marriage and family life, but also to fertility and population in the future.

Policy Responses and Implications

Later marriage and non-marriage in Japan have most likely arisen, at least in part, from growing educational and economic opportunities for young women, coupled with persistently unequal gender relations in the home. If these factors are indeed militating against marriage, and if childbearing outside of marriage remains very low, then Japan's fertility is likely to remain at very low levels for some time to come. This, in turn, will accelerate the pace of Japan's already rapid population aging and population decline.[9] Given the trend in recent decades, educational attainment of young Japanese women is likely to continue to rise. Entry of young women into career-oriented employment is also expected to increase (Retherford et al. 2001), as in the long run the demand for qualified young workers will increase with population aging and decline. Along with these expanding economic opportunities, attitudes are changing about the importance of marriage for women (Bumpass and Choe 2004; Choe et al. 2014; Retherford et al. 1996).

Apart from making gender relations at home more equal, the most promising option for reversing the downward trend of marriage and childbearing in Japan seems to be through policies and programs that help Japanese couples balance their work and domestic roles. Concerned about very low fertility and rapid population aging, the Japanese government has formulated various family policies and programs and promoted them actively since the early 1990s (Tsuya 2005). As in other industrialized countries, these family policies and programs consist of three major components: (1) childcare services; (2) parental leave schemes; and (3) monetary assistance in the form of child allowances.

To bolster fertility, the Japanese government has implemented a succession of childcare-related legislation and programs—the Angel Plan of 1994, the New Angel Plan of 1999, the Plus-One Plan of 2002, the Basic Law to Address Low Fertility (*Shoshika Shakai Kihon Ho*) of 2003, the Strategy to Assist Children and Families (*Kodomo to Kazoku wo Ouensuru Nihon Juten Senryaku*) of 2007, the Vision for Children and Childcare (*Kodomo Kosodate Bijyon*) of 2008, and the 2013 Plan to Accelerate the Reduction of Preschool Children on Waiting Lists (*Taiki Jido Kaisho Kasokuka Puran*). These were all designed to help parents of preschool children balance their work and domestic responsibilities by providing more childcare services and encouraging the workplace to become more family friendly (Naikakufu 2012).

According to the government's annual report on childcare services (Kosei-rodo-sho 2013a; Miura 2001),[10] the number of slots available in daycare centers and the number of children enrolled have both increased since 2000, but the number of

---

[9] According to the medium fertility and mortality variants in Japan's latest official population projection, the country's population is projected to decrease from 128 million in 2010 to around 87 million by 2060. In that year, roughly 40 % of Japan's population will be age 65 and above (National Institute of Population and Social Security Research 2012a).

[10] The Japan Ministry of Health, Labour, and Welfare has conducted a survey on the availability of childcare services (*Hoikusho Nyusho Taiki-jido-su Chosa*) annually since 1994. The survey is based on reports from municipal governments on childcare centers (both public and private) in their jurisdictions.

children on waiting lists has also gone up. This suggests that the demand for childcare services is growing faster than the supply, presumably because of rapidly increasing employment rates among mothers of preschool-age children (Tsuya et al. 2013a). It is also likely that the very increase in availability of childcare services has led to further increases in demand.

There also persist large regional differences in the demand and supply of childcare services. While there tends to be an excess supply (more slots available at daycare centers than applicants) in rural areas, there is an acute shortage of childcare services in large metropolitan areas (Kosei-rodo-sho 2013a; Naikakufu 2003). The increase in employment among mothers with small children has occurred despite the shortage of affordable childcare services of good quality in large metropolitan areas and has, in fact, contributed to the shortage. This has become a major policy concern in Japan in recent years (Kosei-rodo-sho 2010a).

Turning to Japan's parental leave scheme, the government enacted the Maternity and Childcare Leave Law (*Ikuji Kyugyo Ho*) in 1992 and revised it in 1995, 2005, 2007, and 2009 (Kosei-rodo-sho 2010b, 2013b). Since the scheme's beginning in 1992, the duration of leave has been, in principle, 12 months (until the child's first birthday).[11] The leave is applicable to working parents who: (1) are covered by national employment insurance; (2) have been employed for at least 12 months; and (3) have worked at least 11 days in every month during the 2 years prior to the beginning of the leave. To be covered by national employment insurance, employees normally have to work at least 20 h per week and are expected to be employed for at least 31 days prior to taking leave (Kosei-rodo-sho 2013c). In short, parental leave is not applicable to mothers (or fathers) who work less than 20 h per week, or work less than 11 days per month, or have been employed for a short time.

Parental leave was first offered without pay, but in 1995 income compensation was introduced at 25 % of monthly pay prior to the beginning of leave.[12] Of this 25 % compensation, 20 % was payable during the leave and the remaining 5 % payable upon returning to employment. The level of income compensation was raised to 40 % in 2000, with 30 % payable during the leave and the remaining 10 % upon resumption of employment. The level of compensation was raised further to 50 % in 2007, with 30 % payable during the leave and the remaining 20 % payable upon returning to work. Then, as of April 2010, the division of compensation into two parts—one during the leave and the other upon resumption of employment—was abolished. The full 50 % compensation is now paid during the leave (Kosei-rodo-sho 2013b).

---

[11] Under the 2009 revision of the law, the duration of leave can be extended to 14 months when both parents take parental leave together (rather than one parent taking leave alone). The duration of leave can be further extended up to 18 months under certain circumstances such as the lack of available slots at childcare centers or when a parent who is the primary caregiver becomes unable to care for the child due to illness, injury, or marital dissolution. For more specifics, see Kosei-rodo-sho (2010b, 2013b).

[12] While the parental leave scheme is national, municipal governments are responsible for the handling/management of monetary provisions.

The major shortcomings of Japan's parental leave scheme seem to be its limited coverage, a relatively low level of income compensation, and, most importantly, the lack of legally binding authority. The leave has not been applicable to mothers (or fathers) who work, in terms of days or hours, less than one-half the time of full-time employees or who have worked only for a short period. With regard to income compensation, the current level (50 % of pay prior to the beginning of leave) is low compared with the level offered in many Western European countries where the compensation level has generally been 70 % or higher (Tsuya 2005). Further, although it has been required since 1995 for all employers to offer parental leave to all eligible employees, there is no legal sanction against non-compliance. Consequently, the proportion of employers that do not have (or have not yet formulated) specific rules regarding parental leave remains substantial, especially among small organizations. According to the Basic Survey on Equal Employment (*Koyo Kinto Kihon Chosa*) conducted by the government, the proportion of organizations that have formulated specific rules regarding parental leave has been increasing gradually but is not yet universal, particularly among organizations with less than 30 employees. As of 2010, about 70 % of small-sized organizations had rules on parental leave (Kosei-rodo-sho 2013e).[13] To the extent that the formulation of rules pertaining to parental leave indicates compliance with the law, this suggests that a considerable proportion of small-sized organizations are not in compliance. As a result, although use of the parental leave scheme has increased over time, it has not yet become universal: around 84 % of eligible mothers (eligible female employees who gave birth within the past 12 months) took parental leave in 2010 (Kosei-rodo-sho 2013c).[14]

Launched in 1972, the child allowance scheme (*jidou teate seido*) initially covered third and higher-order children in households with incomes below a certain level. The duration of payment was from a child's birth to graduation from junior high school (Tsuya 2005). Since then, although still income tested, the scheme has been expanded to cover lower-order births, and the amount of allowance has increased, especially since 2000. Nonetheless, the amount offered is still relatively small, compared with levels offered in Western European countries (Tsuya 2005). As of 2012, it was 15,000 yen (US$150 at an exchange rate of 100 Japanese yen to 1 US dollar) per month per child for all children under age three. For children from age three until graduation from elementary school, it was 10,000 yen (US$100) per month for first and second children and 15,000 yen (US$150) per month for third and higher-order children. It was 10,000 yen (US$100) per month per child for all children enrolled in junior high school (Kosei-rodo-sho 2013d).

---

[13] The survey draws its sample from organizations with at least five employees. Since organizations with less than five workers are excluded from the survey, the proportion of organizations that have specific rules on parental leave, as reported by the survey, likely overestimates the degree of compliance with the law.

[14] Since the Basic Survey on Equal Employment, from which this information is drawn, excludes organizations with less than five employees (a high proportion of which are most likely not complying with the legal requirement to offer parental leave to all eligible workers), survey results very likely overestimate the proportion of eligible mothers who actually take parental leave.

Despite these efforts, Japan's family policy so far appears to have been largely ineffective, in the sense that strains on parents (especially working mothers) to balance family and work responsibilities have not been significantly alleviated and Japan's fertility has remained very low. Comparing 18 member countries, the Organization for Economic Co-operation and Development (OECD) (2001, chapter 4) ranked Japan second from the bottom in terms of coverage and strength of policies for work-family reconciliation and family-friendly work arrangements.[15] Using indexes measuring the effectiveness of governmental policies for childcare services, childcare leave, and flexible work arrangements, the OECD report points out that Japan's childcare coverage for children under age three and parental leave offered by employers are both especially weak. This suggests that it is vital for the Japanese government to strengthen efforts to help working parents of small children by expanding affordable childcare services. It is also important for both employers and employees to make the workplace more flexible and family friendly and to make efforts to change Japan's traditional corporate culture that places emphasis on long work hours. Given the serious, long-term demographic and socioeconomic consequences of the persistence of very low fertility, Japan has no choice but to strengthen policy and society-wide efforts to help women and couples make work and family life more compatible.

References

Bianchi, S. M., Milkie, M., Sayar, L., & Robinson, J. (2000). Is anyone doing the housework? *Social Forces, 79*(1), 191–228.
Brinton, M. C. (1988). The social-industrial bases of gender stratification: Japan as an illustrative case. *American Journal of Sociology, 94*(2), 300–335.
Brinton, M. C. (1990). Intrafamilial markets for education in Japan. In M. Hechter, K. D. Opp, & R. Wippler (Eds.), *Social institutions: Their emergence, maintenance and effects* (pp. 307–330). New York: Aldine de Gruyter.
Bumpass, L. L., & Choe, M. K. (2004). Attitudes relating to marriage and family life. In N. O. Tsuya & L. L. Bumpass (Eds.), *Marriage, work, and family life in comparative perspective: Japan, South Korea, and the United States* (pp. 19–38). Honolulu: University of Hawaii Press.
Cargill, T. F., Hutchison, M. M., & Ito, T. (1997). *The political economy of Japanese monetary policy*. Cambridge: MIT Press.
Choe, M. K., Bumpass, L. L., Tsuya, N. O., & Rindfuss, R. R. (2014). Nontraditional family-related attitudes in Japan: Macro and micro determinants. *Population and Development Review, 40*(2), 241–271.
Fuwa, M. (2004). Macro-level gender inequality and the division of household labor in 22 countries. *American Sociological Review, 69*(6), 751–767.
Gershuny, J. (2000). *Changing times: Work and leisure in postindustrial society*. Oxford: Oxford University Press.
Hajnal, J. (1953). Age at marriage and proportions marrying. *Population Studies–A Journal of Demography, 7*(2), 111–136.

---

[15] Greece had the lowest scores.

Hirao, K. (2001). Mothers as the best teachers: Japanese motherhood and early childhood education. In M. C. Brinton (Ed.), *Women's working lives in East Asia* (pp. 180–203). Stanford: Stanford University Press.

Igarashi, Y. (2009). Hi-seiki-koyō no genjyo to kadai: Wakamono no mondai wo chūshin-to-shite [Current situations of non-regular employment: Focusing on young persons]. *Rippou to Chosa, 288*, 183–188.

Imai, H. (1999). The employment situation in South Korea. In *Asian economic review*. Tokyo: Japan Research Institute.

International Labour Organization (ILO). (2011). *Global employment trends for youth: 2011 update*. Geneva: International Labour Organization.

Jones, G. W. (1997). The demise of universal marriage in East and Southeast Asia. In G. W. Jones, R. M. Douglas, J. C. Caldwell, & R. D'Souza (Eds.), *The continuing demographic transition* (pp. 51–79). Oxford: Clarendon.

Jones, G. W. (2004). Not "when to marry" but "whether to marry": The changing context of marriage decisions in East and Southeast Asia. In: G. W. Jones & K. Ramdas (Eds.), *(Un)tying the knot: Ideal and reality in Asian marriage* (pp. 3–56). Singapore: Asia Research Institute, National University of Singapore.

Kohara, M. (2010). The response of Japanese wives' labor supply to husbands' job loss. *Journal of Population Economics, 23*, 1133–1149.

Kohler, H. P., Billari, F. C., & Ortega, J. A. (2002). Tempo-adjusted period parity progression measures, fertility postponement, and completed cohort fertility. *Demographic Research, 6*(6), 91–144.

Kosei-rodo-sho [Japan Ministry of Health, Labour, and Welfare]. (2010a). *Hoikusho nyusho taiki jido-su (Heisei-21-nen 10-gatsu) ni tsuite* [On the number of children wait-listed for enrollment in childcare facilities, as of October 2009]. Tokyo: Kosei-rodo-sho.

Kosei-rodo-sho [Japan Ministry of Health, Labour, and Welfare]. (2010b). *Kaisei Ikuji Kaigo Kyugyo Ho no aramashi* [Outline of the revised child and family care leave law]. Tokyo: Kosei-rodo-sho.

Kosei-rodo-sho [Japan Ministry of Health, Labour, and Welfare]. (2013a). *Hoikusho kanren jokyo torimatome (Heisei-25-nen 4-gatu 1-nichi)* [Summary report on the conditions relating to childcare centers in Japan, as of 1 April 2013]. Tokyo: Kosei-rodo-sho.

Kosei-rodo-sho [Japan Ministry of Health, Labour, and Welfare]. (2013b). *Ikuji kyugyo kyufu* [Provisions pertaining to childcare leave]. Tokyo: Kosei-rodo-sho.

Kosei-rodo-sho [Japan Ministry of Health, Labour, and Welfare]. (2013c). *Koyou Hoken Seido* [The national employment insurance system]. http://www.mhlw.go.jp/stf/seisakunitsuite/bunya/koyou_roudou/koyou/koyouhoken/index.html. Accessed 5 Dec 2013.

Kosei-rodo-sho [Japan Ministry of Health, Labour, and Welfare]. (2013d). *Jidou Teate ni tsuite* [On the child allowance scheme]. http://www.mhlw.go.jp/stf/seisakunitsuite/bunya/kodomo_kosodate/jidouteate/index.html. Accessed 5 Dec 2013.

Kosei-rodo-sho [Japan Ministry of Health, Labour, and Welfare]. (2013e). *Heisei-24-nendo Koyo Kinto Kihon Chosa no gaikyo* [Summary of the 2012 basic survey on equal employment]. Tokyo: Kosei-rodo-sho.

Lee, S. S. (2010). *The shift of labour market risks in deindustrializing Asian economies: Taiwan, Japan and the Republic of Korea*. (Barnett papers in social research 2010/2). Oxford: Department of Social Policy and Intervention, University of Oxford.

Lee, K. S., Tufiş, P. A., & Alwin, D. F. (2010). Separate spheres or increasing equality? Changing gender beliefs in postwar Japan. *Journal of Marriage and the Family, 72*, 184–201.

Miura, K. (2001, January 6). Hoikusho taiki sakushun de 33000-nin: 3-nen buri ni zouka, toshibu wa shinkoku, Koseisho chosa [33,000 preschoolers wait-listed for daycare centers as of April 2000: The number increasing after two years of decline with the problem being especially serious in urban areas, a Ministry of Health and Welfare survey reports]. *Kosei Fukushi*, pp. 13–16.

Monbu-kagaku-sho [Japan Ministry of Education, Culture, Sports, Science, and Technology]. (2012). *Monbu-Kagaku Tokei Yoran Heisei 19-nendo ban* [Statistical abstract of education, culture, sports, science, and technology, 2012 edition]. Tokyo: Kokuritsu Insatsu Kyoku.

Naikakufu [Cabinet Office, Government of Japan]. (2003). *Hoiku-sābisu shijyo no genjyo to kadai: Hoiku-sābisu Kakaku ni kansuru Kenkyukai houkokusho* [Current situations and problems of childcare services in Japan: Report from the working group on the costs of childcare services]. Tokyo: Naikakufu.

Naikakufu [Cabinet Office, Government of Japan]. (2012). *Shoshika Shakai Taisaku Hakusho: Heisei-24-nendo shoshika no jokyo oyobi shoshika heno taisho shisaku no gaikyo* [2012 white paper on policy responses to low fertility]. Tokyo: Naikakufu.

National Institute of Population and Social Security Research. (2012a). *Population projections for Japan: 2011–2060 (with long-range population projections: 2061–2110)*. Tokyo: National Institute of Population and Social Security Research.

National Institute of Population and Social Security Research. (2012b). *Report on the fourteenth Japanese national fertility survey in 2010. Volume I: Marriage process and fertility of Japanese married couples*. Tokyo: National Institute of Population and Social Security Research.

National Institute of Population and Social Security Research. (2014). *Latest demographic statistics 2014*. Tokyo: National Institute of Population and Social Security Research.

Oppenheimer, V. K. (1994). Women's rising employment and the future of the family in industrial societies. *Population and Development Review, 20*(2), 293–342.

Oppenheimer, V. K., Kalmijn, M., & Lim, N. (1997). Men's career development and marriage timing during a period of rising inequality. *Demography, 34*, 311–330.

Organization for Economic Co-operation and Development (OECD). (2001). *OECD employment outlook 2001*. Paris: OECD.

Organization for Economic Co-operation and Development (OECD). (2002). *OECD employment outlook 2002*. Paris: OECD.

Raymo, J. M. (1998). Later marriage or fewer? Changes in the marriage behavior of Japanese women. *Journal of Marriage and the Family, 60*, 1023–1034.

Raymo, J. M. (2003). Educational attainment and the transition to first marriage among Japanese women. *Demography, 40*, 83–103.

Retherford, R. D., Ogawa, N., & Sakamoto, S. (1996). Values and fertility change in Japan. *Population Studies–Journal of Demography, 50*(1), 5–25.

Retherford, R. D., Ogawa, N., & Matsukura, R. (2001). Late marriage and less marriage in Japan. *Population and Development Review, 27*(1), 65–102.

Rindfuss, R. R. (2004). The family in comparative perspective. In N. O. Tsuya & L. L. Bumpass (Eds.), *Marriage, work, and family life in comparative perspective: Japan, South Korea, and the United States* (pp. 134–143). Honolulu: University of Hawaii Press.

Rindfuss, R. R., Choe, M. K., Bumpass, L. L., & Tsuya, N. O. (2004). Social networks and family change in Japan. *American Sociological Review, 69*(6), 838–861.

Smith, P. C. (1980). Asian marriage patterns in transition. *Journal of Family History, 5*(1), 58–96.

Somusho Tokeikyoku [Statistics Bureau, Japan Ministry of Internal Affairs and Communication]. (2005). *Annual report on the labour force 2005 (detailed tabulation)*. Tokyo: Somusho Tokeikyoku.

Sorifu Tokeikyoku [Statistics Bureau, Prime Minister's Office of Japan]. (1964). *Kokusei Chosa hokoku 3* [Population census of Japan, Volume 3], part 1. Tokyo: Sorifu Tokeikyoku.

Sorifu Tokeikyoku [Statistics Bureau, Prime Minister's Office of Japan]. (1973). *Kokusei Chosa hokoku 5: Shosai-shukei kekka* [Population census of Japan 5: Results of detailed tabulations], part 1. Tokyo: Sorifu Tokeikyoku.

Sorifu Tokeikyoku [Statistics Bureau, Prime Minister's Office of Japan]. (1984). *1980-nen Kokusei Chosa hokoku dai-4-kan: Shosai-shukei kekka* [1980 population census of Japan, volume 4: Results of detailed tabulations], part 1. Tokyo: Sorifu Tokeikyoku.

Tsuya, N. (2005). Shoshika to jyosei/gendaa seisaku [Fertility decline and gender policy in Japan]. In: H. Ohbuchi & M. Atoh (Eds.), *Shoshika no seisaku-gaku* [Studies of policies relating to fertility decline to below-replacement levels] (pp. 157–87). Tokyo: Hara Shobo.

Tsuya, N. (2009). Gakureki to koyou-anteisei no paatonashippu keisei heno eikyo [Education, regular employment, and partnership formation in Japan]. *Jinko Mondai Kenkyu* [Journal of Population Problems], *65*(2), 45–63.

Tsuya, N. O. (2010). Gender relations and family forms: Japan as an illustrative case. In Asian Research Institute (Ed.), *Gender relations in the 21st century Asian family* (pp. 49–108). Singapore: National University of Singapore.

Tsuya, N. O. (2012, May 25–27). *Education, employment, and first marriage in Japan.* Paper presented at the Shanghai Forum/IUSSP seminar on patterns of economic development, social change, and fertility decline in comparative perspective, Shanghai.

Tsuya, N. O., & Bumpass, L. L. (2004). Introduction. In N. O. Tsuya & L. L. Bumpass (Eds.), *Marriage, work, and family life in comparative perspective: Japan, South Korea, and the United States* (pp. 1–18). Honolulu: University of Hawaii Press.

Tsuya, N. O., & Choe, M. K. (2004). Investments in children's education, desired fertility, and women's employment. In N. O. Tsuya & L. L. Bumpass (Eds.), *Marriage, work, and family life in comparative perspective: Japan, South Korea, and the United States* (pp. 76–94). Honolulu: University of Hawaii Press.

Tsuya, N. O., & Mason, K. O. (1995). Changing gender roles and below-replacement fertility in Japan. In K. O. Mason & A. M. Jensen (Eds.), *Gender and family change in industrialized countries* (pp. 139–167). Oxford: Clarendon.

Tsuya, N. O., Bumpass, L. L., Choe, M. K., & Rindfuss, R. R. (2013a). Employment and household tasks of Japanese couples, 1994–2009. *Demographic Research, 27,* 705–718.

Tsuya, N. O., Choe, M. K., Rindfuss, R. R., & Bumpass, L. L. (2013b, April 11–13). *Low fertility in Japan: Desires and behavior, 2000–2009.* Paper presented at the annual meeting of the Population Association of America, New Orleans.

Turner, R. (1960). Modes of social ascent through education: Sponsored and contest mobility. *American Sociological Review, 25,* 212–239.

United Nations (UN). (1991). *The world's women, 1970–1990: Trends and statistics.* New York: United Nations.

United Nations (UN). (1995). *The world's women, 1995: Trends and statistics.* New York: United Nations.

United Nations (UN). (2010). *The world's women, 2010: Trends and statistics.* New York: United Nations.

United Nations Economic Commission for Europe (UNECE). (2013). *Gender statistics database: Fertility, families, and households.* http://www.unece.org/stats/gender.html. Accessed 3 Dec 2013.

Chapter 6
Lowest-Low Fertility and Policy Responses in South Korea

Samsik Lee and Hyojin Choi

Over the past half century, South Korea has experienced rapid economic growth accompanied by dramatic fertility decline. In the early 1960s, South Korea's economic development began to speed up, standards of living improved, infant and child mortality declined, levels of education rose dramatically, and women's participation in the labor force increased. As a result, the traditional value placed on having many children began to wane. In the early 1960s, explosive population growth was expected to become a major obstacle to economic development, leading to a vicious cycle of poverty. In response, the government initiated a strong family planning program, and fertility began to decline sharply. To the surprise of many observers, the total fertility rate (TFR) plummeted from 6.0 children per woman in 1960 to 1.3 children per woman in 2001, making South Korea one of the countries with the lowest fertility in the world.

Statistics Korea predicts that this extreme level of low fertility, together with a continued rise in life expectancy, will result in a very old population. The proportion of elderly people (age 65 and above) is predicted to increase from 10 % in 2009 to 20 % in 2026, 30 % in 2037, and 40 % in 2060 (Statistics Korea 2011a). In fact, South Korea's population is aging more quickly than the population of any other country in the world.

This chapter will examine the pace and magnitude of South Korea's fertility decline, along with the accompanying rate of population aging. We then examine the effects of low fertility and demographic change on Korea's future economy and society and the factors that have contributed—and continue to contribute—to Korea's fertility decline. Finally, we will discuss the government's policy response to these issues.

S. Lee (✉) • H. Choi
Korea Institute for Health and Social Affairs (KIHASA), Seoul, South Korea
e-mail: lss@kihasa.re.kr

© Springer International Publishing Switzerland 2015
R.R. Rindfuss, M.K. Choe (eds.), *Low and Lower Fertility*,
DOI 10.1007/978-3-319-21482-5_6

Trends in the Fertility Rate

The total fertility rate (TFR) in South Korea was as high as 6.0 children per woman in 1960 but decreased to the population-replacement level of 2.1 by 1983. Between 1984 and 1997, the TFR fluctuated within a narrow range between 1.5 and 1.8 children per woman. Then in 1998, immediately after the 1997 financial crisis, fertility declined to less than 1.5. South Korea's TFR declined further to 1.3 in 2001 and 1.08 in 2005. Since then, the TFR has fluctuated at around 1.2 (Statistics Korea 2014).

The fertility decline in South Korea differs from the pattern in many other countries in three important ways—the speed of the decline, the magnitude of the decline, and the duration in which fertility has remained at a very low level. A comparison with the pattern in other Organization for Economic Cooperation and Development (OECD) member countries illustrates these points (Fig. 6.1).

At 6.0 children per woman, South Korea's TFR was particularly high in 1960, well above fertility levels in all other OECD countries except Mexico and Turkey. From that point, fertility in South Korea dropped extremely quickly, dipping to below 1.3 in 50 years. By 2012, South Korea had gone from the third highest fertility level in the OECD to one of the very lowest. Fertility also dropped rapidly in Mexico and Turkey, but has not dipped below 2.0 children per woman in either country. Between 1960 and 2012, the TFR in South Korea dropped by 4.77 children per woman. Among OECD member countries, only Mexico experienced a fertility decline of greater magnitude. Some other Asian countries, such as Taiwan and Singapore, experienced a similar pattern of very high fertility in 1960 dropping to very low levels by 2012 (Fig. 6.2). The difference in TFR over the 52-year period was 4.48 for Taiwan and 4.47 for Singapore. Nevertheless, the magnitude of South Korea's fertility decline was the greatest in the region.

The third special feature of fertility in South Korea is that the TFR has remained at a very low level—less than 1.3 children per woman—for many years. As of 2012, only nine of the 34 OECD member countries, plus Singapore and Taiwan, had ever experienced fertility less than 1.3 (Table 6.1). Fertility remained at this low level for 12 years (2001–2012) in South Korea, compared with 11 years in Italy (1993–2003) and Slovenia (1995–2005), 10 years in Singapore (2003–2012), 9 years in Taiwan (2004–2012), 4 years in Germany (1992–1995), and 3 years in Japan (2003–2005).

Demographic and Socio-Economic Implications of Very Low Fertility

Demographic Implications

Statistics Korea (2011a, b) has projected the size of South Korea's population under various fertility and mortality scenarios. Under the medium scenario, Statistics Korea assumes that TFR will increase from 1.23 in 2010 to 1.42 in 2045 and then

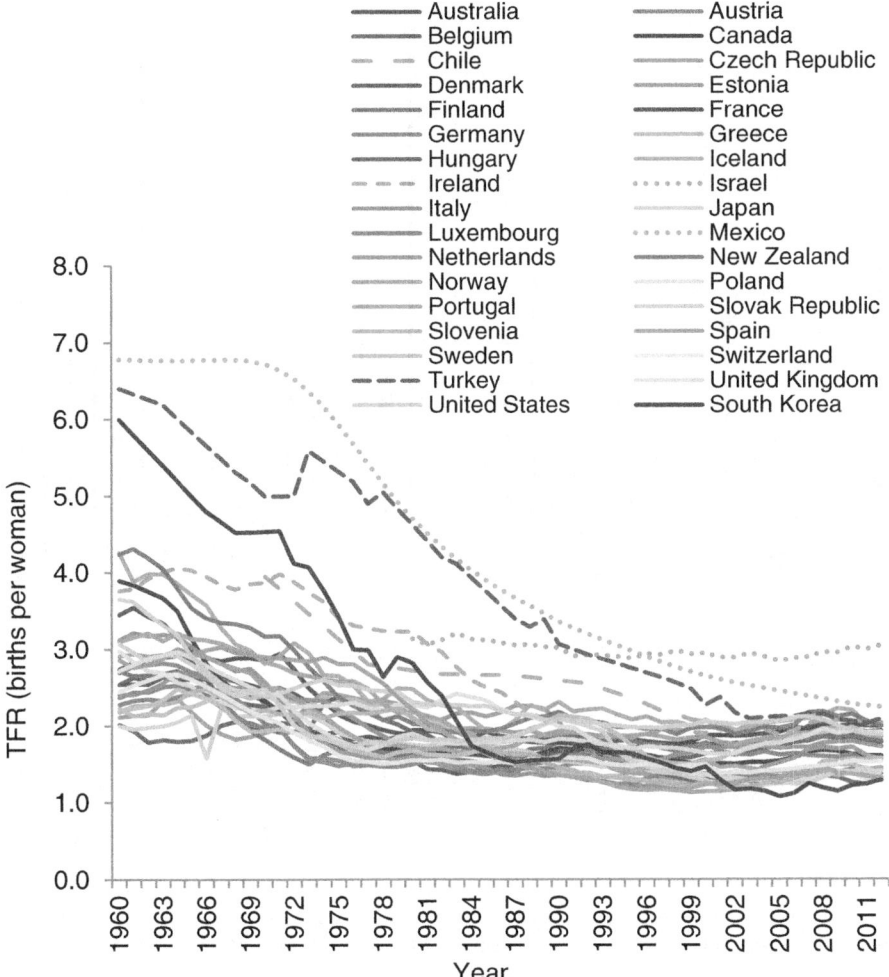

Fig. 6.1 Trends in the total fertility rate (TFR) for Organization for Economic Cooperation and Development (OECD) member countries, 1960–2012 (OECD 2014a)

remain at that level. Between 2010 and 2060, life expectancy at birth is assumed to increase from 77.2 to 86.6 years for men and from 84.1 to 90.3 years for women. Over the same period, the net annual immigration rate is assumed to decrease from 1.67 to 0.53 per thousand. Given these assumptions, South Korea's population is projected to reach a peak of 52 million in 2030 and then start to decline, falling to 44 million in 2060.

We extended this population projection from 2060 to 2100, assuming that fertility and net immigration rates will remain constant at 2060 levels and that life expectancy at birth will increase by 2100 to 89.3 years for men and 93.2 years for women. Given these assumptions, South Korea's population will shrink to 28 million by 2100.

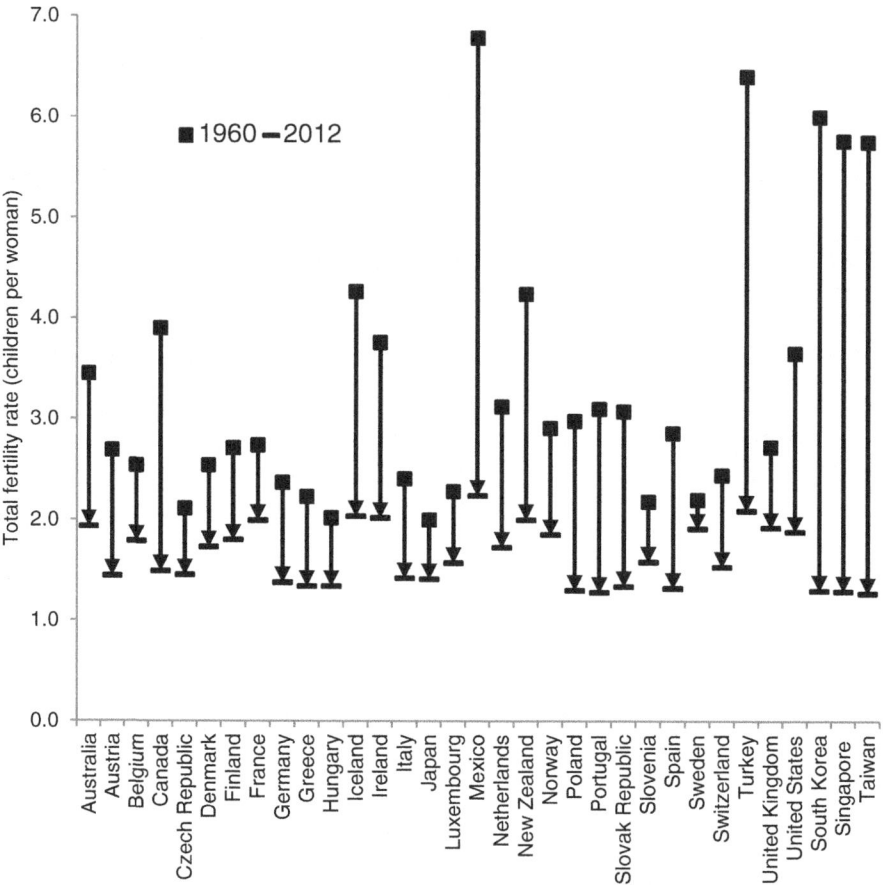

Fig. 6.2 Difference in TFR between 1960 and 2012 for selected OECD countries (OECD 2014a), Singapore (Department of Statistics, Singapore 2013), and Taiwan (Ministry of the Interior, Republic of China 2014)

A breakdown of these forecasts by age group reveals a pattern of extreme population aging (Fig. 6.3). The population of young people, age 0–14, will decrease from about 8.0 million in 2010 to 4.5 million in 2060 and 2.8 million in 2100. The working-age population, age 15–64, will peak at about 37 million in 2016 and then fall to 22 million in 2060 and 13 million in 2100. Beginning in 2020, the elderly population will increase rapidly, as the baby-boomer generation, born in the 5-year period around 1960, reaches age 60 and above. South Korea's population age 65 and above will increase from 5.5 million in 2010 to about 12.7 million in 2030 and 18.0 million in 2049. At that point, the size of the elderly population will start to fall along with the decline of South Korea's population overall. The population age 65 and above is projected to drop to 11.9 million by 2100. By contrast, the proportion of elderly people in the total population is projected to increase steadily throughout

6 Lowest-Low Fertility and Policy Responses in South Korea

Table 6.1 Number of years, as of 2012, with TFR at less than 1.3 children per women, selected OECD and Asian countries

Country	Years with TFR less than 1.3	Time period
South Korea	12	2001–2012
Italy	11	1993–2003
Slovenia	11	1995–2005
Spain	10	1993–2002
Singapore	10	2003–2012
Taiwan	9	2004–2012
Greece	8	1996–2003
Slovak Republic	8	2000–2007
Germany	4	1992–1995
Poland	4	2003–2006
Japan	3	2003–2005

OECD (2014a), Department of Statistics, Singapore (2013), and Ministry of the Interior, Republic of China (2014)

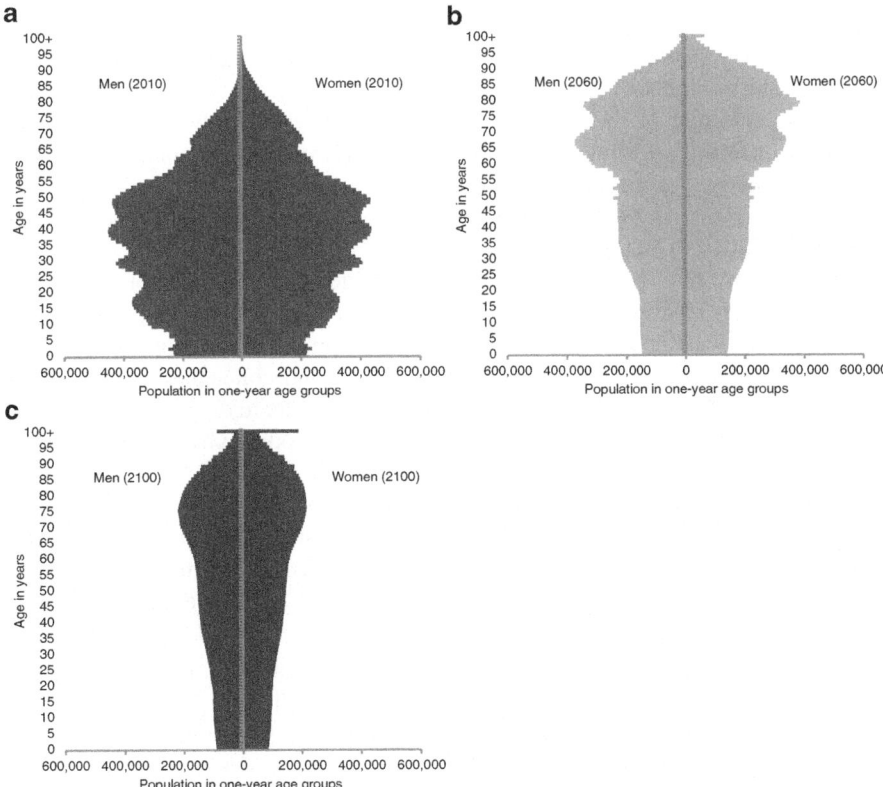

Fig. 6.3 Age structure of South Korea's population in 2010 (**a**) and projections for 2060 (**b**) and 2100 (**c**) (Statistics Korea 2011a)

the twenty-first century, rising from 10 % in 2009 to 20 % in 2026, 30 % in 2037, 40 % in 2060, and approaching 50 % in 2100. This pace of population aging is one of the fastest in the world.

Economic Implications

As the working-age population is predicted to increase until 2017 and then start to decline, the size of the labor force in South Korea will rise from 23.5 million in 2008 to 24.8 million in 2019 and then drop to 17.0 million in 2050. Between 2000 and 2010, South Korea's labor force increased at an annual rate of 0.97 %, making a strong contribution to economic growth. By contrast, the labor force is projected to decrease by an annual rate of −0.60 % between 2020 and 2030, by −1.31 % between 2030 and 2040, and by −1.65 % between 2040 and 2050 (Moon et al. 2004). The impact on the labor force of very low fertility in the 2000s will appear in earnest from 2020 onward. The first baby boomers number 7.1 million, including 5.3 million in the labor force, and they started retiring in 2010. Between 2010 and 2018, 3.1 million workers will retire, but only 0.6 million will enter the working-age population. The resulting labor shortage is estimated at 0.6 million in 2015 and 1.5 million in 2020 (Bang et al. 2004).

The age structure of the working-age population will also be affected by the rapid pace of fertility decline. The proportion of the working-age population at age 50–64 will increase from 24.7 % in 2010 to 37.0 % in 2030 and 39.1 % in 2050 (Fig. 6.4). Accordingly, the average age of South Korean workers will increase from 39.1 years in 2010 to 42.0 in 2030 and 43.0 in 2050.

The aging of South Korea's labor force is expected to decrease labor productivity. Some studies have shown that labor productivity peaks between age 30 and 50 and then goes down due to physical decay, human-capital depreciation, and obsolescence (Vandenberghe and Waltenberg 2010). Moon and colleagues (2004) found that after controlling for human and physical capital, an increase of 1 % in the proportion of workers age 55 and above decreases labor productivity by an estimated 0.09–0.17 %.

Declining fertility is also expected to reduce domestic demand for a variety of goods and services. The Korean Medical Association (2008), quoting from the Health Insurance Review and Assessment Service, notes that the number of obstetrics and gynecology hospitals and clinics decreased by 8.5 % between 2003 and 2007, and the number of pediatric hospitals decreased by 7.8 %. In addition, retirement of the baby-boom generation will decrease the demand for housing and other goods and services. In South Korea, only a small proportion of workers receive a pension. Rather, the elderly tend to hold a large proportion of their assets as home equity, and they are likely to sell their homes to fund their retirement. As these houses come on the market, Bae and colleagues (2007) predict that the number of new houses to be constructed annually will decrease from 471,000 units in 2008 to 451,000 in 2020 due to rising supply and falling demand.

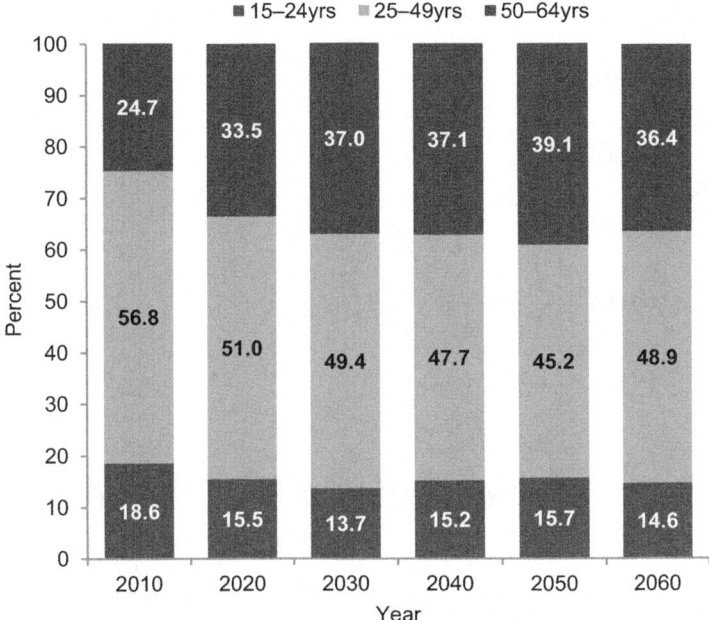

Fig. 6.4 Projected age structure of South Korea's working-age population, 2010–2060 (Statistics Korea 2011a, b)

The predicted drop in domestic demand may lead to a decrease in jobs, imbalance across industries, and an economic recession. Hwang (2009) estimates that changing consumption due to low fertility and population aging could lead to a loss of about 90,000 jobs in 10 years. The average annual growth of South Korea's gross domestic product (GDP) may well slow down—from 4.0 % in 1995–2011 to a predicted 1.0 % in 2030–2060 (Johansson et al. 2012). The pace of the economic slowdown will accelerate from about 2020 onward, when South Korea's baby boomers start retiring in large numbers.

South Korea's national pension program has recently expanded, but the number of contributors is expected to shrink in the long term, given the prolonged period of low fertility. Contributors are projected to increase from 20.4 million in 2013 to a peak of 20.6 million in 2015 and then start to decrease, down to 11.0 million in 2078. Over the same period, the number of pensioners will increase from 1.8 million in 2013 to a peak of 14.0 million in 2065 and then decrease to 11.8 million in 2083. Thus the proportion of pensioners compared with contributors will rise dramatically, from 13.0 % in 2013 to peak at 112.9 % in 2068 and then decline slightly to 111.9 % in 2083.

The pension fund is forecast to peak at South Korean won (KRW) 2,561 trillion (US$2.35 trillion at 5 Feb 2015 exchange rate) in 2043 and then start to shrink, with annual earnings less than expenditures, beginning in 2044 (Fig. 6.5). At current rates, the fund will be exhausted in 2060. To keep the fund solvent, contributions

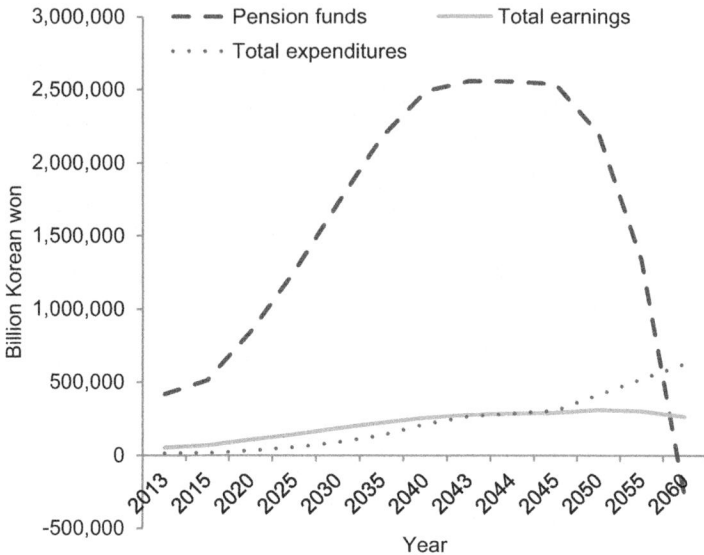

Fig. 6.5 Projection of pension funds for South Korea, 2013–2060, billion KRW (National Pension Finance Estimate Committee 2013)

will need to increase from the current rate of 9 % of reported income to 12–16 % (National Pension Finance Estimate Committee 2013).

Similarly, the number of contributors to South Korea's national medical insurance program will go down, and the number of beneficiaries will go up, so that the ratio of expenditure to revenue will increase from 1.00 in 2012 to 1.53 in 2030. Total expenditure already exceeds total revenue, and the deficit is predicted to rise from KRW 2.8 billion (US$2.58 million) in 2012 to KRW 47.7 billion (US$43.90 million) in 2030. It is estimated that the premium rate for medical insurance will need to increase from 5 % in 2012 to 12 % in 2030 (Park and Kim 2010).

As expenditures increase for pensions, medical insurance, long-term care of the elderly, and other areas of social welfare, the ratio of South Korea's total social expenditure to GDP will increase (Fig. 6.6). In 2013, public social expenditure accounted for 9.8 % of GDP; in 2060 this proportion is expected to rise to 29.0 % (Social Security Committee 2014).

Factors Contributing to South Korea's Fertility Decline

Rapid social and economic development in South Korea has ushered in major improvements in the standard of living, but development has also brought changes that make it more expensive for Koreans to raise and educate children. Other factors contributing to low fertility include rising uncertainty about employment and

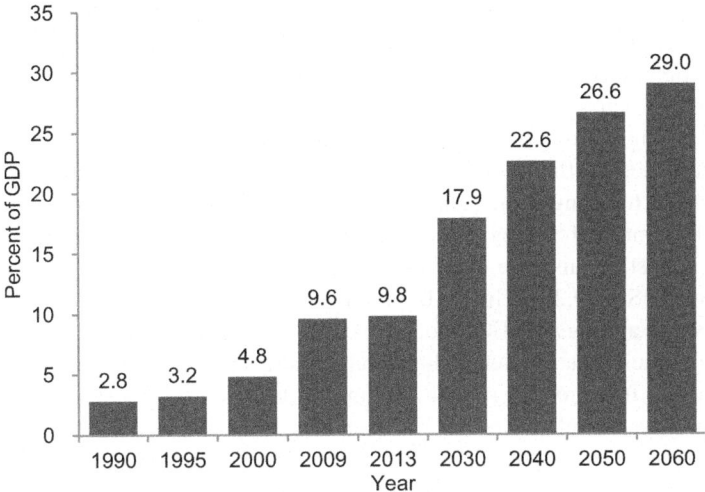

Fig. 6.6 Public social expenditure as percentage of gross domestic product (GDP) for South Korea, 1990–2060 (Social Security Committee 2014)

income that has accompanied global economic change, the difficulty of balancing work and family obligations, and changing values within Korean society.

The High Cost of Housing and Education

One impediment that young people face if they wish to marry and have children is the high cost of housing. Since the property bubble in the early 2000s, the price of either purchasing or renting a house has increased sharply. South Korea has a unique system for house rentals, called *jeonse*, which is based on a long-term lease with a large down payment and no monthly rent. Under the *jeonse* system, interest payments from the down payment go to the landlord as a type of "rent," and the down payment is returned to the renters when they vacate the dwelling unit. Because of high prices, it is difficult for young people to purchase a house when they marry. If they wish to rent a house, however, the initial cost under the *jeonse* system is nearly as high as the purchase price. As a result, most young people have to obtain a mortgage, even to rent a house.

Another impediment is the rise in expectations related to education. In particular, there has been a dramatic increase in enrollment in colleges and universities. Today, about 80 % of South Koreans enroll in tertiary education after completing high school. Gains in enrollment have been particularly large for young women—beginning in 2009, enrollment ratios have been higher for women than for men. In a period of economic uncertainty and job insecurity, a degree, particularly from a prestigious university, is viewed as an important prerequisite for success in the labor market.

The increase in college and university enrollment has affected fertility in two ways. For one thing, the cost of tertiary education raises the long-run costs that parents anticipate when deciding whether to have a child. In addition, as young women become more educated, they obtain higher-paying jobs, so the opportunity cost of dropping out of the labor market to raise a child increases. This dilemma is exacerbated by the difficulty of achieving a balance between work and family obligations, which has long been a characteristic of the South Korean labor market.

The 2012 National Survey on Fertility, Family Health, and Welfare reported that the average cost of raising a child from birth to college graduation is about KRW 260 million (US$239,287). In 2010, private expenditure on education was highest in South Korea among all OECD countries (Table 6.2). Note that private funding for education in the United States includes scholarships provided by academic institutions, whereas in Korea all private funding is provided by the students' families. Young Koreans are well aware of these high education costs. The 2012 survey asked married women why they might not want (more) children. Slightly more than one-half gave economic reasons, including unstable employment, low income, and the cost of a child's education (Kim et al. 2012).

Economic Uncertainty

Young people tend to postpone or even give up the prospect of marriage in times of economic crisis. South Korea experienced such a crisis in 1997–1998. The unemployment rate soared from 2.0 % in 1997 to 7.0 % in 1998. Another global financial crisis hit the South Korean economy in the late 2000s.

As young people faced these periods of high economic uncertainty, they delayed leaving their parents' home and marrying. In 1990, 9.5 % of men age 30–39 were unmarried. By 2010, the proportion of unmarried men in this age group had risen to 37.9 % (Fig. 6.7). Among women age 30–39, the proportion unmarried increased from 4.1 % in 1990 to 20.4 % in 2010 (Statistics Korea 2011b). According to the 2009 National Survey on Marriage and Fertility Dynamics (Lee et al. 2009), about 50 % of unmarried men reported financial reasons for not marrying, such as uncertainty related to income or employment and the cost of housing. Unmarried women reported concerns about the cost of marriage and the difficulty in balancing work and family obligations.

Table 6.2 Expenditure on education as a percentage of GDP, by source of funds, 2010

	OECD average	South Korea	United States	Canada	Sweden	United Kingdom	France	Japan
Public	5.4	4.8	5.1	5.0	6.3	5.9	5.8	3.6
Private	0.9	2.8	2.2	1.6	0.2	0.6	0.5	1.5
Total	6.3	7.6	7.3	6.6	6.5	6.5	6.3	5.1

OECD (2013)

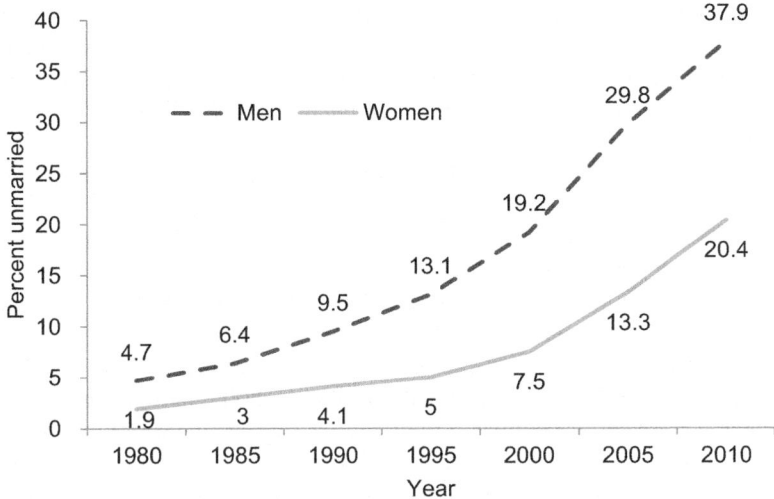

Fig. 6.7 Percent unmarried among South Korean men and women age 30–39, 1980–2010 (KOSIS 2014)

The marriage rate has a strong effect on the fertility rate in South Korea because only about 2 % of all births occur outside of marriage (Statistics Korea 2014). Such births are rare because Korean children born outside of marriage suffer considerable discrimination, both institutionalized and social.

It is notable that fertility trends in South Korea seem to be inelastic—the TFR goes down sharply in times of economic hardship but does not increase to the same degree when the economy improves. This is in contrast to the pattern in several other countries, for example, in Sweden. Fertility behavior in South Korea is probably so sensitive to economic shocks because of the lack of a social safety net for raising children.

Difficulty in Balancing Career and Family

In recent years, most young women have sought full-time employment when they completed their education. About 50 % of working women, however, quit their jobs when they have their first child (Lee et al. 2009). There are several reasons for this: (1) traditional gender roles still prevail in South Korea, with women fully responsible for household work and childcare; (2) most South Korean workplaces are not family-friendly and do not provide flexible work conditions; (3) support from family members such as grandparents or other relatives has been weakened as more couples live on their own in nuclear households; and (4) there is a shortage of institution-based childcare and other child-related infrastructure.

Men work long hours and spend very little time on childcare or house work. In 2011, South Korean men spent an average of 46.7 h per week at their main job (OECD 2014b). No doubt related to these long work hours, South Korean men contribute very little to household chores or childcare. The Time Use Survey of South Korea (Statistics Korea 2009) reported that men spent on average about 42 min a day on household chores and childcare, while women spent on average 3 h and 35 min.

There are many ways in which the workplace in South Korea is unfriendly to families. Women tend to be discriminated against in terms of employment, wages, and promotion when they marry or have a child. The biggest problem in maintaining a family-work balance is the shortage of daycare, but Korean firms are reluctant to provide infrastructure or services to help working mothers. Although Korea's Infant Care Act stipulates that firms with more than 500 employees or more than 300 female employees are obligated to provide workplace childcare facilities, only about 50 % of such firms had childcare facilities in 2013 (Ministry of Health and Welfare 2014). For this reason, many married women drop out of employment when they have children. This pattern drives down both fertility and female participation in the labor market. The result is an "M-shaped curve" for women's labor-market participation by age—they tend to work during their young-adult years, leave employment to stay home and raise children, and then return to the work force later in life. A similar, but less pronounced, pattern is found in Japan, but it is no longer the case in Western countries (Fig. 6.8).

Given the difficulty of balancing careers and motherhood, it is not surprising that women in South Korea tend to have few children and tend to have them relatively

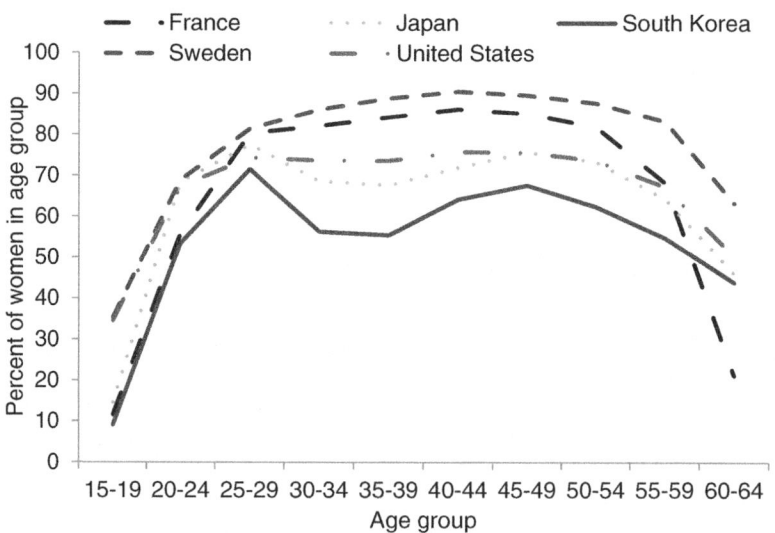

Fig. 6.8 Female labor-force participation rates by age for five OECD member countries (OECD 2014b)

late in life. Women who quit their jobs to raise children are severely disadvantaged when they seek to reenter the work force, which contributes to the high opportunity cost of raising a family. Women with higher educational attainment are more likely to have more prestigious and higher-paying jobs— increasing the opportunity costs of having children.

Changes in Family Values

The social environment in South Korea has changed dramatically along with rapid economic growth. As more and more young women receive university degrees, they are increasingly motivated to join the work force. This has created a conflict between women's aspirations and traditional Korean patriarchal culture, which specifies that men should work outside the home for money and women should stay at home to take care of housework and children. Such gender-specific cultural expectations have persisted even as more women have started working outside the home, resulting in a heavy dual burden on women.

Family values are changing, however, including views on marriage and parenthood. According to the 2009 National Survey on Marriage and Fertility Dynamics (Lee et al. 2009), only 23.4 % of single men and 16.9 % of single women age 20–44 consider that it is necessary to marry. Among currently married women, the proportion who agrees that "having a child is a must" dropped from 73.7 % in 1997 to 46.3 % in 2012 (Kim et al. 2012).

Although family incomes have increased with economic growth, the difficulties in balancing work and family life have also increased, along with the high opportunity cost of having a child, particularly for women with higher-level education and socio-economic status. Increasingly, the emphasis has shifted toward maximizing the "quality" of each child, entailing large investments in childcare and education, rather than the "quantity" of children produced in a family.

Policy Response

Individuals and couples decide whether to have children based on their circumstances and a calculation of the costs and benefits of parenthood. Taken together, however, individual-level fertility decisions affect the size and age structure of a population and thus have an impact on society as a whole. For this reason, governments are sometimes willing to implement policies aimed at influencing marriage, fertility, mortality, and migration, either directly or indirectly.

Concerned about rapid population growth, the South Korean government initiated a national family planning program in 1962. By 1996, the fertility rate had plummeted and appeared to be stationary at well below the replacement level, so the government abolished its family planning program and adopted a new policy emphasizing population quality. The focus was on problems such as the unbalanced sex ratio at birth, the high prevalence of sex-selective abortions, the deterioration of reproductive health, and the rapid pace of population aging. As fertility remained at extremely low levels, the government passed a series of plans aimed at tackling the problems of an aging population. The Basic Plan for Low Fertility and Aging Society, which is to be renewed every 5 years, aims to increase South Korea's fertility rate and respond to the challenges of population aging (Lee et al. 2013). The Framework Act on Low Birth Rates in an Aging Society stipulates that both the central government and local governments establish an action plan every year. The results of these action plans have to be evaluated and submitted to the National Assembly Budget Settlement Committee and the Ministry of Security and Public Administration, to be taken into account in formulating the action plan for the following year.

In an attempt to raise the fertility rate, the government has adopted three strategies. These are: improving support for childbirth and child rearing; fostering a family-friendly and gender-equal culture and society; and raising a healthy future generation.

To improve support for childbirth and child rearing, the South Korean government provides either fees for center-based daycare and kindergarten or an allowance for childcare at home. The government also provides a free after-school education program. Families with children receive tax exemptions and means-tested loans for purchasing or renting a house. The government also provides health and medical services before and after childbirth and supports the costs of in-vitro fertilization for couples who have difficulty conceiving.

The South Korean government has also made an effort to help parents balance work and family obligations. The government provides 90 days of maternity leave at 100 % of salary plus 1 year of childcare leave at 40 % of salary, although both of these benefits are capped at KRW 1,000,000 (US$919) per month. In addition, employers must give male employees whose wives give birth 5 days of parental leave, including 3 days at 100 % of salary and 2 days unpaid. Employers must also keep jobs open for their female employees who take maternity or childcare leave. Employers who break these rules will be fined up to KRW 5,000,000 (US$4,598).

The government has also attempted to expand workplace daycare centers, shorten work hours, and increase the flexibility of working conditions. Finally, the government has initiated education and publicity campaigns to expand gender equality within families and the broader society and to encourage family-friendly companies, which are to be given a certificate with a special logo.

The South Korean government's response to low fertility and population aging has also included an emphasis on child health. In order to ensure safe environments for children and adolescents, the government has initiated programs to prevent accidents, strengthen the protection of children from abuse and neglect, and prevent violence in schools. Programs to support the healthy development of children and adolescents include setting up community centers for children, after-school programs, and small community libraries as well as establishing a system to protect children's rights, protect children from harmful influences, and improve child healthcare by linking public health centers with schools.

To address the needs of an aging population, the government has made efforts to promote income security, healthcare, and an active lifestyle for the elderly. Policy measures designed to improve the income security of older citizens include providing diverse employment opportunities such as reemployment after retirement, assistance to start a new career, and support to start a business, as well as enhancing public and private pension systems. Expanding employment opportunities for the elderly is intended to help them play a role as productive members of society, rather than merely as recipients of social security. Policy measures to enhance the health of Korea's elderly population also include establishing a preventive care system, stabilizing medical costs, and improving medical insurance coverage. Other policy measures include providing the elderly with opportunities for volunteer work and leisure activities, improving social infrastructure for the elderly such as housing and transportation, and putting in place a social-protection system for vulnerable elderly people who live alone or are at risk of being abused.

Conclusion

Although South Korea only reached its current level of extreme low fertility in the 2000s, fertility has been declining steeply for about 30 years. To ensure South Korea's future social and economic development, policies and programs must be put in place to raise fertility and to support the country's aging population. The experience of several European countries, however, suggests that low fertility rates can persist for years in spite of government policy efforts.

Experience in many countries has shown that reversing the trend toward low marriage rates and very low fertility is extremely difficult. Fertility behavior is closely intertwined with overall socio-economic conditions, which means that efforts to raise fertility need to address aspects of the economy and society that either encourage or discourage marriage and parenthood. Government efforts should include programs to help men and women balance work and family life, improvements in maternity and childcare leave, expansion of flexible working conditions, and programs that foster family-friendly work environments, alleviate the economic burden of child rearing, support safe and healthy pregnancy and childbirth, establish a system of diverse and high-quality childcare, and provide safe environments for children—all in an integrated manner. Nothing, however, is more important than recognizing that the current low level of fertility is not a transitory phenomenon, but rather is a long-term feature of South Korean society that must be addressed with a broad response.

After experiencing a quarter century of low fertility, it seems unreasonable to expect South Korea's fertility rate to rise to anywhere near the replacement level in the foreseeable future. Instead, given its current demographic structure, it is inevitable that South Korea will experience further population aging. Even if fertility were to start rising today, it would take a long time to have a tangible effect on the country's population age structure. For this reason, the focus of policy should be not only on raising fertility levels, but also on improving social and economic conditions to minimize the problems associated with an aging society.

Policy responses to changes in population age structure will need to include a wide range of sectors, such as education, housing, and finance. Making such policy responses effective will require not only the commitment of the South Korean government, but also the cooperation of the private sector and current and future generations of the Korean people.

References

Bae, S. S., Kim, G. Y., Jeon, S. J., Kim, H. S., Bong, Y. S., & Ryokichi, E. (2007). *New directions in the housing supply system: Responding to the structural changes of housing demand* [in Korean]. Anyang-si: Korea Research Institute for Human Settlements.

Bang, H. N., Shin, D. G., Kim, D. H., & Shin, H. G. (2004). *Population aging and the labor market* [in Korean]. Seoul: Korea Labor Institute.

Department of Statistics, Singapore. (2013). *Yearbook of statistics Singapore.* http://www.singstat.gov.sg/publications/publications_and_papers/reference/yearbook_of_stats.html. Accessed 29 July 2014.

Hwang, S. P. (2009). *The impacts of changes in the structure of consumption on the structure of industry* [in Korean]. Seoul: Institute for Monetary and Economic Research, Bank of Korea.

Johansson, A., Guillemette, Y., Murtin, F., Turner, D., Nicoletti, G., de la Maisonneuve, C., Bagnoli, P., Bousquet, G., & Spinelli, F. (2012). *Looking to 2060: Long-term global growth prospects* (OECD Economic Policy Papers No. 03). Paris: Organization for Economic Cooperation and Development (OECD).

Kim, S. G., Kim, Y. K., Kim, H. R., Park, J. S., Son, C. G., Choi, Y. J., Kim, Y. U., Lee, G. E., & Yoon, A. R. (2012). *The 2012 national survey on fertility, family health, and welfare in Korea* [in Korean]. Seoul: Korea Institute for Health and Social Affairs (KIHASA).

Korean Medical Association. (2008). *The rate of closure of primary healthcare facilities* [in Korean]. Seoul: Korean Medical Association.

KOSIS (Korean Statistical Information Service). (2014). *Statistical database* [in Korean]. http://kosis.kr. Accessed 29 July 2014.

Lee, S. S., Choi, H. J., Oh, Y. H., Seo, M. H., Park, S. K., & Do, S. R. (2009). *The 2009 National survey on marriage and fertility dynamics* [in Korean]. Seoul: Korea Institute for Health and Social Affairs (KIHASA).

Lee, S. S., Kim, I. K., Choi, H. J., Du, P., Lu, J., Okuyama, S., & Takahashi, I. (2013). *Population change and future strategies in China, Japan, and Korea* [in Korean]. Seoul: Korea Institute for Health and Social Affairs (KIHASA).

Ministry of Health and Welfare, Republic of Korea. (2014). *Statistics on workplace childcare facilities* [in Korean]. Seoul: Ministry of Health and Welfare.

Ministry of the Interior, Republic of China. (2014). *Statistical yearbook of interior.* http://www.moi.gov.tw/stat/english/year.asp. Accessed 1 Aug 2014.

Moon, H. P., Kim, D. Y., Kim, D. S., Kim, S. Y., Park, C. G., & Ahn, J. B. (2004). *Socio-economic impacts of population aging and policy issues* [in Korean]. Sejong: Korea Development Institute (KDI).

National Pension Finance Estimate Committee, Republic of Korea. (2013). *Long-term projections for national pension finance and future directions* [in Korean]. Seoul: National Pension Finance Estimate Committee.

OECD (Organization for Economic Cooperation and Development). (2013). *Education at a glance 2013: OECD indicators.* http://www.oecd.org/edu/eag2013%20(eng)--FINAL%2020%20June%202013.pdf. Accessed 1 Aug 2014.

OECD (Organization for Economic Cooperation and Development). (2014a). *OECD family database*. http://www.oecd.org/social/soc/oecdfamilydatabase.htm. Accessed 1 Aug 2014.
OECD (Organization for Economic Cooperation and Development). (2014b). *StatExtracts*. http://stats.oecd.org. Accessed 29 July 2014.
Park, I. S., & Kim, D. H. (2010). *Long-term prospects for the finance of health insurance* [in Korean]. Seoul: Health Insurance Policy Research Institute.
Social Security Committee, Republic of Korea. (2014). *Long-term prospects for social expenditure* [in Korean]. Seoul: Social Security Committee.
Statistics Korea. (2009). *2009 time-use survey of South Korea* [in Korean]. Daejeon: Statistics Korea.
Statistics Korea. (2011a). *Future population projection* [in Korean]. Daejeon: Statistics Korea.
Statistics Korea. (2011b). *The results of the 2010 census* [in Korean]. Daejeon: Statistics Korea.
Statistics Korea. (2014). *Birth statistics* [in Korean]. http://kosis.kr/statisticsList/statisticsList_01List.jsp?vwcd=MT_ZTITLE&parentId=A. Accessed 11 Aug 2014.
Vandenberghe, V., & Waltenberg, F. D. (2010). *Ageing workforce, productivity, and labour costs of Belgian firms* (Discussion Paper No 2010-3). Louvain-la-Neuve: Institut de Recherches Économiques et Sociales de l'Université catholique de Louvain.

Chapter 7
Variation in U.S. Fertility: Low and Not so Low, but Not Lowest-Low

S. Philip Morgan

In a discussion of low fertility and population aging, the United States stands out with a level of fertility hovering around the replacement level (substantially higher than that of most economically advanced countries) and a corresponding, modest pace of aging. As a result, government policy is not directed toward increasing or decreasing overall levels of fertility (United Nations 2011). Thus to contribute to a discussion of below-replacement fertility, the most relevant questions are: What accounts for the relatively robust U.S. fertility rate? And how does the U.S. experience contribute to our understanding of the determinants of low and very low fertility in other contexts?

We address these questions by describing fertility levels and variation in the United States. For some groups, fertility is quite low, well below replacement. Other groups have fertility well above the replacement level. In order to understand this variation, we begin by introducing two compatible theoretical frameworks. The first posits a set of intermediate variables: the level of desired/intended fertility and factors that constrain (e.g., sub- or infecundity) or augment (e.g., unwanted fertility) fertility relative to these intentions. These "intermediate" variables (that characterize a "fertility regime") are anchored in culture and social structure, and we also offer a conceptualization of these more distal causes. Both frameworks aid discussions of low fertility in the United States and, I argue, are useful for thinking about low fertility and policy options in all contexts.

S.P. Morgan (✉)
Carolina Population Center and Sociology Department, University of North Carolina at Chapel Hill, Chapel Hill, NC, USA
e-mail: pmorgan@unc.edu

Conceptual and Theoretical Frameworks

The usefulness of intermediate-variable frameworks for the study of fertility is unquestioned. Bongaarts and Potter's (1983) and Bongaarts' (1978) proximate-determinant frameworks proved valuable for conceptualizing and empirically decomposing the causes of high fertility and the fertility transition.[1] Once fertility falls to moderate or low levels, however, the Bongaarts/Potter model is much less useful. The reason is that in low-fertility contexts the fundamentally important proximate determinants are always contraception and abortion. This makes other aspects of the Bongaarts/Potter model (such as the biological maximum fertility level and length of breastfeeding) largely irrelevant. Thus, in economically developed contexts, low fertility is the result of persons' desires to have small families and the use of contraception and abortion.

Bongaarts (2001) proposed an alternative model that we have found very useful for studying low fertility and its variations. This model has two broad components: (1) the desired family size characterizing a population; and (2) the factors that either enhance or reduce aggregate fertility relative to these fertility preferences. As described by Bongaarts (2001, see Figure 4 and discussion), this model could be useful at early stages of the fertility transition. He points out that early in the fertility transition, fertility often exceeds desired family size. On the other hand, once fertility falls to low levels, the opposite is often the case—desired levels of childbearing exceed the levels observed. We explore this later case. Once the fertility transition is well underway, individuals are explicitly strategizing about appropriate family size, and birth control is widespread. Specifically, this model has proven useful as a conceptual model (for instance, many articles have focused on single components of this model—the effects of tempo, desired family size, or unwanted fertility) and occasionally as a general framework for studying low fertility (see Morgan et al. 2009; Morgan and Rackin 2010; Dharmalingam et al. 2014).

As noted above, the low-fertility model has at its core the incongruence between population-level stated preferences and actual observed fertility (Bongaarts 2001; Morgan and Taylor 2006). The framework can be represented as in Eq. (7.1):

$$\text{TFR} = \text{DFS} * \left(F_U * F_R * F_{SP} \right) * \left(F_T * F_I * F_C \right) \tag{7.1}$$

Aggregate period fertility, the total fertility rate (TFR), equals women's desired family size (DFS) increased or decreased by factors and circumstances that are not or cannot be incorporated when women report their childbearing desires. If all women realized their DFS (and if tempo distortions were eliminated; see Bongaarts and Feeney 1998), then period fertility would equal DFS. The factors that increase fertility relative to desires are: unwanted fertility (F_U), replacement of child deaths (F_R), and gender preference (F_{SP}), which in the case of the United States is a preference for a son and a daughter. The effects of these factors in Eq. (7.1) would be

---

[1] Bongaarts and Potter (1983) build on the classic Davis and Blake (1956) framework.

greater than 1.0, and thus they increase fertility relative to desires (Hagewen and Morgan 2005; Dharmalingam et al. 2014). The factors that decrease fertility relative to desires are the tempo effect of fertility postponement to later years/ages (F_T), sub- or infecundity (F_I), and desires/intentions that compete with the desire for children (F_C) (Bongaarts 2001). These factors would be expected to have values of less than 1.0 in Eq. (7.1), and thus they decrease fertility compared with intentions. In the United States, aggregate intentions approximate the TFR, and both are near replacement. This is because factors that increase and decrease fertility relative to intentions are largely offsetting, not because most women individually realize their desired family size (Morgan and Rackin 2010). In most developed countries, intentions approximate replacement, but actual fertility falls far short of the replacement level (Bongaarts 2001; Hagewen and Morgan 2005). This is true because factors reducing fertility relative to intentions are stronger than factors that raise fertility.

Equation (7.1) can be used to capture the "fertility regime" in a particular population (see Morgan 2003; Morgan and Hagewen 2005; Dharmalingam et al. 2014). On the left, the TFR captures the level of actual fertility and, on the right are intermediate variables that produce this level. The fertility regime for the United States as a whole is estimated in Morgan and Hagewen (2005): Replacement-level fertility is produced by preferences for small family sizes with a general reluctance to be childless or to have only one child. These preferences, modestly above the replacement level, are augmented by: (1) high levels of unplanned pregnancies and unwanted births (i.e., they increase the TFR by 10–15 %); and (2) very modest effects of additional births to balance the gender composition of offspring (having an additional child to have a daughter or son increases fertility by about 2 %).

Opposing forces reduce fertility relative to intentions. To explain, the timing of childbearing is relatively young (compared with the situation in many European countries), but it has been increasing steadily for more than three decades. This fertility postponement has lowered the TFR by about 10 % over the period that age at childbearing was increasing. Later ages at childbearing lead to "fertility foregone" because of sub- and infecundity (reduces the TFR by 2–4 %) and because of competition between fertility and other valued activities that becomes more intense or more visible as persons age. This second factor (competition) is difficult to estimate, but the "residual" produced by assuming that this factor equals 1.0 (no effect) implies an effect on the order of a 10–15 % reduction in the TFR over the past few decades. The fertility regime based on this pattern of intermediate factors has been in place for more than four decades.[2] There is no reason to believe that it is not sustainable in the future.[3] Of course, this is not to say that it will be sustained.

---

[2] If one combines the estimated effects of the factors F_U, F_R, F_{SP} and F_T, F_I, F_C, then their cumulative effect is approximately 10 %—TFR/DFS = .90. This is what one observes in the NLSY-79 data. Young women intend an average of approximately 2.2 children but have only 2.0.

[3] An exception is F_T. Logically, the postponement of fertility cannot be maintained forever. Over the past few decades, however, ages at first and second birth have increased by only about 0.1 year, and this increase could easily be maintained for several more decades. Other parameters are often expected to change. F_U, the level of unwanted births, is often assumed to be anachronistic in a context of wide availability of effective contraceptives. This parameter is largely unchanged over

The weakness of intermediate-variable explanations is that they beg questions about the more fundamental causes of fertility: Why are fertility intentions clustered at two children per woman? Why have they remained stable? Why is unwanted fertility so high in the United States, and why has it not declined? What causes fertility postponement? Answers to these questions require consideration of more distal/fundamental causes. Asking these questions takes us to the aggregate level and focuses attention on social structure: Are there regularities at this level? Can we identify the mechanisms that produce them? In looking for explanations of aggregate differences, we are not denying micro-level variation or decision making. Rather, we view macro-level dynamics as a product of the interaction of micro- and macro-level processes (Johnson-Hanks et al. 2011). We assert, however, that major influences on aggregate fertility levels/differences should be conceptualized and operationalized at the aggregate level. Thus, emphasis moves away from individual decisions to the structures in the world that motivate and constrain behavior (Bachrach and Morgan 2013).

Relying on a Theory of Constructural Action (TCA, see Johnson-Hanks et al. 2011), we define social structures as durable forms of organization, patterns of behavior, or systems of social relations (Greenhalgh 1990; see also, e.g., McNicoll 1980). The fertility regime, its fertility level, and a set of intermediate variables make up one such social structure. Social structures are dual in nature (Sewell 1992, 2005; Johnson-Hanks et al. 2011). They emerge from the interplay of observable material structures (e.g., objects, speech, observable behaviors, and built environments) and the schematic meanings that material forms instantiate (e.g., values, beliefs, norms, scripts, and ways of categorizing). Thus, low-fertility regimes are produced by schemas that legitimate small families as "good" and fertility control as "appropriate for responsible parents," as well as material aspects of the environment that make small families advantageous, such as the expense of childcare for working mothers and the "second shift" of housework and childcare that women often disproportionally assume (see Johnson-Hanks et al. 2011, Chapter 4). While the aggregate measurement of DFS operationalized above is the mean of individual responses, the concept we seek to measure is the DFS that is "in the world." What family size is judged as most desirable and appropriate in a particular population?

Aggregate family-size desires are strongly correlated with observed fertility in many contexts (Bongaarts 1992; Morgan 2001). I am interested in identifying factors that can account for observed differences between the mean desired family size and observed fertility and in locating the more distal causes of these differences. For instance, in the United States there is a well-documented preference for couples to have both a son and a daughter. Couples without this balance are more likely to have an additional child (Pollard and Morgan 2002). These regularities reflect the importance of the institution of gender and the different roles expected of sons/daughters (or boys/girls). In situations where the sex of children cannot be controlled, this

---

the past three decades, however, indicating that it is not driven by the availability of contraception but rather by effective contraception use and the acceptability of abortion should it fail. See discussion in Technical Panel on Assumptions and Methods (2011).

preference leads some persons to revise their fertility desires upward based on their fertility history and to have more children than previously intended.[4] More generally, all of the intermediate variables, such as the gender composition of current children, are anchored in aspects of the social structure (in its virtual/schematic and/ or material components).

Social structure influences behaviors "one at a time" as persons live their lives. Situations (or conjunctures) require action, and this action may include active decision making. Variation in behavior among individuals and across groups reflects not only variation in structure (schemas and materials) but also variation in the social ecology (both experienced and observed). Different social niches (e.g., those with more or less poverty and insecurity) make some conjunctures much more likely than others. Social policy should be designed to influence actions in particular situations (or conjunctures).

U.S. Fertility Variation

How useful are these layered frameworks for understanding variation across and within populations? The more useful they are for understanding observed variation, the more confident we can be in using them to pose counterfactuals linked to policy interventions or to make predictions about the fertility regimes of the future. In other papers, we have examined cross-country variation (Morgan 2003; Morgan et al. 2009) and within-country variation elsewhere (Dharmalingam et al. 2014 on fertility variation in India). Here we examine the substantial fertility variation within the United States using the intermediate variables and TCA frameworks. Fertility regimes vary considerably across subsets of the U.S. population, and we trace this variation to their more distal determinants.

Regional Fertility Variation

U.S. regional fertility variation is substantial. Vital registration data for 2011 show TFRs for U.S. states as low as 1.6 (Massachusetts, Maine, Rhode Island, Vermont) and as high as 2.3 (Alaska, South Dakota) and 2.4 (Utah). Given an aggregate TFR of 2.0, variation on the order of 0.5–0.7 is substantial (0.7/2.0 = 35 %).

Lesthaeghe and Neidert (2006, 2009) examine this contemporary U.S. regional (state) variation and link it to voting/political partisanship. Specifically, they use state-level data (N = 50) and show a correlation of 0.78 between the percent voting

---

[4] Pollard and Morgan (2002) argue that this preference for a balanced gender composition has declined in recent decades. A recent paper by Tian and Morgan (2014) extends the time series of estimates and provides further support for the declining significance of gender-balance preference in the United States.

for George Bush (versus Kerry) in the 2004 presidential election and the TFR for white non-Hispanics (Lesthaeghe and Neidert 2006, Figure 8). This is one of the most interesting findings about U.S. fertility in the past few decades, although we will take issue with aspects of the authors' interpretation. Specifically, Lesthaeghe and Neidert (2006, pp. 695, 696) argue that the United States provides a "textbook example" of the second demographic transition. They say it is "abundantly clear that the United States is a heterogeneous country, with even more variation within its borders than within the EU-25" (p. 671). Further, they document a clear "family/fertility regime" referred to as "the second demographic transition" (including low fertility, fertility and marriage postponement, and substantial nonmarital childbearing) that characterizes some states (and counties) and not others.

Lesthaeghe and van de Kaa, who coined and developed the concept of the second demographic transition (van de Kaa 2001), see the driving force of the transition as "postmodernist" values of self-expression, self-fulfilment, and self-actualization. The term "transition" implies that there is a secular change in the direction of these values and that demographic change reflects/responds to this change. In short, postmodernist values and a package of family/fertility behaviors are the future. In both Europe and the United States, they predict that there will be populations that are leaders and laggards. But the end result (with an undefined time line) will be the same. In terms of the structural theory we propose, these postmodernist values are incorporated into schemas (frames) that are certainly visible in contemporary society. We think that Lesthaeghe and Neidert have fallen victim to "reading history sideways" (see Thornton 2001, 2005), however, and the oft-made mistake of thinking that the most socioeconomically advanced populations reveal the future of less-developed ones.

We do not deny the visibility of postmodern values in the United States—as noted above they are components of many contemporary schemas. But a key part of our TCA theory is that schemas are "multiple" and can be used selectively in different situations. Of course, schemas are not selected randomly. A person's identity provides consistency to the schemas that he or she employs. Regional and political identities are intertwined in the United States, captured by the terminology of "Red States" and "Blue States" (signalling, respectively, a conservative versus liberal social and political orientation). Note Lesthaeghe and Neidert's attempt to project the second demographic transition onto the United States:

> Yes, there is an "American exceptionalism" among a non-negligible section of the population. That section is mainly located in the Midwest, the Great Plains, and the South. It is on average much more rural than metropolitan, less well educated, adheres more to Evangelical Christianity or Mormonism.... No, there is little or no "American exceptionalism" in the remainder of the United States (Lesthaeghe and Neidert 2006, p. 694).

The characterization of the Midwest, the Great Plains, and the South in terms of lower development and less secularization makes them sound as if they are simply laggards in the long slog toward postmodernism and lowest-low fertility. But in their article's concluding paragraphs, Lesthaeghe and Neidert (2006, p. 694) give some ground and propose an "American bipolarity" (as opposed to an American exceptionalism), saying:

What makes the United States particularly interesting in the overall Western context is that the conservative and religious right is openly and vocally trying to fight back (e.g., with amendments seeking to ban same-sex marriage, closure of abortion clinics). This has not happened in Europe, Canada, or Australia.

Lesthaeghe believes that this "fighting back" is a rear-guard, last gasp. We are much less convinced of the invincibility of postmodern ideology. In our TCA frame, this fighting back reflects different schemas and identities and the structures that support them. These elements of structure have shown substantial vitality on a decadal time scale. The link that Lesthaeghe and Neidert make between U.S. politics and fertility is very interesting. But note that few persons in the U.S. see the Red/Blue divide as a thing of the past. If the partisan ideology has staying power and is linked to fertility differentials, why would one expect the fertility differentials to wane?

The Lesthaeghe and Neidert (2006, 2009) work does not provide full details of the regional regime/intermediate variables. We expect that the higher fertility in the Red (versus Blue) States is a combination of factors: higher intended fertility, higher unwanted fertility, less fertility postponement, and less "competition" (in terms of revising fertility intentions downward in the face of nonfamilial opportunities). Lesthaeghe and Neidert provide evidence of less postponement in Red (versus Blue) States but are silent on the remaining intervening variables.

Religious Fertility Variation

Hayford and Morgan (2008, Table 2) show that contemporary U.S. fertility variation is primarily traced to religiosity, not to a particular religion or denomination. A simple question asked in the 2002 National Survey of Family Growth (NSFG) captures substantial fertility variation: How important is religion in your life? Responses are very important, somewhat important, or not important. The TFRs estimated for those giving these responses (in the 5 years prior to the 2002 survey) were 2.3, 2.1, and 1.8, respectively. A similar religiosity gradient in fertility is observed in a number of European countries (see Frejka and Westoff 2008). Hayford and Morgan use the low-fertility intermediate-variable framework proposed above to examine the religiosity gradient in U.S. fertility. They find clear evidence that fertility intentions are higher for the more religious but find little difference in the other intermediate variables (including unwanted fertility and fertility postponement).[5] To explore more distal causes, Hayford and Morgan turn to NSFG items that measure respondent's attitudes toward various aspects of family formation and sexuality. NSFG attitude variables are included in their analyses by constructing an additive index representing traditional family ideology. They show that the higher fertility intentions of the more religious disappear if one controls for traditional family ideology.

---

[5] Frejka and Westoff (2008) do not explore the proximate causes of the European religious gradient.

Thus the authors identify both the key intermediate variable (higher intentions) and its origin in more distal social structure (the schemas and materials of religious and family life). As Hayford and Morgan (2008, p. 1180) say, religion, family values, and politics have been conjoined by the "culture wars" of the past few decades. This association can be seen in aggregate voting and demographic behavior and in the identity of individuals.

In sum, religiosity (measured at the individual level) shows a differential fertility pattern similar to the aggregate, state-level variation that was discussed above. To a large extent, being conservative in the contemporary United States means being religious. And being conservative and religious means supporting family values that place importance on children and parenthood. Thus individuals are "Red" or "Blue" and tend to reside in communities (and states) that include similar-minded persons. This partisan "color" is amplified and reified by material symbols in places more deeply "Red" or "Blue."

Educational Fertility Differences

Morgan and Rackin (2010) use data from the 1979 National Longitudinal Survey of Youth (NLSY-79) that follows women (and men) throughout the childbearing years. Results discussed here compare intended parity[6] at age 22–24 with completed parity at age 40–44 (in 2006, see Morgan and Rackin 2010, Table 4). Those with less than a high-school education at age 22–24 have a mean completed fertility (by age 40) of 2.55, compared with only 1.67 for those with a college education. Thus, there is a clear negative fertility gradient with more education at age 22–24 (i.e., more schooling associated with lower completed fertility). But this difference is not due primarily to different levels of fertility intentions at ages 22–24. Rather, the more educated "miss their fertility target" on the low side—by an average of more than one-half a birth (−.54). In contrast, the least educated exceed their fertility target slightly (by .09 births). Taking another contrast, the intended parity of high school and college graduates (at ages 22–24) is estimated to be exactly the same (2.2 children per woman). But the former have completed fertility of 2.05 compared with 1.67 for the latter.

Educational attainment can be thought of as a proxy for the types of jobs available to young women and men and the corresponding workplace environments that they will occupy during their childbearing years. These workplace demands and norms shape both fertility intentions and fertility decisions over time and thus influence whether an individual will achieve her/his fertility intentions. Postponement of fertility is a common strategy used by highly educated women to deal with long and demanding work schedules and a normative environment that does not tend to be supportive of childbearing. Once Morgan and Rackin include variables that measure postponement—childlessness and marital status, both at age 24—the effects of

---

[6] Intended parity is the sum of children one has and the number of additional children intended.

education are sharply attenuated. Thus much of the educational effect on under-achieving fertility intentions is explained by the continued postponement of marriage and fertility; many of these postponed births become fertility forgone.

In sharp contrast, more-educated men and men currently enrolled in school at age 24 are not more likely to under-achieve their fertility intentions compared with less-educated men. Once postponement is taken into account, highly educated men (compared with the least educated) are actually less likely to under-achieve their fertility intentions. To be specific, college-educated men are only one-half (a factor of .50) as likely to underachieve their fertility intentions compared with men with the least education. Morgan and Rackin attribute these different effects to the gender-based division of labor with respect to children. Men can combine enrolment in higher education or demanding careers with having children because they bear less of the responsibilities and time demands of childcare. Of course, the gender structures producing these differences are not immutable, and more recent cohorts may confront a situation with less different constraints for men and women.[7]

The Morgan and Rackin paper shows the importance of postponement as a strategy for dealing with the competition (F_C) that arises between valued roles and opportunities. Again a "demographic regime" anchored in distal structural determinants (conceptualized as in the TCA) provides a useful framework for explaining the educational gradient in fertility.

Race-Ethnic Fertility Differences

A common claim is that the higher fertility of U.S. racial/ethnic minorities explains the robust fertility rate of the nation as a whole. The historically higher fertility of African Americans is now a modest difference. For cohorts recently completing childbearing (using estimates from Morgan and Rackin 2010, as discussed above), white women had 1.93 children on average and African Americans had 2.18. African Americans have a much earlier pattern of childbearing and are both more likely to have fewer and more children than intended (versus the exact number) compared with whites. Using 2011 vital registration period estimates (see Martin et al. 2013b), the rates for all whites and African Americans are 1.91 and 1.92, respectively. If we focus on non-Hispanic whites and African Americans, the TFRs are 1.77 and 1.92. This difference of 8 % (1.77/1.92 = 1.08) could be largely accounted for by differing levels of unwanted fertility (F_U).[8]

---

[7] Alternatively, the experience of the cohorts in the NLSY 1979 (the birth cohorts born in the 1955–1964 decade) may have become calcified, a stalled gender revolution (England 2010).

[8] Mosher et al. (2012, Table 1) show the percentage of unwanted births among non-Hispanic whites and African Americans as 6.4 % and 11.7 %, respectively, a difference of 5.3 %. African American fertility is 8 % higher than that of whites. Thus, unwanted fertility can account for 66 % of the higher African American TFR.

The Hispanic TFR was estimated at 2.24 in 2011, but was as high as 2.86 in 2006.[9] The Mexican-origin population's TFR was 2.14 in 2011, but was as high as 3.00 in 2006. Both these higher rates and their dramatic decline can be explained by immigration and the timing of fertility vis-à-vis migration (see Parrado 2011; Parrado and Morgan 2008). Immigrants tend to be young adults; they partner and have children soon after arrival in the United States. This makes their fertility appear to be quite high when measured on a period basis. The lifetime fertility of most immigrant groups is unlikely to be much above replacement, however. The recent dramatic decline in Hispanic (and especially Mexican) fertility is due to the sharp decline in immigration resulting from the Great Recession. This decline in immigration dramatically and swiftly changed the proportion of recent migrants in the United States (i.e., those in the United States 0–5 years who have much higher fertility than longer-term residents).

Vital registration data (see Martin et al. 2013a) show that the Asian and Pacific Islander population had a 2012 TFR of 1.8 (little different from the 2012 estimate for whites and African Americans at 1.9). Some Asian American groups (Japanese and Chinese, for instance) have fertility that is substantially below replacement levels. Using data from the American Community Survey, Yong Cai estimates that ethnic Chinese and Japanese TFRs in the 2008–12 period were 1.5 and 1.6, respectively.[10] There is little work on ethnic Asian fertility in the United States, but these low levels resemble patterns in China and Japan. Preference for sons may place some upward pressure on Chinese fertility (F_{SP}), but the counterforces are obviously strong. We suspect that levels of fertility postponement (F_T) are dramatic and that some postponed births are foregone to invest in existing children (F_C). Levels of unwanted fertility (F_U) are very low. These proximate variables, in turn, are anchored in a greater "rationality," or degree of planning (compared with U.S. whites), characterizing a highly rational cultural logic that determines family size in these populations (for Chinese diaspora populations see Greenhalgh 1988). This cultural logic includes less stigma toward abortion.

Discussion

When we introduced the (low-fertility) intermediate-variable framework above, we identified the parameters (the fertility regime) that lead to replacement-level fertility in the United States. In our discussion of fertility differentials, we identified the most likely intermediate variables responsible for variation. Table 7.1 summarizes our claims about variation. For instance, variation by state is caused by different levels of desired fertility (DFS) that are altered by differential levels of unwanted fertility (F_U) and postponement/competition (F_T and F_C). In contrast,

---

[9] To illustrate the diversity within the Hispanic population, Cuban Hispanics' 2011 TFR was only 1.43, while that for "other Hispanics" was 2.87.

[10] Personal correspondence, 13 Jan 2014.

Table 7.1 Intermediate variables responsible for fertility variation in the United States

Variation by:	Desired family size (DFS)	Level of unwanted fertility (F_U)	Effect of sex preference (F_{SP})	Effect of fertility postponement (F_T)	Effect of competition with other desires/intentions (F_C)[a]
State	X	X		X	X
Religiosity	X				
Education				X	X
Race/ethnicity					
Black/white		X			
Hispanic/non-hispanic				X	
Asian/white		X	X	X	X

[a]Effect of competition with other desires/intentions that reduces fertility intentions over the life course

education differentials can be accounted for by variation in postponement/competition (F_T and F_C) alone.

Identifying the demographic regime and its variations is only the first step. Documenting the difference in, for instance, unwanted fertility begs the question of why these levels of unwanted fertility vary. Answering this question requires attention to fundamental/distal causes embedded in social structure. In our (TCA) conceptualization of social structure, we look to key conjunctures, the situations where actions occur. What are the materials available to realize action or to suggest it? What is the nature of the available schemas? We will provide two examples of the kind of analysis we propose.

Unplanned Pregnancies

The first conjuncture is an unplanned pregnancy. Unplanned pregnancy is common in the United States. Roughly 50 % of pregnancies are unintended, as are 37 % of all births (Mosher et al. 2012). Ten to fifteen percent of all births are unwanted births (F_U), with little evidence of secular change in the past few decades (Mosher et al. 2012).

Unintended pregnancy is a classic conjuncture: It is a situation that must be resolved. The schemas for construing the situation are well known by all in the United States and are highly politicized—they are "in the world." There is a pro-choice schema that stresses the importance of planned pregnancies. One should be ready, economically and emotionally, to have children. This schema accepts postponement of childbearing as a way to meet these goals. This pro-choice schema legitimates the option of ending an unplanned pregnancy. An opposing anti-abortion schema views life as beginning at conception and views abortion as morally problematic. Further, this schema valorizes the choices of those who "do the right thing" and have the child. This schema holds that such choices produce maturity and that being a parent provides stability and order to otherwise chaotic lives.

How one construes a woman's situation (the schema she uses to motivate/justify her decision) may be contested. It is influenced by significant others (including parents, friends, and romantic partners) and by the availability of materials (including abortion services and information) that make enacting one decision easier/more difficult than another. Edin and Kefalas (2005) describe U.S. women living in poverty for whom many of the role models embody the anti-abortion schema. Many of the stories told in these environments suggest that having children early (even if unintended) does not ruin lives; rather, these children bring order, meaning, and stability. Mothers, even the economically disadvantaged, can provide children what they most need—love and support. Such mothers say that they make "promises I can keep" to "be there" for their children. This pro-life schema is not embraced only by the poor. The Republican Vice-Presidential candidate in 2008, Sarah Palin's daughter's much-discussed pregnancy and her decision to have the child received widespread media attention in 2007. Conservative political views and many religious leaders valorized her and her family's choice (see Morgan 2011, pp. 61–63).

Of course, there are many abortions in the United States as well. Edin and Kefalas's sample consists of young mothers living in poverty. Abortion is common even within these communities, and presumably those choosing not to have children at young ages would justify their decision using the opposing schema. In other communities—among the wealthier and better-educated segments of the population—early and unintended childbearing is less common. In these settings, abortions are justified in terms of allowing persons to fulfill their goals and dreams and/or to advantage existing children or potential future ones.

The contrasting responses to unwanted pregnancy in the United States explain the high level of unplanned/unwanted births. Variation in the construal of this conjuncture across physical and social space explains variation in this intermediate variable across these same dimensions. Contrasts with East Asia seem noteworthy. The anti-abortion schemas are not legitimated there, and the dominant concern is with not diluting the resources that would allow existing children to thrive. This conjuncture would be consistently construed in favor of abortion in East Asia. Unwanted fertility is rare in East Asia compared with the United States – so rare that measurement of the phenomena is frequently not even attempted.

Second Births

Since births are inherently sequential, persons can make decisions to have or not have an additional birth.[11] A second key conjuncture is the decision/intent to have a second birth. The schemas that are "in the world" and thus accessible to women are many. Having a second child is often justified/rationalized as providing a sibling for

---

[11] The obvious exception is the relatively rare case of multiple births.

the first born. Having a sibling is argued to be advantageous in terms of the first child's development and providing an important relative throughout life. Some parents are also concerned that having a single child puts them at risk of having no children given the small chance that something happens to the first born. Finally, with one child already born, the "marginal cost" of a second is reduced in several ways: Some toys/clothes are already purchased; the parents already have experience with children, etc. Alternative schemas in the United States (reasons to stop at one child) are less visible than in East Asia. Having a difficult or disabled child is a possible reason and implies that the investment in the first child (because of the unusual circumstances) limits the couples' ability to invest in a second. Other reasons include union dissolution, again a factor that limits resources (such that a second child would threaten the ability to care for the first).

The progression to second birth is high in the United States across time and social space; one-child families are relatively rare. Again the contrast with East Asia is informative. There, concerns about the cost of education and the competitive nature of admission to the best schools legitimate rationales that postpone or forego the second child in order to advantage the first born. In the East Asian context, good parents are expected to provide "intensive parenting," including cram courses after school in English and math. These courses matter for admission to the best schools and colleges. In turn, graduation from the best colleges provides the greatest access to the most secure and best-paying jobs. Tan et al. (2014) describe this intense competition as a dysfunctional "arms race" that encourages ever greater investments in existing children.

U.S. Policies

As noted at the outset, U.S. fertility has approximated the replacement level for four decades. The U.S. government sees the current fertility rate as adequate and has no policies aimed at changing the aggregate rate (United Nations 2011). Policymakers are concerned about the high level of adolescent childbearing, however, and about the large proportion of births that are unintended or unwanted (compared with the situation in many other highly developed countries). Healthy People 2020[12] set a goal of increasing the use of highly effective contraceptives, and the United States has policies aimed at reducing unintended and unwanted childbearing, especially among the young and the unmarried where unintended childbearing is greatest. Federally supported abstinence-only education programs have grown rapidly since 2008. The recent decline in U.S. adolescent pregnancy rates follows the patterns observed in other developed countries, however—improved contraceptive use, not increasing abstinence, has been the primary determinant of declining rates (Santelli et al. 2007). Much evidence indicates that government funding for family planning

---

[12] See http://www.healthypeople.gov/2020/topicsobjectives2020/overview.aspx?topicid=13

services reduces unintended pregnancies among the poor and near poor (Cleland et al. 2011).

There is also a large set of policies that likely have inadvertent effects on fertility. Some of these policies are aimed at poor children and families. Moffitt (2014) argues that changes in these policies in the past two decades have favored the working poor and near poor,[13] as opposed to those most disadvantaged. These families, as the result of having some earned income, likely get the full benefit of programs such as the annual child tax credit (at $1,000 per child) and a substantial credit through the Earned Income Tax Credit (EITC, a maximum annual tax credit of $3,305 or $5,460 for one or two qualifying children, respectively). Married couples (with two children) making over $50,000 do not qualify for any payments from the large EITC program,[14] and the $1,000 child tax credit is phased out as income for a married couple moves above $100,000.[15] These policies are aimed at poverty reduction and assisting the middle class, but there is evidence that they have some pronatalist impact (Whittington 1992).

Other policies are no doubt relevant, although their connection to fertility is less direct. For instance, monetary policies aimed at making homes more affordable through government-backed mortgages may contribute to family formation at earlier ages. On the other hand, macro-economic policies that lead to a globalized work force and globalized production reduce job and income security for much of the U.S. working and middle class. This insecurity likely postpones family formation.

In short, the tapestry of public policy likely has pervasive inadvertent effects on U.S. family formation. Unraveling these effects is a very difficult task. The more valuable lessons from policy interventions are more likely to come from intentional interventions in low-fertility countries (see McDonald 2006).

Conclusion

According to Lesthaeghe and Neidert (2006), the United States has more internal fertility variation than the EU-25. We have examined this variation and identified important intermediate variables that are responsible. These intermediate variables are anchored in a social structure that makes them sustainable. Thus, very low fertility is a possibility in the United States, but the more likely scenario is fertility slightly to modestly below replacement level. The U.S. case does not provide strong or clear lessons for those with much lower fertility. The fertility regime in the United

---

[13] The U.S. poverty line in 2014 is an annual income of $24,000 for a family of four. The working poor and near poor would consist of families that earn approximately $10,000 to $45,000 a year for a family of four.

[14] For limits to the EITC in 2014, see: http://www.irs.gov/Individuals/Preview-of-2012-EITC-Income-Limits,-Maximum-CreditDOUBLEHYPHENAmounts-and-Tax-Law-Updates

[15] For limits to the child tax credit in 2014 see: http://www.irs.gov/uac/Ten-Facts-about-the-Child-Tax-Credit

States does produce replacement-level fertility, but the intermediate variables involved are not sustained by explicit policy. Rather they are sustained by historical and cultural continuity. We do argue, however, that the approach to explaining fertility levels and variation in the United States is transportable. That is, a first step is to identify the "fertility regime": What is it that needs to be explained? Which intermediate variables account for low fertility? The second step is to locate the origins of these intermediate variables in social structure and examine the conjunctures in which this structure is reproduced. The conjunctures described above, focusing on abortion and having a second child, provide examples.

Understanding the social structures that determine the intermediate variables (that, in turn, determine the level of fertility) requires imagining the conjunctures that individuals face. This includes consideration of the materials that suggest or enable courses of action and the "local logics" (the schemas available to actors). Effective policy must be designed to alter the way conjunctures are construed. Social scientists often see policy as altering the materials present in a conjuncture. But altering the ways people think about their options is also a plausible strategy. Considering policies that provide innovative ways of thinking about a situation (conjuncture) and providing resources that enable new choices can lead to new social structures, including those that produce replacement-level fertility.

References

Bachrach, C. A., & Morgan, S. P. (2013). A cognitive–social model of fertility intentions. *Population and Development Review, 39*, 459–485.
Bongaarts, J. (1978). A framework for analyzing the proximate determinants of fertility. *Population and Development Review, 4*, 105–132.
Bongaarts, J. (1992). Do reproductive intentions matter? *International Family Planning Perspectives, 18*(3), 102–108.
Bongaarts, J. (2001). Fertility and reproductive preferences in post-transitional societies. *Population and Development Review, 27*(Supplement: Global Fertility Transition), 260–81.
Bongaarts, J., & Feeney, G. (1998). On the quantum and tempo of fertility. *Population and Development Review, 24*(2), 271–291.
Bongaarts, J., & Potter, R. G. (1983). *Fertility, biology and behavior*. New York: Academic.
Cleland, K., Peipert, J. F., Westhoff, C., Spear, S., & Trussell, J. (2011). Family planning as a cost-saving preventive health service. *New England Journal of Medicine, 364*(18), e37.
Davis, K., & Blake, J. (1956). Social structure and fertility: An analytical framework. *Economic Development and Cultural Change, 4*, 211–235.
Dharamalingam, A., Rajan, S., & Morgan, S. P. (2014). The determinants of low fertility in India. *Demography, 51*(4), 1451–1475.
Edin, K., & Kefalas, M. (2005). *Promises I can keep: Why poor women put motherhood before marriage*. Berkeley: University of California Press.
England, P. (2010). The gender revolution: Uneven and stalled. *Gender and Society, 24*(2), 149–166.
Frejka, T., & Westoff, C. F. (2008). Religion, religiousness, and fertility in the US and in Europe/ Religion, religiosité et fécondité aux Etats-Unis et en Europe. *European Journal of Population, 24*(1), 5–31.

Greenhalgh, S. (1988). Fertility as mobility: Sinic transitions. *Population and Development Review, 14*(4), 629–674.
Greenhalgh, S. (1990). Toward a political economy of fertility: Anthropological contributions. *Population and Development Review, 16*(1), 85–106.
Hagewen, K. J., & Morgan, S. P. (2005). Intended and ideal family size in the United States, 1970–2002. *Population and Development Review, 31*(3), 507–522.
Hayford, S., & Morgan, S. P. (2008). Religiosity and fertility in the United States: The role of fertility intentions. *Social Forces, 86*(3), 1163–1188.
Johnson-Hanks, J., Bachrach, C., Morgan, S. P., & Kohler, H.-P. (2011). *Understanding family change and variation: Structure, conjuncture, and action.* New York: Springer.
Lesthaeghe, R., & Neidert, L. (2006). The second demographic transition in the United States: Exception or textbook example? *Population and Development Review, 32*, 660–698.
Lesthaeghe, R., & Neidert, L. (2009). U.S. presidential elections and the spatial pattern of the American second demographic transition. *Population and Development Review, 35*(2), 391–400.
Martin, J. A., Hamilton, B. E., Osterman, M. J. K., & Mathews, T. J. (2013a). Births: Final data for 2012. *National Vital Statistics Reports, 62*(9).
Martin, J. A., Hamilton, B. E., Ventura, S. J., Osterman, M. J. K., & Mathews, T. J. (2013b). Births: Final data for 2011. *National Vital Statistics Reports, 62*(1).
McDonald, P. (2006). Low fertility and the state: The efficacy of policy. *Population and Development Review, 32*(3), 485–510.
McNicoll, G. (1980). Institutional determinants of fertility change. *Population and Development Review, 6*(3), 441–462.
Moffitt, R. (2014, 1–3 May). *The deserving poor, the family, and the U.S. welfare system.* Presidential address at the annual meeting of the Population Association of America, Boston.
Morgan, S. P. (2001). Should fertility intentions inform fertility forecasts? In *Proceedings of U.S. Census Bureau Conference: The direction of fertility in the United States.* Washington, DC: U.S. Census Bureau.
Morgan, S. P. (2003). Is low fertility a twenty-first-century demographic crisis? *Demography, 40*(4), 589–603.
Morgan, S. P. (2011). Thinking about demographic family differences. In M. J. Carlson & P. England (Eds.), *Social class and changing families in an unequal America* (pp. 50–67). Palo Alto: Stanford University Press.
Morgan, S. P., & Hagewen, K. (2005). Is very low fertility inevitable in America? Insights and forecasts from an integrative model of fertility. In A. Booth & A. C. Crouter (Eds.), *The new population problem: Why families in developed counties are shrinking and what it means* (pp. 3–28). Malwah: Lawrence Erlbaum Associates.
Morgan, S. P., & Rackin, H. (2010). The correspondence of fertility intentions and behavior in the U.S. *Population and Development Review, 36*(1), 91–118.
Morgan, S. P., & Taylor, M. G. (2006). Low fertility at the turn of the twenty-first century. *Annual Review of Sociology, 32*, 375–400.
Morgan, S. P., Guo, Z., & Hayford, S. (2009). China's below replacement fertility: Recent trends and future prospects. *Population and Development Review, 35*(3), 605–630.
Mosher, W. D., Jones, J., & Abama, J. C. (2012). Intended and unintended births in the United States: 1982–2010. In: *National health statistics reports* (Vol. 55, pp. 1–27). Hyattsville: National Center for Health Statistics.
Parrado, E. A. (2011). How high is Hispanic/Mexican fertility in the United States? Immigration and tempo considerations. *Demography, 48*, 1059–1080.
Parrado, E., & Morgan, S. P. (2008). Intergenerational fertility among Hispanic women: New evidence of immigrant assimilation. *Demography, 45*(4), 651–671.
Pollard, M. S., & Morgan, S. P. (2002). Emerging gender indifference: Sex composition of children and the third birth. *American Sociological Review, 67*, 600–613.
Santelli, J. S., Lindberg, L. D., Finer, L. B., & Singh, S. (2007). Explaining recent declines in adolescent pregnancy in the United States: The contribution of abstinence and improved contraceptive use. *American Journal of Public Health, 97*(1), 150–156.

Sewell, W. H. (1992). A theory of structure: Duality, agency, and transformation. *American Journal of Sociology, 98*(1), 1–29.

Sewell, W. H. (2005). *Logics of history*. Chicago: University of Chicago Press.

Tan, P. L., Morgan, S. P., & Zagheni, E. (2014). *A case for "reverse one-child" policies in East Asia? Examining the link between education costs and lowest-low fertility*. Unpublished manuscript. Durham: Duke University.

Technical Panel on Assumptions and Methods. (2011). *2011 technical panel on assumptions and methods: Report to the social security advisory board*. Washington, DC: Social Security Advisory Board.

Thornton, A. (2001). The developmental paradigm, reading history sideways, and family change. *Demography, 38*(4), 449–467.

Thornton, A. (2005). *Reading history sideways: The fallacy and enduring impact of the developmental paradigm on family life*. Chicago: University of Chicago Press.

Tian, F. F., & Morgan, S. P. (2014, May 1–3). *Sex composition of children and third birth in the United States: Further evidence for emerging gender indifference*. Paper presented at the annual meeting of the Population Association of America, Boston.

United Nations. (2011). *World fertility policies wallchart 2011*. http://www.un.org/en/development/desa/population/publications/fertility/world-fertility-policies-2011.shtml. Accessed 14 Oct 2014.

van de Kaa, D. J. (2001). Postmodern fertility preferences: From changing value orientation to new behavior. *Population and Development Review, 27*(Supplement: Global Fertility Transition), 290–331.

Whittington, L. A. (1992). Taxes and the family: The impact of the tax exemption for dependents on marital fertility. *Demography, 29*(2), 215–226.

Chapter 8
The Evolution of Population and Family Policy in Australia

Peter McDonald

Population Growth, 1788–1945

Population growth was a prominent focus for policy debate from the beginning of the settlements in the new-world countries—the United States, Canada, and Australia. All saw themselves as creating a new society that would be superior to the first world (Europe) from which they had come. Healthy population growth often was used as evidence of the success of the new societies. In the United States, these views were expressed by prominent people in the independence movement, such as Benjamin Franklin and John Adams, and the rapid growth of America's population is said to have contributed to the onset of the revolution (Hoff 2012, Ch. 1). In the nineteenth century, Malthusian theory was often debated in the United States with advocates on both sides of the debate. According to Hoff (2012, Ch. 2), population again played a role in the Civil War. Throughout the nineteenth century, the United States population grew rapidly through largely unrestricted migration but also through high rates of fertility associated with early marriage.

As early as the 1830s, Britain and the colonies of Australia and Canada came to an agreement that the excess poor populations of Britain would be provided with assisted passages so as to boost labor supply in the colonies, while at the same time relieving poverty in Britain (Robinson 2002).[1] Since the 1830s, migration to Australia has always been policy driven, with the single exception of the spontaneous wave of migration in the 1850s, stimulated by the discovery of gold in Victoria.[2]

---

[1] Many of the author's ancestors arrived in Australia as poverty-stricken assisted-passage immigrants between 1839 and 1854.

[2] Australia's population trebled in the single decade, 1850–1860, as a result of the Victorian gold rush.

P. McDonald (✉)
Crawford School of Public Policy, The Australian National University,
Canberra, ACT, Australia
e-mail: Peter.McDonald@anu.edu.au

Labor demand has always been the most important determinant of migration to Australia, and successive governments have ramped up or curtailed immigration according to the perceived level of labor demand at the time. When the Australian federation was created in 1901, one of the first acts of the new Parliament was to close the border to free movement as was done in the United States at the same time. This was not designed to limit population growth which, at the time, was seen to be unacceptably low. Instead, border closure was essentially a move to prevent Asian migration, in what became known as the White Australia Policy. In general, migration to Australia was low in the first half of the twentieth century except for surges immediately before and after the First World War (Fig. 8.1).

As in the United States, fertility in mid-nineteenth century Australia was very high, at around eight births per married woman who completed the childbearing years. Australia also participated fully in the decline in fertility that swept across the English-speaking countries in the latter part of the nineteenth century (Ruzicka and Caldwell 1977). This decline was expertly documented in an important early study by Timothy Coghlan (1903), who had been appointed in the mid-1880s as the Government Statistician of New South Wales. Coghlan was not a Malthusian and was a strong advocate of the theory that population growth was a reflection of prosperity (Hicks 1981). Coghlan's observations on the decline of fertility led to the establishment of the Royal Commission on the Decline of the Birth-Rate and on the Mortality of Infants in New South Wales, the first major enquiry into falling birth rates held anywhere in the world. The Commissioners concluded that the decline

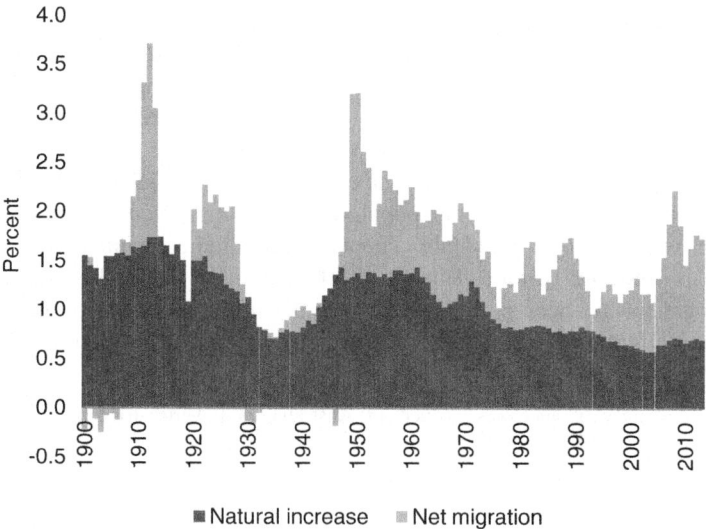

Fig. 8.1 Percentage annual rate of population growth showing components due to natural increase and net international migration, Australia, 1900–2013 (For 1900–2008, Australian Bureau of Statistics 2008; for 2009–2013, Australian Bureau of Statistics 2013)

8 The Evolution of Population and Family Policy in Australia

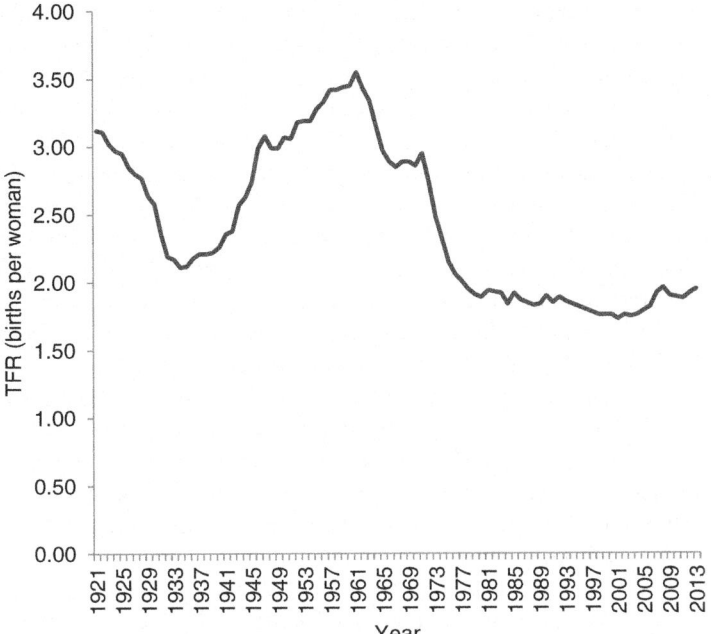

Fig. 8.2 Total fertility rate, Australia, 1921–2013 (For 1900–2008, Australian Bureau of Statistics 2008; for 2009–2013, Australian Bureau of Statistics 2013)

was due to an outbreak of materialism (couples preferring to accumulate the good things of life rather than providing more children for the nation) and to the selfishness of women wanting to avoid the "discomforts" of frequent pregnancies. There were also references to the recourse to immoral and illegal means of preventing births (viz. contraception).

Despite the call of the all-male commissioners for citizens to end these deviant behaviors and contribute to nation building, the birth rate continued to fall. By the early 1930s, with the country in deep depression, the Australian fertility rate had fallen to replacement level (Fig. 8.2). Throughout the 1930s and the years of the Second World War, net migration was close to zero. In the period 1930–1945, annual population growth averaged 0.85 %, the only sustained period in Australian history when the growth rate has been lower than 1 % per annum.

Family Support Policy, 1907–1945

The genesis of family policy in Australia was the Basic Wage Case (the Harvester Judgment) in 1907, in which Justice Higgins established a basic wage that was sufficient for a man to support a wife and three dependent children at a modest but adequate level.³ Higgins had drawn his inspiration from the study of adequate wages conducted by Seebohm Rowntree in York, England in the late nineteenth century. Thereafter, wage negotiations and the various awards for different adult male workers took the basic wage as their starting point. The basic wage applied to all adult males irrespective of their family circumstances on the assumption that all males were potentially husbands with a dependent wife and three children. Wages for women and for minors were set at much lower levels on the basis that they were not husbands supporting families—even if they were women with an unemployed husband and three children. Thus, the origins of family policy were in the legal system and the industrial courts, not in the government. The basic wage continued as the foundation of wages policy in Australia until it was abolished in the early 1970s, when it was replaced by a system of equal pay for equal work.

With some memory of the 1903 Royal Commission in mind, but also with an emphasis on the costs of maternity, the Commonwealth Labour government introduced a maternity allowance in 1912. The allowance was a lump-sum cash grant of five pounds, payable to a mother on the birth of a child. This was equivalent to 2 weeks' wages for an unskilled worker at the time. It was payable to single mothers but not to indigenous mothers.

With a much greater emphasis on the wellbeing of families, the Labour Government of New South Wales introduced a range of policies in the late 1920s that were supportive of families with children. These included a cash payment made to the mother for each child, known as child endowment, abolition of fees for students in government secondary schools, workers' compensation for injury sustained at work, reduction of the standard working week from 48 to 40 h, and a pension for widows with children under the age of 15 years. A Commonwealth Royal Commission on Child Endowment was set up in 1927 but, at its conclusion in 1929, three out of the five commissioners recommended that child endowment should not be introduced at the national level.⁴

In 1935, the Commonwealth Minister for Health, William Morris Hughes, concerned about the low level of fertility in Australia, made a speech in which he used a phrase that has reverberated in Australian population policy debate ever since. In the speech, he drew linkages between population and defense, saying that Australia must "populate or perish." In campaigning against the falling birth rate, Hughes became known informally as "the minister for motherhood." Partly in response, in 1941, the Commonwealth Government, led by Prime Minister Robert Menzies, extended child endowment to all children in a family beyond the first child and, as in New South Wales, the payment was made to the mother of the child. While under the Australian constitution children are the responsibility of the state governments, the transfer of the income-tax power to the federal government during World War

---

³ Australia's social-welfare system is based on a system of guaranteed "safety-net" payments made by the government from consolidated revenue rather than upon a social-insurance system. Its development is described in Castles and Mitchell (1993).

⁴ In the minority, John Curtin, later war-time Prime Minister of Australia, supported the introduction of child endowment along with the only female commissioner, Mildred Muncio.

Two meant that control of the funding for cash transfers or tax allowances related to children shifted to the federal government, and it has remained with the federal government ever since.

Population Growth, 1946–2013

By the end of the Second World War, the "populate-or-perish" imperative had taken on increased force. A population projection made in 1947 indicated that, with zero net migration, Australia's population would rise from 7.7 million in 1950 to only 8 million by the year 2000 (Kippen and McDonald 2000). This was a frightening prospect for those concerned with post-war reconstruction. From that point, Australia embarked upon a post-war migration program that aimed to sustain the rate of net migration at 1 % of population per annum. When to the surprise of most contemporary demographers, the fertility rate began to rise on its way to creating the post-war baby boom (Fig. 8.2), an informal target population growth rate of 2 % per annum, 1 % from natural increase and 1 % from net migration, became the basis of the population policy underpinning reconstruction of Australia. While the 2 % target disappeared from policy rhetoric long ago, the reality in the 68 years from 1946 to 2013 has not been far away from the early post-war target level. The average annual rate of population growth in Australia in that 68-year period has been 1.62 %, 0.97 % from natural increase and 0.65 % from net migration.

Despite the high average rate of population growth across this time period, all three demographic parameters underwent significant changes in trend or approach. The first and most obvious was the movement from comparatively high fertility during the baby-boom years to below replacement fertility (Fig. 8.2).[5] This change happened in the 1970s. The baby boom was driven to a large extent by a tempo effect resulting from increasingly early marriage and early childbearing (McDonald and Kippen 2011). Under the influence of higher education levels for women, higher female labor-force participation, and better access to reliable contraception, the pattern of early childbearing reversed rapidly in the 1970s, with marriages and childbearing being substantially delayed. This trend produced a tempo effect on fertility in the opposite direction, with cross-sectional fertility being lower than the underlying cohort fertility until about 2006.

By the early 2000s, the slow but persistent decline of fertility in the 1990s had created a concern that Australian fertility might continue to fall to the very low levels that were then evident in several European countries. Certain policy initiatives were undertaken, in part, to halt this decline, while at the same time supporting mothers to combine work and childbearing. Indeed, the total fertility rate rose after these policy initiatives were introduced in 2004, but McDonald and Kippen (2011) have demonstrated that this rise was due to the cessation of the tempo effect on fertility, that is, to the end of further delay of childbearing and the occurrence of

---

[5] Fertility reached a peak of 3.55 births per woman in 1961 and a trough of 1.73 in 2001.

births at older ages that had been previously delayed. Today, the cross-sectional rate is in accord with the underlying completed cohort fertility at around 1.9 births per woman. In the past 35 years, Australian fertility has fluctuated in a relatively narrow band between a low of 1.73 births per woman in 2001 and a high of 1.96 in 2008. Policy interest in measures to support fertility has almost disappeared as a result of the recent relatively high fertility levels.

The second change of trend relates to mortality. As in other developed countries, the rate of improvement in Australian mortality levelled off during the 1960s, and there was a sense that further improvements in mortality would be small. However, since 1970, improvements in mortality rates, especially at older ages, have been substantial and continuous. Today, Australia has one of the highest expectations of life of any country.

The third major change was in the approaches to overseas migration. The many changes are described in detail in Markus et al. (2009). Following the Second World War, Australia accepted a very large number of displaced persons, especially from East and Central European countries. Then, from the 1950s, international migration to Australia was founded upon an assisted-passage scheme where migrants, particularly migrants from the United Kingdom but also from many European countries and especially from Southern Europe, received highly subsidized passages to settle in Australia. This approach was brought to an end in 1982, and from that time onwards, travel to Australia for migration has been funded by the immigrants themselves. In the earlier period, it was necessary to provide incentives for people to move to Australia from other countries. However, from 1982 onwards, reflecting Australia's steadily increasing attractiveness as a destination country for migrants, it has not been necessary to provide subsidies. Also, in 1982, the Trans-Tasman Travel Agreement was signed with New Zealand, an agreement that enables free and open movement between the two countries. Today, some 15 % of all New Zealand citizens live in Australia.

The attractiveness of Australia as a migrant destination enabled Australia from the mid-1990s to select its new settlers on the basis of their ages and skills. Family migration has been restricted, so that its ratio to skilled migration is one to two. Today, most new settlers are skilled persons under the age of 40. Furthermore, most family migrants are the spouses/partners of Australian citizens and permanent residents, and this group also tends to be highly skilled (McDonald et al. 2013). The mid-1990s also ushered in a new approach that transformed the nature of settler migration to Australia in the 2000s. Migrants were permitted to enter Australia on a temporary basis and later to convert to permanent residence on-shore. Today, almost two-thirds of all new skilled permanent residents are already working in Australia when their permanent residence is granted. They are recruited from among temporary residents who entered Australia on long-stay business visas, international student visas, or working holiday-maker visas. The system is designed to be responsive to labor demand. From 2006 onwards, net migration to Australia has been running at an average of 230,000 persons per annum, a numerical level that far exceeds any other period in Australian history.

Family Policy, 1947–2003

Child Endowment, Tax Deductions, and Family Allowance

Robert Menzies, Prime Minister of Australia from 1949 to 1963, saw himself as a champion of government support for families with children. In the early 1950s, the Menzies Government extended the child-endowment payment to all children including the first child. Motivated by a strong belief in tax equity for families with children, Menzies introduced generous tax deductions later in the 1950s for children and for certain child-related expenses such as education and health. As tax deductions, the benefits were largely in the hands of fathers. This was in harmony with the reassertion of the male-breadwinner ideology of the family in the 1950s, and Menzies was a great believer in this ideology. The Menzies tax deductions also included a deduction for a dependent spouse, again in accord with the male-breadwinner ideology. Because the benefits took the form of tax deductions in a progressive income-tax system, these measures valued children and wives in wealthier families at a higher absolute level than children and wives in poorer families. As such, they violated the principle of vertical equity, which stipulates that the tax-transfer system should be used as an instrument to narrow differences in disposable incomes across the community. Indeed, it was quite inconsistent to combine tax schedules that supported the principle of vertical equity with child- and spouse-related deductions that violated this principle. This anomalous situation continued until 1975 when, for 1 year, the tax deductions were converted to tax rebates.

Throughout this era, child endowment payments continued to be paid, but its value was allowed to languish. It had been "grandfathered," rather than abolished, and was popularly regarded as "pin money" for mothers. In 1975, the year before they were abolished, child endowment payments had fallen to the grand amounts of 50 cents per week for the first child, $1 for the second, and $2 for the third and subsequent children.[6] The $3.50 per week for a three-child family contrasted poorly with the tax deductions provided for a dependent spouse and three children, which totaled $20 per week, leaving aside the deductions that were available for the education and health costs of children (McDonald et al. 1989).

By the end of the 1960s, Australian family policy consisted of the basic wage, child endowment, and the Menzies tax deductions. These measures had been introduced on top of each other with little consideration for their consistency, a "bolt-on" approach to policy that has characterized Australian family policy ever since. From the 1980s onwards, the bolt-ons continued but became progressively smaller and more complex, but this was after major reforms in the 1970s. By the end of the 1960s, it was evident that the basic wage had lost its family-support origins and had become simply a wages policy for men. This made the injustice of the unequal

---

[6] All dollar amounts in this chapter are Australian dollars. From the time the Australian dollar was introduced in 1966, its value has fluctuated widely against the United States (US) dollar, but in recent years, the Australian and US dollars have been close to parity.

wages of women for equal work with men particularly evident. In a case beginning in 1969 and ending in 1972, the Industrial Court declared the basic wage to be anachronistic and introduced equal pay for equal work. The Industrial Court was thus finally freed from its responsibility to consider the adequacy of family income, leaving it more open to shift its attention in subsequent years to the working conditions of workers with family responsibilities. Around the same time, all restrictions upon the employment of married women (the hallmark of male-breadwinner policy) were removed.

A radical change to the family-support system was made by the conservative Coalition parties in 1976, when the tax deductions for children and child-endowment payments were abolished simultaneously and replaced with a universal per-child cash payment to the mother (or principal caregiver), called family allowance. The introduction of the family allowance was a strong endorsement of the principal of horizontal equity. The payment was made in equal measure to families irrespective of the level of family income. This meant that the family allowance was worth more to lower-income families than to higher-income families, and so it had a moderately positive effect upon vertical equity, unlike the tax deductions that it replaced. This was one of the few moments of clear-headed rationalization of family policy in Australian history. The inconsistencies and inefficiencies of the basic wage, child endowment, and tax deductions for children were swept away in one bold move.

To this point, the central theme for the formulation of family-support policy had been equity, both horizontal and vertical. The ending of bans on the employment of women, the introduction of equal pay, the demands of the feminist movement, the control over fertility provided by modern contraception, the increased emphasis on the education of women, and labor shortages—all these contributed to the emergence of a new policy direction, the balancing of work and family responsibilities. There were small but promising beginnings in the 1970s with the introduction of operating subsidies for community-based childcare centers (1975), paid maternity leave in the public sector (1973), and 1 year of unpaid maternity leave for permanent workers who had worked for an enterprise for at least 12 months (1979). The dependent-spouse rebate continued throughout this period of change in the 1970s but, in the 1980s, its role as a work disincentive for women in couple families was increasingly recognized. This gave rise to a new political battleground that has continued through the 1980s to the early 2000s, the battle between those who argued for family policies that enabled mothers to stay at home and those who argued for policies that supported the combination of women's paid work with family responsibilities. Before detailing the elements of this battle, we will discuss another debate that has continued from the 1980s onwards, that between vertical and horizontal equity.

Vertical and Horizontal Equity in Family Payments

After the introduction of the family allowance in 1976, there was a two-tiered child-payments system in Australia: the high child-related payments made to government-income-support recipients and the lower family-allowance payments made to all other parents. The payments made to government-income-support recipients were income tested when a person moved off income support. It was argued that the loss of this child supplement operated as a work disincentive for government-income recipients and, in 1982, a new, income-tested supplement for low-income working families with children was introduced, the Family Income Supplement (FIS). In 1987, FIS was replaced by a more generous payment, the Family Allowance Supplement (FAS) that was also income tested but had the same rationale as FIS, to function as a work incentive for low-income people.

At the same time, the payment of the original (base rate) family allowance to high-income parents was questioned by the then Labour Government, and the policy decision was taken that the base level of family allowance should be removed from families above a specified income level. At the time, this led to about 10 % of high-income families losing the base rate of family allowance. These changes transformed the family allowance from a payment that was largely invariable as parental income changed to one that varied over a considerable range of incomes. In other words, what had been consolidated as a horizontal equity program in 1976 had become largely a vertical equity program by 1990. This trend was reinforced by the failure over most of the 1980s to index family-allowance payments to changes in prices or incomes. By 1989, family allowances had lost 43 % of their 1976 value in real terms. In contrast, between 1983 and 1989, the payments to low-income families increased in real terms by 45 % for children less than 13 years of age and by 86 % for children age 13–15 years (McDonald et al. 1989). The large relative shifts in the value of the payments to low-income families and the payments to middle-income families meant that the FAS, originally introduced as a work-incentive payment for low-income families, was converted into a strong work disincentive. Subsequently, FAS and family allowance (and their successor, Family Tax Benefit Part A) and their thresholds have been indexed to changes in the Consumer Price Index but, because family incomes have risen faster than prices, the proportion of families who receive no child payments has increased from 10 % in 1989 to 25 % today, and this percentage continues to increase. Almost as a formalization of the demise of horizontal equity, FAS and family allowance are now combined into a single payment called Family Tax Benefit Part A (FTBA) that is income tested over most of the range of family incomes.

A small but meaningful shift in the opposite direction occurred in 1995 when a flat, lump-sum Maternity Allowance was introduced to cover the costs of childbirth. Initially, this payment was not income tested, but a few years later, with a change of government, it was phased out at the same income level as the FTBA.

The introduction of a 10 % goods and services tax (GST) in 2000 provided a further blow to the horizontal equity of child payments. Families with children were compensated for the additional costs of children through a 10 % increase in FTBA. For low-income families, this meant a 10 % increase in the maximum rate of FTBA (formerly FAS). This was a fairly sizeable amount of money compared to the additional expenditure that parents incurred as a result of the GST. For families receiving the base rate of FTBA, however, it meant an increase of just 90 cents per child per week. Effectively, the policymakers had assumed that the base rate of FTBA was the total money that parents spent on their children. Of course, the 25 %

of families who received no FTBA received no compensation at all for the increased costs of their children related to the introduction of the GST. As all other sections of the community received much larger compensation through the reduction of the taxes they paid or the increases in government pensions or benefits they received, the totally inadequate compensation for middle- and high-income families for the increased costs of their children with the imposition of the GST was yet another blow to the principle of horizontal equity. In effect, the GST returned most of the child payments made to middle-income families to the government in the form of increased consumption tax. While middle-income families with children were substantial losers from the introduction of the GST, the "no-losers" principle did not apply because the losses were hidden by the complexity of the GST and its compensation package.

Family Support Policy and Women's Roles

In the 1980s, the Labour Government made several reforms to support the labor-force participation of women with children. The central policy area for this support was childcare. In 1983, an income-tested Child Care Assistance was introduced to help working families pay for the costs of childcare in recognized community-based centers (essentially those that had been receiving federal government operational subsidies) or by registered family daycare workers. The Industrial Court made a return to family policy by including the addition of new approved childcare places as part of the wage/tax trade-off agreements made through the centralized wage-fixing process. Later, the income thresholds for the withdrawal of Child Care Assistance were raised so that this form of support was available to more middle-income families. Because community-based childcare centers were few and far between, many parents used private, for-profit childcare centers and consequently were ineligible for Child Care Assistance. This anomalous situation was ended in 1990, when eligibility for receipt of Child Care Assistance was extended to parents using private centers. This was accompanied by a new system of quality accreditation for centers. Community-based centers continued to receive the operational subsidies that had been introduced in the 1970s, but these subsidies were not extended to private centers.

There were also some notable changes in industrial conditions for families with children. The year of unpaid leave for mothers following the birth of a child was extended to fathers, and parents became eligible for up to 5 days of paid family-caregiver leave each year. Firms were also encouraged to implement their own "family-friendly" policies, and a system of national awards was introduced for the family-friendliest firms.

These changes were accompanied by considerable increases in the labor-force participation rates of mothers during the 1980s. The participation rate of mothers with a child less than 5 year old rose from about 30 % in 1981 to about 50 % in 1991, but the increased participation was almost exclusively in part-time work.

8 The Evolution of Population and Family Policy in Australia

The centralized wage-fixing system was brought to an end in 1993, effectively introducing labor-market deregulation. This meant that it was no longer possible to tie advances in family-support arrangements for workers to changes in wages, as had been the case in the 1980s. As a consequence, most work-family arrangements became negotiable only at the enterprise or individual level, rather than at the national level. Nevertheless, the Industrial Court still retained powers to implement broad-based work-family benefits through test cases. For example, the right to 12 months of unpaid parental leave was extended by the Court to casual workers, with the support of the employer organizations.

In 1995, the then Labour Government introduced a new payment for low-income, single-income families with children, called the Parenting Allowance. This payment was introduced as part of a package to encourage unemployed families back into the workforce, but it had the effect of providing an incentive for women with low-income husbands to reduce their labor-force participation, and they did.

With the election of the Howard Coalition Government in 1996, conservative forces had a ready ear for the view that the changes during the previous 13 years of government by Labour had favored mothers who worked at the expense of mothers who stayed home. In opposition, Howard had espoused the virtues of a family taxation system that involved the splitting of income for tax purposes between husbands and wives. The central argument used by the reformers was that two-income couples received two tax-free thresholds,[7] while single-income couples received only one. In fact, the tax-free threshold had been introduced in recognition of the standard minimum costs of working and because it made the administration of the tax system considerably simpler since most workers would not have to claim the costs of working as tax deductions. In any case, the Dependent Spouse Rebate, the last remnant of the Menzies family tax deductions, remained in place effectively, providing a second tax-free threshold for single-income families. Nevertheless, the argument that "stay-at-home" mothers had been disadvantaged carried the day, and in 1999, all previous single-income family payments were rationalized into a single, larger payment that was heavily income tested, based on the income of the lower-earning partner (usually the mother), but not income tested on the income of the higher-earning partner (usually the father). This payment is known as the Family Tax Benefit Part B (FTBB).

Tipping the balance even further away from mothers who worked, the Howard Government abolished the operating grants made to community-based childcare centers on the grounds that these grants were not made to private centers and there should be a competitive, level playing field in the industry. The government also introduced a more stringent income test for Child Care Assistance and froze the amount available to working families to subsidize childcare. Because it was not recognized that childcare demand was very price sensitive, these changes had the effect of reducing demand and sending many centers into liquidation, creating a

---

[7] The tax-free threshold is the income level below which no income tax is payable by an individual. The threshold had remained at about $5,000 to $6,000 for decades before it was increased to $18,200 on 1 July 2012.

crisis in the availability of center-based childcare. Many workers left the industry. The government was eventually forced to respond through the creation of a new and better Child Care Benefit (CCB) that remains in place today.

As another gesture to "stay-at-home" mothers, the Howard Government introduced a new payment during the 2001 election campaign, known as the Baby Bonus, which was tested away as a mother increased her work-force participation. This payment was not gender-neutral as was the case with FTBA and FTBB. The entitlement was determined by the amount of tax paid by the *mother* in the year prior to having the baby. The payment fell into disrepute because of its complexity and its high administrative costs. Recent information suggested that only about 60 % of people who were eligible for this payment had actually taken it up. As part of the 2004 reforms (see below), this form of Baby Bonus was abolished.

Family Policy 2004–2013

Late in 2002, the conservative Prime Minister, John Howard, by then a convert to the work-family perspective, created an Inter-Departmental Task Force on Work and Family Policy to report on "all of the options that might better facilitate choice for parents in balancing their work and family lives" (Heard 2006).

As part of its May 2004 budget, the Howard Government announced major changes to the family-payments system. Most significant was the abolition of the means-tested Baby Bonus and its replacement with a large and universal payment at each birth. This was initially called the Maternity Payment, but in time it also became known as the Baby Bonus. The new Baby Bonus was introduced at a value of $3,000 per annum, with a rise over a few years to $5,000. It was not taxable. Subsequently, it was to be indexed by the Consumer Price Index, as is the case with all family payments but, later indexation of the payment was ended, and its value was pegged at $5,000. In 2010, an income test was applied by the Labour Government to the Baby Bonus,[8] meaning that it was no longer a universal payment. Then in July 2013, the Labour Government reduced its value from $5,000 to $3,000 for all but the first child. Initially, the Baby Bonus was paid as a lump-sum payment. This was later changed to 13 installments paid at intervals of 2 weeks. Payment of the Baby Bonus was also affected by the introduction of universal paid parental leave in 2012 (see below). From 1 April 2014, the Baby Bonus has been replaced by a Newborn Upfront Payment and Newborn Supplement. This is paid as an addition to the Family Tax Benefit Part A at a maximum rate of $2,056 for the first birth and $1,028 for second and higher-order births. Effectively, this is a substantial reduction in comparison with the previous Baby Bonus.

The Baby Bonus was introduced in 2004 with overtones of pro-natalism. The initiative for the payment came from the Prime Minister but was announced by

---

[8] Those with a family taxable income of $75,000 or more in the six months following the birth of the child do not receive the payment.

the Treasurer who had opposed the payment.[9] He did so jocularly, saying that parents should have three children: one for the father, one for the mother, and one for the country. He was then famously photographed surrounded by babies. Later, when the birth rate rose, the Treasurer was inclined to take the credit. All of this made the payment an object of ridicule and, besides its cost, helped to explain its later trimming.

In addition, as part of the 2004 Howard Government reforms, the Family Tax Benefit Part A, the per-child payment, was increased by more than 50 %. This increase essentially restored the value of this payment to what it had been when it was first introduced in 1976 as the Family Allowance, and belatedly, it partly compensated middle-income families for the increased costs of children that they had incurred with the introduction of the Goods and Services Tax. Also, the income thresholds for the FTBA and FTBB were raised so that the benefits extended over a wider range of middle-income families. Although reduced somewhat, the work-disincentive effects of Family Tax Benefit Part B remained.

Until 2012, there had been no universal, paid parental-leave scheme in Australia. Many employers provided paid parental leave for various periods of time, however, as a benefit to their employees. Public employers and most large firms provided this benefit because it was seen as a way for firms to attract and retain the best workers. In 2012, however, the then Labour Government introduced a new, universal, paid parental-leave scheme consisting of 18 weeks of leave paid at the rate of the minimum wage ($622.10 per week from 1 July 2013 or $11,197.80 for 18 weeks). Those already receiving paid parental leave from their employers were permitted to continue to receive the employer entitlement without penalty except for the fact that the benefit from the new scheme was taxable. Those giving birth were provided with the option of taking either the new paid parental leave or the pre-existing Baby Bonus. Obviously those not eligible for paid parental leave (because of their employment history) would opt to take the Baby Bonus. The availability of government-funded paid parental leave and the replacement of the Baby Bonus by the Newborn Upfront Payment have shifted the balance in family payments a long way in favor of employed mothers compared with those who are not employed, especially for those receiving a parental leave payment from their employers as well. From 1 January 2013, a new payment, entitled Dad and Partner Pay, has been introduced for the fathers or partners of women giving birth. The payment is 2 weeks at the minimum wage, but it is only paid to those who are on unpaid leave or are not working when they take the payment.

The parental leave story is not over yet, as the recently elected, conservative Abbott Government has promised to abolish the former Labour Government's paid parental-leave scheme and replace it with a new scheme that provides 6 months leave with full pay capped at a payment of $50,000. The details of this scheme are yet to be determined.

Returning to the 2004 Howard Government reforms, a new Child Care Tax Rebate was introduced that operates in association with the pre-existing Child Care

---

[9] A few weeks previously, the payment had been announced as an Opposition policy initiative.

Benefit. The Child Care Benefit is a payment scaled according to family income that meets as much as 90 % of the costs of childcare for those on a low income but only a small fraction of the costs of those on high incomes. The Child Care Tax Rebate initially provided a tax rebate of 30 % of the costs of childcare that had not been covered already by the Child Care Benefit. The 30 % rebate was later increased to 50 % by the Rudd Labour Government. A maximum value is attached to the rebate (currently $7,500 per child per annum). In combination, the two payments mean that all families using approved forms of childcare get a return from government of 55–90 % of their childcare costs if the costs are at a standard level. In addition, childcare provided by employers to their employees was deemed to be exempt from fringe-benefit tax.

As childcare workers are poorly paid and there is a high staff turnover, there are problems in the viability of the childcare industry from the perspectives of both quality and cost. The largest private childcare provider in Australia (ABC Learning) was forced to cease operations due to bankruptcy. Today, community (not-for-profit) childcare centers are generally of better quality and more expensive than private childcare centers, although the quality of all centers is vetted by the government. Private childcare centers cover about 75 % of the full-day childcare market. Some large employers provide childcare at the workplace, but this is relatively rare. Reportedly, there are supply problems in the industry, with excesses of supply in some areas and deficits in others. The low wages paid to childcare workers have led to labor-supply problems that can only be overcome through large increases in the fees payable. Such increases would, in turn, create access problems if the costs are to be met by parents. The present government has initiated an Inquiry into Child Care and Early Childhood Learning conducted by the Productivity Commission.

The details of all Commonwealth (national) Government family-support schemes can be found at www.familyassist.gov.au. The site includes a calculator that enables families to estimate the benefits to which they are entitled. The system is very complicated and tends to change frequently, however, particularly when the government changes.

At the 2007 election, the winning Rudd Labour Party promised a program of free and universal early-childhood education for all 4-year-olds. Labour had made a similar promise during the 2004 election, which it lost. As early-childhood education involves negotiation between the Commonwealth (national) and the State and Territory governments, its implementation has been problematic. At the 2013 election, the winning Abbott-led opposition made a commitment to provide 15 h per week of preschool for all 4-year-olds at no extra cost to parents. This would be provided for a minimum of 40 weeks per year and delivered by early-childhood teachers qualified with 4-year degrees. Supported by both sides of the Parliament, this is an extremely important area of reform, but it has been on the policy agenda for 10 years with little progress.

There are other policy approaches that are supportive of workers with family responsibilities. For example, all workers are eligible for 10 days of family caregiver's leave per annum, for use when children or other relatives are sick or to attend school functions. So-called "flextime" is also widely available in Australia. By working longer hours (without pay), workers can build up future leave credits. Women often use flextime credits to cover the longer leave required during school holidays. More broadly, it has been common in Australia for decades for workers, especially parents, to negotiate with their employers about specific work hours on an individual basis (Gray and McDonald 2002). Finally, Australia has relatively low tax rates that have the effect of placing money in the hands of parents to apply to the costs of their children (see McDonald and Moyle 2010).[10]

Contemporary Population Debate and Policy in Australia

The Department of the Treasury's publication, in February 2010, of the periodic Intergenerational Report (Department of the Treasury 2010) gave rise to an intense debate about Australian population growth and the need for an Australian population policy. This was in large part generated by a statement by the then Prime Minister, Kevin Rudd, that he supported a "big Australia." His view was criticized by lobby groups who were opposed to further population growth for environmental reasons. The debate heated up during 2010 and was very hot by the time of the 2010 federal election. The new Prime Minister, Julia Gillard, having deposed Kevin Rudd prior to the 2010 election,[11] argued that population growth needed to be slowed down and that she did not agree with Rudd's "big Australia." The then opposition, wishing to avoid making population an issue that differentiated the two sides of politics, also made statements that were in opposition to population growth. In the details of their immigration policy, both the government and the opposition proposed levels of migration that were consistent with the status quo.

Wishing to take the heat out of this debate, the Gillard Government set up an enquiry into sustainable population growth in Australia. The report was published in the first part of 2012 as *Sustainable Australia—Sustainable Communities: A Sustainable Population Strategy for Australia* (Department of Sustainability, Environment, Water, Population, and Communities 2011). Rejecting any notion of an "optimum" population level, the key conclusion of the report was the following:

> It is more useful for governments, businesses and communities to focus on ways of improving our wellbeing, protecting our environment and making better use of the resources we have, rather than trying to determine an absolute limit to our population and focusing efforts on restricting growth in order to not exceed this "limit" (Department of Sustainability, Environment, Water, Population and Communities 2011, p. 25).

---

[10] Among 34 OECD countries, Australian has the fifth lowest tax-to-gross-domestic-product (GDP) ratio, only higher than Mexico, Chile, the United States, and South Korea.

[11] The Prime Minister can be replaced at any time if a majority of members of the two houses of Parliament from the Prime Minister's party vote for another Member of the House of Representatives to become Prime Minister.

With the prior stabilization of Australian fertility at a moderately high level (1.8–1.9 births per woman), the level of fertility was hardly mentioned in the enquiry report, and certainly there was no evidence of pro-natalism. In fact, the level of fertility has largely remained off the political agenda. The one exception was the creation of the Stable Population Party that ran candidates in the 2013 federal election. Along with zero net migration, this party advocated limiting government birth payments to each woman's first two children. The party was almost totally ignored by the electorate, receiving just 3,954 primary votes (0.0 %) in the House of Representatives election. In the Senate election, where it fielded a candidate in every state and territory, it only received 12,687 primary votes, with an average ranking of 24th out of 28 parties. Compared with the 2010 election, there was little public interest in population policy in 2013.

Today, as in most past years in Australia's history, population policy effectively is policy about the size and nature of the migration program. This makes Australia somewhat unusual among low-fertility countries.

References

Australian Bureau of Statistics. (2008). *Australian historical population statistics, 2008*. http://www.abs.gov.au/AUSSTATS/abs@.nsf/ProductsbyCatalogue/632CDC28637CF57ECA256F1F0080EBCC?OpenDocument. Accessed 25 July 2014.

Australian Bureau of Statistics. (2013). *Australian demographic statistics, Dec 2013*. http://www.abs.gov.au/AUSSTATS/abs@.nsf/ProductsbyCatalogue/BCDDE4F49C8A3D1ECA257B8F00126F77?OpenDocument. Accessed 25 July 2014.

Castles, F., & Mitchell, D. (1993). Three worlds of welfare capitalism or four? In F. Castles (Ed.), *Families of nations*. Brookfield: Dartmouth.

Coghlan, T. (1903). *The decline of the birth rate in New South Wales and other phenomena of childbirth: An essay in statistics*. Sydney: NSW Government Printer.

Department of Sustainability, Environment, Water, Population, and Communities, Australian Government. (2011). *Sustainable Australia—sustainable communities: A sustainable population strategy for Australia*. Canberra: Commonwealth of Australia.

Department of the Treasury, Australian Government. (2010). *Australia to 2050: Future challenges*. Canberra: Commonwealth of Australia.

Gray, E., & McDonald, P. (2002). *The relationship between personal, family, resource and work factors and maternal employment in Australia* (Organization for Economic Cooperation and Development (OECD), Labour Market and Social Policy, Occasional Paper No. 62). Paris: OECD.

Heard, G. (2006). Pronatalism under Howard. *People and Place, 14*(3), 12–25.

Hicks, N. (1981). Australian dictionary of biography. In *Coghlan, Sir Timothy Augustine (1855–1926)* (Vol. 8). Melbourne: Melbourne University Press.

Hoff, D. (2012). *The state and the stork: The population debate and policy making in US history*. Chicago: University of Chicago Press.

Kippen, R., & McDonald, P. (2000). Australia's population in 2000: The way we are and the ways we might have been. *People and Place, 8*(3), 10–17.

Marcus, A., Jupp, J., & McDonald, P. (2009). *Australia's immigration revolution*. Melbourne: Allen and Unwin.

McDonald, P., & Kippen, R. (2011). *Forecasting births* (Feature Article, ABS Catalogue 2051.0). Canberra: Australian Bureau of Statistics.

McDonald, P., & Moyle, H. (2010). Why do English-speaking countries have relatively high fertility? *Journal of Population Research, 27*(4), 247–273.

McDonald, P., Brownlee, H., Burbidge, A., Gondor, G., & Maas, F. (1989). *Families and tax in 1989* (Australian Family Income Transfer Project, Bulletin No. 5). Melbourne: Australian Institute of Family Studies.

McDonald, P., Khoo, S.-E., & Edgar, B. (2013). *The role of family migration in Australia's permanent migration program*. Canberra: Department of Immigration and Citizenship.

Robinson, W. (2002). Population policy in early Victorian England. *European Journal of Population, 18*(2), 153–173.

Ruzicka, L., & Caldwell, J. (1977). *The end of demographic transition in Australia*. Canberra: Department of Demography, Australian National University.

Chapter 9
The Dutch Fertility Paradox: How the Netherlands Has Managed to Sustain Near-Replacement Fertility

Melinda C. Mills

Fertility research in Europe and East Asia has often focused on the "lowest-low fertility" (Kohler et al. 2002; Jones 2007; Balbo et al. 2013). Less attention has been placed on the lessons we might learn from countries that have maintained fertility at near the replacement level of 2.1 children per woman. The exception has been research on Scandinavia, where the focus has been on the link between fertility and higher-level parity with emphasis on the role of strong family-leave policies and explicit gender-equality goals (e.g., Duvander et al. 2010). There is a country in Western Europe, however, that has sustained near-replacement fertility for many years. But in this country there has been virtually no direct family or fertility policy, more than 60 % of the population state no religious affiliation, and gender equity is not a driving factor. This country is the Netherlands.

This chapter will argue that an historical path dependency and unique constellation of inadvertent national institutions have created what could be termed the "Dutch fertility paradox." It is a paradox in the sense that many institutional factors, upon first sight, appear to contradict one another, yet together they have operated to enable near-replacement fertility. For instance, it appears to be contradictory that there is near-replacement fertility in the absence of any active fertility policies. Or that one of the most non-religious, secular societies in Europe has such strong norms for primary mother care combined with an aversion to formal childcare. The aim of this chapter is to unravel this paradox and attempt to understand how various direct—but, even more important, inadvertent—national policy constellations have created the Dutch fertility regime. We then conclude by examining the lessons we might learn from the Netherlands.

The first section of the chapter presents an overview of the main population trends in the Netherlands, with a focus on fertility. This is followed by a brief elaboration of the theoretical framework—Coleman's (1990) macro-micro-macro

M.C. Mills (✉)
Department of Sociology, Nuffield College, University of Oxford, Oxford, UK
e-mail: melinda.mills@sociology.ox.ac.uk

theory—that is used as a heuristic to link institutional policies and constellations to fertility decisions and behavior at the individual level and to determine how these lead to the macro-level fertility outcomes we observe at the national level. Family policies are then examined in more detail, with the recognition that due to a fear of overcrowding and high population density, the Dutch have been less concerned than policymakers in some other European countries about dropping fertility levels. Other related factors often considered in fertility research are then described, such as family planning, childcare, child allowance, and parental leave. The final part of this section discusses the strong cultural and normative values about parental—but particularly maternal—care in the Netherlands and the aversion to women working full-time.

Until now, the majority of demographic fertility research has focused on fertility primarily in relation to family policies and institutional or macro-level factors such as economic trends and welfare regimes (for reviews see Balbo et al. 2013; Mills et al. 2011). Not only direct family policies, however, shape fertility intentions and behavior. For this reason, the second half of the chapter is devoted to the impact of inadvertent national constellations and historical path dependency. The section starts with a description of the paternalistic welfare state and political history to understand how Dutch gender roles have emerged with the prominent male-breadwinner and one-and-a-half-earner model. Labor-market flexibility and the right to part-time work are also addressed, since these are core features of the Dutch labor market that strongly affect women and their ability to combine work and family. This is followed by an overview of not only how higher levels of education affect family formation, but also the role of educational field of study, education systems, and the cost of higher education. The Netherlands is one of the most non-religious, secular societies in Europe, and this fairly recent phenomenon has influenced fertility, particularly at higher-level parities. The section ends with a reflection on how housing systems and immigration affect fertility. It concludes with a summary of the most prominent aspects of the Dutch fertility regime, a reflection on whether the Dutch system is sustainable, and the lessons that we might learn from the Dutch case.

A Brief Demographic Overview of the Netherlands

The demographic landscape of the Netherlands has several striking and interrelated characteristics: an extremely high population density, an aging population coupled with increasing life expectancy, a rapid decline and postponement of fertility, and a shift to unmarried consensual unions. Located to the west of Germany and with Denmark and Norway to the north, the Netherlands has a small population—around 16.8 million people in 2013—but with 484 persons per square kilometer, it has one of the highest population densities in Europe. Since 2000, the Netherlands has experienced continued and rapid population decline, which has been linked to falling birth rates. Due to persistent in-migration, however, population numbers are now expected to remain stable until 2035. At that time, the population is projected to begin declining again (Garssen and Van Duin 2006; Fokkema et al. 2008). As in many Western European countries, the Dutch population is also aging. The number of persons age 65 and above has increased by 1.2 percentage points per decade, and the proportion of the population age 65 and above is projected to increase until 2040, when it will reach 24 % and remain stable at this level (Garssen and Van Duin 2006).

A remarkable change since the 1950s has been the rapid decline in fertility. The tempo-adjusted total fertility rate (TFR) from 1951 to 2009/2010 is shown in Fig. 9.1 for selected countries. Until the early 1960s, the Netherlands stood out for its relatively high fertility rate, comparable with high-fertility countries such as Ireland, Portugal, and Poland. The figure shows that the Netherlands experienced a "baby boom" from around 1953 to 1964, followed by rapid fertility decline, with the TFR dropping from 3.1 in 1964 to 1.7 in 1977. In 1974, the TFR fell below the replacement level of 2.1, and it has remained below replacement ever since. Just below the levels of the United States and Sweden, the Netherlands is considered a "middle-range" fertility regime, with higher levels than in Eastern European countries such as the Russian Federation and Asian countries such as Japan. One reason

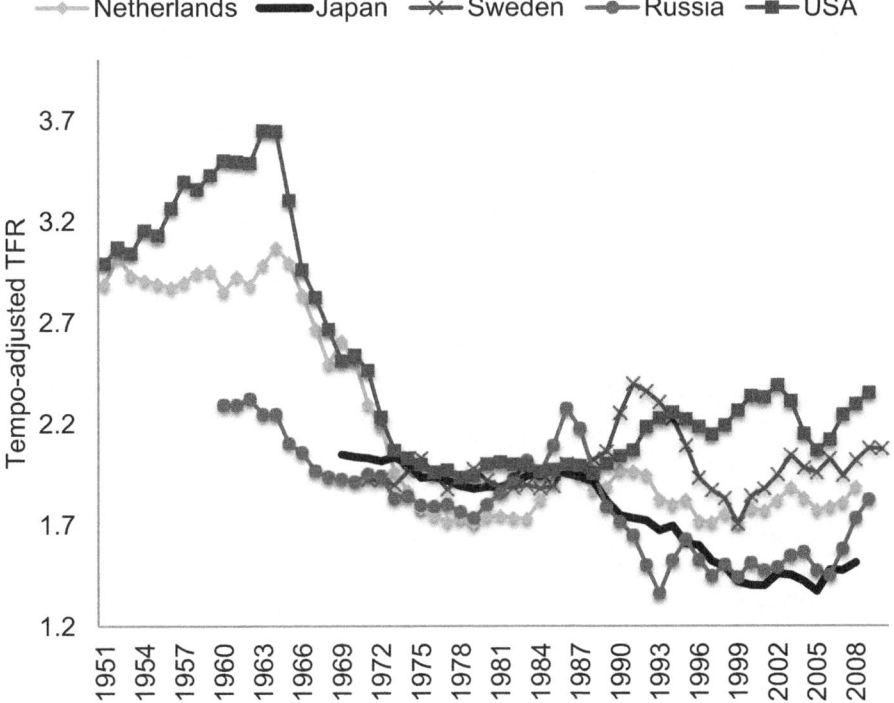

Fig. 9.1 Tempo-adjusted total fertility rates, Bongaarts-Feeney method, selected countries (Max Planck Institute for Demographic Research/Vienna Institute of Demography 2014; dates vary depending on data availability)

for the decrease in fertility was the drop in third and higher-order births. By contrast, until about 1938, about 40 % of Dutch women had three or more children.

The Netherlands is also characterized by very late fertility, ranking among the societies with the oldest first-time mothers in the world. Figure 9.2 shows that the average age at first birth for women in the Netherlands is now above 29, having increased steadily since the 1970s. This is similar to increases in the age at first birth for women in countries such as Sweden, Japan, and Italy. Another characteristic is that Dutch women have compressed fertility and generally have their second child soon after the first. Women who are now in their late 40s have an average of almost two children (about 1.87 for women born in 1957 and 1.85 for women born in 1960) (Fokkema et al. 2008).

Partnership formation has likewise undergone significant changes over the past decades (Dykstra and Komter 2006). This includes the postponement of entry into first partnership, postponing and forgoing marriage, and differences in the level of symbolic and legal commitment by relationship type (Liefbroer and Dykstra 2000; Poortman and Mills 2012). Between the late 1980s and the late 1990s, the share of people aged 25 and above who entered consensual unions without being married more than doubled (CBS 2011), a trend that has continued in the past decade. Another striking development is that not only are more and more people living together without being married, but they also do so for longer periods of time (Fokkema and Liefbroer 2008; Poortman and Mills 2012). The Netherlands has experienced not only an increasing number of couples who postpone marriage, but a smaller proportion who eventually marry. This is attributed to changes in Dutch partnership laws, such as registered partnerships and cohabitation contracts that

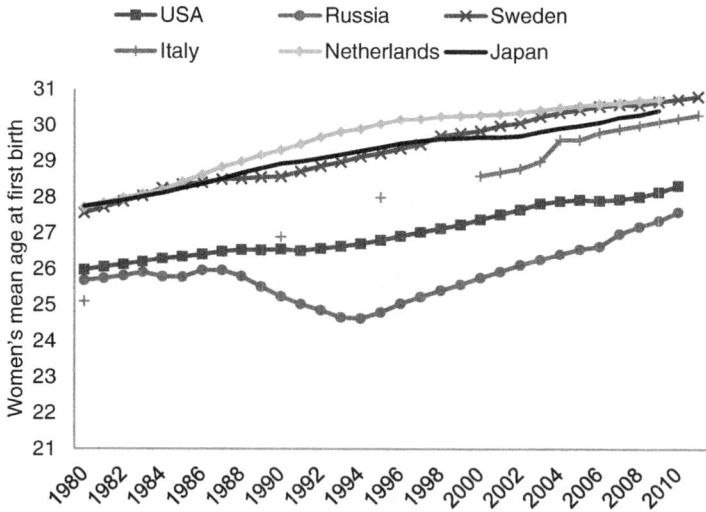

Fig. 9.2 Women's mean age at first birth, 1980–2010, selected countries (UNECE 2014 for Italy; Max Planck Institute for Demographic Research/Vienna Institute of Demography 2014 for remaining countries, which shows the period mean ages at first birth by age 40)

were introduced in the late 1990s, which mean that individuals no longer need to get married for legal reasons or to clarify the rights of children. This has also meant a surge in the number of children born in "out-of-wedlock" consensual unions, which is now more than one in five, with almost 90 % legally acknowledged (*erkend*) by the father (CBS 2012).

Toward a Multilevel Theory of Fertility Change

In order to understand how different national policy constellations and cultural schemas might affect population and fertility levels, the theoretical model shown in Fig. 9.3 serves as a useful guiding heuristic. It is implausible to assume that macro-level (or institutional, national) policies lead directly to the macro-level fertility rates that we observe (the dotted line). It is therefore useful to adopt Coleman's (1990) macro-micro-macro model to understand the link between macro-level systems, micro-level intentions, decision-making processes, and behavior, and in turn, macro-level national fertility levels.

Following Coleman (1990), the macro-level consists of the social system, which is made up of various institutional policies and also more general cultural schemas and values that often underlie policies. What is central in this model is that the different levels of the analyses are causally linked, which is useful for understanding how macro-level systems, institutions, or cultural norms and values at the national level serve as an antecedent to micro- and macro-level consequences. It also clarifies that macro-level fertility outcomes can only be described by linking them to a micro-level analysis—albeit an often daunting empirical task. Macro-level policies and schemas operate in the form of a contextual mechanism or national filter that enables or constrains decision-making and fertility behavior. In other words, the institutional and normative context discussed in the pages that follow is envisaged to shape the way that Dutch people think about families and children and their "action formation," or how they are able to realize their fertility desires. This, in turn, either sustains or transforms the macro-level fertility trends that we observe. The remaining discussion goes into more detail about how these direct and inadvertent policies, institutional changes, and cultural norms have developed in the Netherlands.

Family Policies

Although the Dutch government has never promulgated direct fertility policies, there are a myriad of institutional features that affect fertility in either an intended or unintended manner. These include family-related policies, often aimed at work-family reconciliation and aiding women to enter the labor market, but there are also indirect national-level policies such as employment-protection legislation and the cost of higher education that either enhance or hamper fertility.

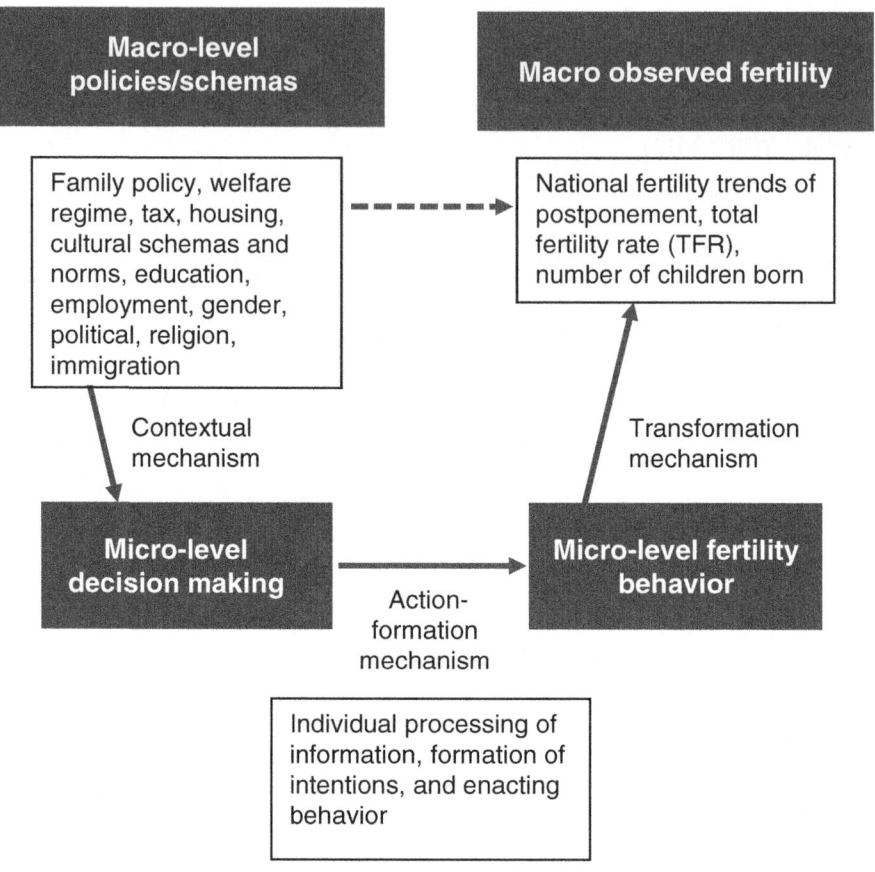

Fig. 9.3 Multilevel theoretical framework to illustrate how national-level institutions affect observed fertility levels

"The Netherlands Is Full": Fear of Overcrowding and Fertility

Although several European countries have been concerned about low fertility levels for some time, the Dutch government has never perceived the fertility level as too low, nor has it ever initiated any pro-natalist policies. Rather, due to high population density and disturbing population forecasts that were made in the 1970s, the government became concerned about overpopulation. As Fokkema et al. (2008) chronicle, a Royal Commission on Population in 1977 concluded that natural population growth should be halted and argued for the advantages of a stable population size. This view was repeatedly supported in Parliament, and official government statements argued that "in the longer run a stationary population is viewed as desirable" (Government of the Netherlands 1999, p. 135). The last formal Royal Speech of Queen Juliana of the Netherlands in September 1979 showed the spirit of the times with the now often-repeated words: *"Ons land is vol, ten dele overvol* (Our country is full, partially overcrowded)." This fear of overcrowding has remained in the Dutch public debate, with the slogan "The Netherlands is full" adopted by various anti-immigration parties. The focus on overpopulation has been fuelled by large-scale non-Western immigration (Bail 2008) and a surge in ethnically and culturally diverse minorities, in particular Muslim groups. Survey data show that the Netherlands is the only European country in which the majority would like to have a smaller population (e.g., Kontula and Miettinen 2005; Dorbritz et al. 2005), with only one-fifth perceiving a drop in birth rates as negative.

Family Planning: Contraceptive Use and Abortion

As in most Western countries, contraceptive use was forbidden and largely taboo in the Netherlands until the 1960s. The prohibition on contraceptives was removed in 1969, and they began to be covered by national health insurance in 1971, which ensured the widespread usage that still persists today (Fokkema et al. 2008). It should be noted, however, that in 2004, national health insurance rules changed, and contraceptives are no longer provided free to women above the age of 22. Nevertheless, the use of reliable birth control became common practice in the Netherlands and still persists today. The pill is the most common method used, followed by voluntary sterilization, IUDs (intrauterine devices), and, to a much lesser extent, condoms (Fokkema et al. 2008). The peak ages of pill use are from 16 to 28, clearly intended for effective birth control.

The Netherlands has one of the lowest rates of legal induced abortion in Western Europe, and this has been true for some time. In 2003, for example, the annual rate of legal abortion was 8.6 per 1,000 women of reproductive age, compared with 18.7 in Sweden, 16.5 in France, and 68.4 in the Russian Federation (Frejka 2008, Table 3). The Netherlands also has the lowest rate of teenage pregnancies in the world (CBS 2010), which has been attributed to various factors such as open sexuality and sex education and high and early use of effective oral contraceptives (Ivanova et al. 2014). Abortion and teenage pregnancy rates range from 3 to 10 times higher among the four main ethnic minority groups, originating from Surinam, Netherlands Antilles, Turkey, and Morocco, compared with the non-minority population (Beerthuizen 2003; Fokkema et al. 2008; CBS 2010).

Childcare: Use It, But Not Too Much

The Netherlands has a complicated relationship with formal childcare. Due to the political climate, historical development of the welfare state, and religious legacy, there is a strong cultural norm for at least one of the biological parents to care for children, preferably the mother (Portegijs et al. 2006; Mills and Täht 2010). In fact, it was not until the early 1990s that formalized public childcare became accessible. In the past decades, the government has made multiple changes in childcare policies, and since 2007, and particularly since 2011, there have been substantial reductions in state support.

The Central Childcare Act, introduced in 2005, recommended that the government, employers, and parents share the costs of childcare (Den Dulk 2001). Since employers were only urged to participate voluntarily and were not formally required to contribute to childcare costs, many did not. The rules were changed in 2007 because it had become apparent that many employers were not helping to pay for childcare, and serious administrative problems had arisen. In 2007, the Dutch government began paying one-third of childcare costs, but payments were income adjusted. Employers continued to resist paying their share, but in 2012, after demonstrations and lobbying by large labor unions (FNV Bondgenoten 2014) and opposition parties, employers were formally required to pay one-third of childcare costs. The childcare sector received four substantial financial cuts in 2011 and three additional cuts from 2012 to 2015. These cuts included lowering the amount provided for second children in 2012 and ending childcare subsidies to parents who together earn more than US$160,660 (€118,000) in 2013.

Compared with the rest of Europe, children in the Netherlands spend a very limited number of hours in formal childcare, which is related to the large number of Dutch women who work part time. Childcare centers are generally open during standard business hours only, and women often adapt their work hours around the school times of their children (Mills and Täht 2010). Children start school at age four, but many come home for lunch and are out of school on Wednesday and Friday afternoons. Although in-school lunches and after-school care have been increasing since the early 2000s, particularly in urban areas, school schedules still appear to limit the hours that Dutch women work. It is important to note, however, that grandparents and other informal caregivers play a key role in childcare. More than 40 % of children under the mandatory school age are cared for, on average, for one day a week by grandparents or other family members (Mills et al. 2013).

Childcare became a central issue in many European countries after the introduction of the Barcelona Targets in 2002. The Barcelona Targets provide a prime example of how the family policies of European countries might be influenced by supra-national entities such as the European Commission or the European Union. Specifically, the intention was to encourage member states to "remove disincentives to female labor-force participation and strive, taking into account the demand for childcare facilities and in line with national patterns of provision, to provide childcare by 2010 to at least 90 % of children between 3 years old and the mandatory school age and at least 33 % of children under 3 years of age" (European Council 2002). Although measurement remains challenging, a recent report showed that the Netherlands meets the Barcelona objective of 33 % childcare coverage for children under three, but the use of formal childcare is predominantly part-time (Mills et al. 2013). In this respect, the Netherlands and the United Kingdom, with high rates of female part-time employment, differ dramatically from other European countries.

Figure 9.4 compares full-time employment rates for mothers of 0–2 year olds with full-time formal childcare coverage rates for European countries in 2010. In

9 The Dutch Fertility Paradox: How the Netherlands Has Managed to Sustain...

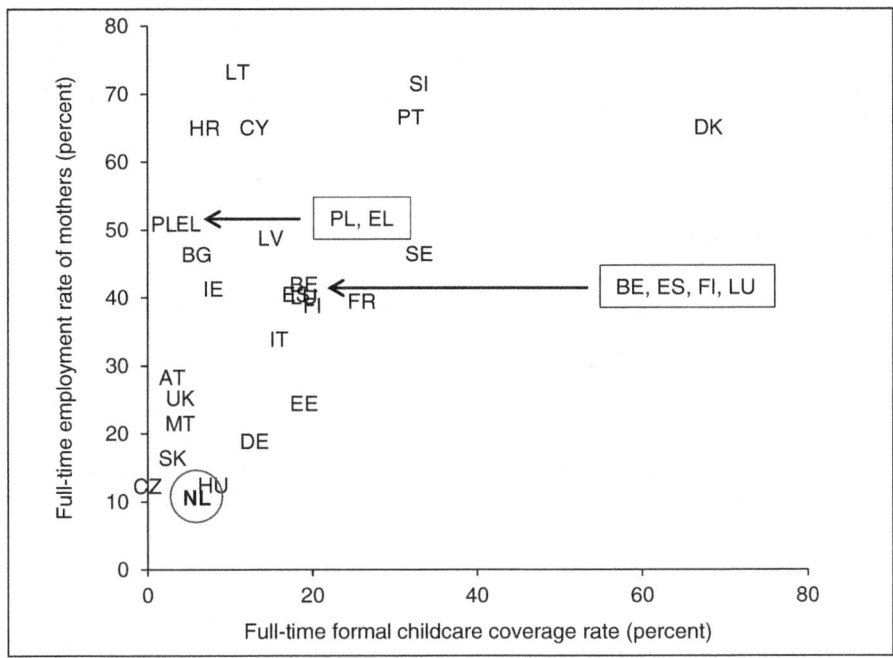

Country Code	Country name	Country Code	Country name
AT	Austria	IT	Italy
BE	Belgium	LT	Lithuania
BG	Bulgaria	LU	Luxembourg
CY	Cyprus	LV	Latvia
CZ	Czech Republic	ME	Montenegro
DE	Germany	MK	Macedonia
DK	Denmark	MT	Malta
EE	Estonia	NL	Netherlands
EL	Greece	NO	Norway
ES	Spain	PL	Poland
FI	Finland	PT	Portugal
FR	France	RS	Serbia
HR	Croatia	SE	Sweden
HU	Hungary	SI	Slovenia
IE	Ireland	SK	Slovakia
IL	Israel	TR	Turkey
IS	Iceland	UK	United Kingdom

Fig. 9.4 Full-time employment rates of mothers and full-time (30+ hours per week) formal childcare rates for children up to 3 years old in European countries, 2010 (Data from European Union Labour Force Survey (EU LFS) and European Union Statistics on Income and Living Conditions (EU SILC), see Mills et al. 2013)

general, we see a weak relationship between mother's full-time employment rates and full-time childcare coverage. The association is strong in the Netherlands, however, with low full-time childcare coverage and very low rates of full-time mother's employment.

Child Allowance

A means-tested child allowance has been provided in the Netherlands since 1946, not as a pro-natalist policy, but to support family welfare. The minimum level for the first child is almost US$82 (€60) per month (Fokkema and Esveldt 2006). Benefits are paid until age 17, increasing with the age of the child from ages 6 to 12. Before 1995, child allowances were paid according to the age and number of children in order to provide higher benefits to large families. During this period, the larger the family size, the higher the benefit level for each child. After 1995, however, this seemingly pro-natalist policy was discontinued, and the allowance was paid only according to the age of the child. After the recent financial crisis, the generous spending on child benefits was cut by about US$1 billion (€700 million) in 2013, from an annual total of US$13.6 billion (€10 billion) to US$12.6 billion (€9.3 billion) (Rijksoverheid 2014). The cut in benefits was also designed to encourage poorer parents to work. The annual child allowance (*kinderbijslag*) for children age 12–17 is scheduled to go down from about US$1,270 (€932) in 2013 to US$1,045 (€768) by 2016. The annual allowance for children age 6–11, which was US$1,491 (€1,096) in 2013, is scheduled to be reduced in a similar manner over time (for a detailed summary in Dutch, see Rijksoverheid 2014).

Parental Leave: Maternity and Paternity Leave

Women in the Netherlands have a legal entitlement to 16 weeks of maternity leave at 100 % pay. The Labor Act of 1919 and the Working Hours Act of January 1996 stipulated that women should not work for at least 8 weeks after childbirth and 2 weeks before their due date. Today, maternity leave falls under the Sickness Benefits Act, with employees entitled to a total of 16 weeks, including 4–6 weeks to be taken before a birth (*zwangerschapsverlof*) and the remainder after the birth (*bevallingsverlof*). This provision for fully paid maternity leave is typical of many European countries such as Germany (14 weeks at 100 % pay), Switzerland (14 weeks at 80 % pay), and Austria and France (16 weeks at 100 % pay) (ILO 2013). Women in Sweden are entitled to more than 1 year (480 days) of maternity leave at up to 80 % of salary, with the possibility of transferring some of the leave to the father. Other countries have 52 weeks at either full or partial pay (e.g., United Kingdom at 90 % and Denmark at 100 %) (ILO 2013).

In the Netherlands, mothers and fathers are also entitled to parental leave to care for young children. This varies by employer. Some trade-union or collective-bargaining agreements stipulate some pay for a specified number of hours, generally up to 1 day during the first year after the birth of a child. A father also had the right to paternity leave immediately after a child is born. This increased from 2 to 5 days in 2014.

Cultural and Normative Values about Parenthood and Childcare

The previous figures suggest that other factors beyond the availability and use of childcare are related to women's decisions to participate in the labor force or have children. Using the European Social Survey, which was collected in 2006/2007, it is possible to situate the Netherlands in a comparative context in relation to cultural and normative values about parenthood and childcare. Figure 9.5 provides a comparative European view of the level of approval, ambivalence (neither approval nor disapproval), or disapproval of whether a woman with a child under 3 years old should have a full-time job.

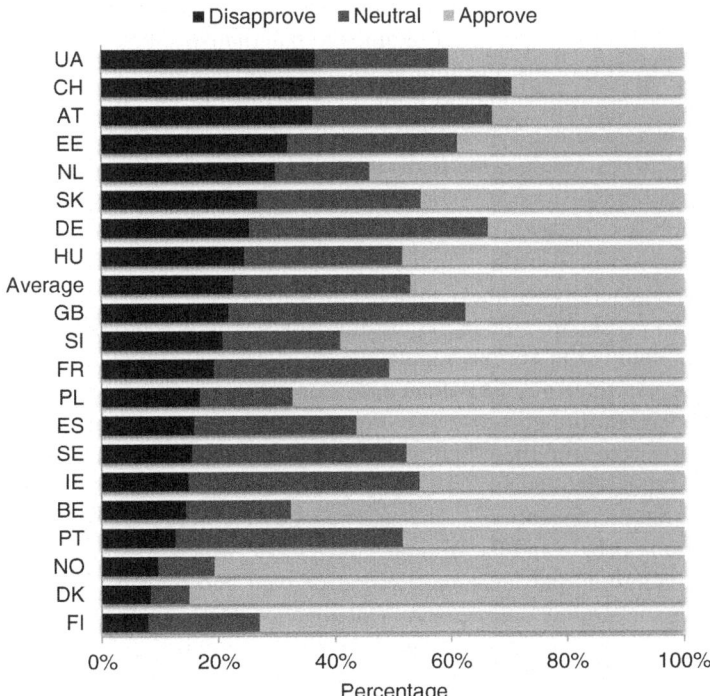

Fig. 9.5 Approval or disapproval of a woman with a child under age three working full-time, selected European countries (European Social Survey (ESS) 2006/2007, author's calculations; see note to Fig. 9.4 for a key linking country codes to full names)

In more than half of the countries, only 50 % approve of a woman with a child under three having a full-time job. There is a striking similarity between the level of approval of women with young children working full-time and the actual levels of childcare enrollment and employment shown in the previous figures. The low levels of approval in countries such as the Netherlands, Switzerland, Austria, and Germany suggest why these countries have non-existent or ineffective policies on childcare and female employment. The negative views on full-time female employment may help explain the lack of momentum to create policies on women's employment and childcare.

Inadvertent National Constellations That Affect Fertility

The Paternalistic Welfare State and Importance of Political Regimes

The Dutch welfare state emerged out of Keynesian economic policies, which were introduced in the 1950s and 1960s, focusing on the role of the state and corporate institutions. During this time, life-course risks (e.g., unemployment, disability) were transferred from citizens and families to paternalistic state institutions, often (co)governed by corporatist institutions such as trade unions or employer's organizations. The government sought to implement an ideal of the "the good life," with signals that were a mixture of accepted practices, such as married women staying out of the labor market, and the realization of social and political ideals, such as state pensions and insurance against unemployment and disability, a healthcare plan, and policies to increase educational attainment (Wielers and Mills 2011). These policies were codified in a number of laws that assigned citizens more rights, to which they, generally willingly, adapted their lives.

During this period, the role of the full-time housewife was promoted by the government and codified in various regulations (e.g., taxes). Although this traditional division of gender roles was not enforced, the constellation of social-security arrangements made certain life choices more attractive and thus prevalent, and there was little public resistance to these options. Although there were women with full-time jobs in the 1960s, they were generally unmarried without children. The political, cultural, and moral implications of the paternalistic state were put into question in the 1960s by young people and the women's movement, which organized itself around the issue of abortion and later the division of paid and unpaid labor (Kool-Smit 1967). The Social-Democratic[1] government changed its position toward more moral liberalism, which was staunchly resisted by the large political group of Christian Democrats, who disagreed with the idea of individual freedom on moral issues.

---

[1] The term "Social Democrats" refers to a political stance that emerged in the latter half of the twentieth century in Western and Northern Europe from democratic socialism. It is often equated with "social democracy" or Scandinavian welfare regimes. It is characterized by collective bargaining and a broadly based welfare state, yet still within the framework of a capitalist economy.

One consequence of the government's paternalistic policies was very low flexibility in the Dutch labor market, which made it vulnerable to economic shocks. The economic crises in the 1970s, and particularly the 1980s, fueled a growing recognition that the welfare state could not fund long durations of unemployment or disability (Mooi-Reci and Mills 2012). These crises were followed by considerable job growth, relative stability in job quality, a clear rise in labor-market participation (particularly of women), and increased flexibility in the labor market by means of temporary jobs, part-time employment, and the growth of temporary employment agencies.

From about 1918 to 1994, the Christian Democrats took part in all elected governments, in which they upheld many traditional views and laws related to the family and individual rights. In 1994, a new government was formed, consisting of Social Democrats and Liberals.[2] Several cultural issues that had been pending for decades could now be resolved, and the new government implemented multiple pieces of social legislation that had been held back on "moral" grounds, such as legalizing gay marriage, prostitution, and euthanasia. The main goal of the new cabinet was, like that of its predecessors, to increase labor-market participation. It was only in the mid-1990s that new policies related to the family were introduced such as fiscal equality between men and women, expansion of childcare, the extension of shop opening hours, and the right to part-time work.

Dutch Gender Roles: The Right to Part-Time Work and the One-and-a-Half-Earner Model

In the middle of the 1990s, employment in the Netherlands started to grow rapidly, particularly the number of part-time jobs and the number of hours worked in part-time jobs. The stagnant Dutch labor market improved its flexibility and became highly successful (Visser and Hemerijck 1999). This created a tight labor-market situation, with improvements for workers in flexible jobs. The government developed legislation to drive out wage discrimination in part-time jobs and to provide a legal "right to part-time work," under which every employee was granted the right to reduce his or her number of work hours (Visser 2002). This right was championed by Dutch "part-time feminists" as a way for women to remain at home and still participate in the labor market. Importantly, part-time workers had the same benefits as full-time workers, such as healthcare coverage and pensions. These new laws were enacted in 1997 and 2000 (Wielers and Mills 2011). In addition, legislation was introduced to reduce the risks of temporary jobs. An employer can extend a temporary contract with an employee only twice and, at maximum, for a period of 6 years. After that, the employer has to offer the employee a longer-term contract (Remery et al. 2002).

---

[2] In the Dutch system, several parties often group together to form ruling and opposition coalitions. In 1994, the "Purple Cabinet" was formed by the VVD (equivalent to a conservative or Republican party), the D66 (a more center-left party), and the PvDA (Labor Party).

Increased flexibility in the labor market has had mixed effects on the life courses of individuals in the Netherlands, with detrimental effects on some groups such as new labor-market entrants and women (Remery et al. 2002; de Vries and Wolbers 2005). Although the growth of fixed-term contracts and part-time work has permitted young people and women to enter the labor market in large numbers, these have often been "stop-gap" jobs for young people or unequal or dead-end jobs for women. At the same time, the persistence of the "modern male breadwinner" or "one-and-a-half-earner" model, where the man works full time and the female partner works part time, has meant that men's careers have remained relatively stable (de Vries and Wolbers 2005). The degree of employment security, the ability to enter or re-enter the labor market, and the possibility to balance work with family responsibilities—all these are pivotal conditions for individuals to make long-term commitments to have children (Mills and Blossfeld 2005).

Unequal Pay for Unequal Work

Feminism in the Netherlands has historically focused on the right to part-time work or to remain out of the labor force and less on equal wages or career opportunities. The Netherlands is truly exceptional in international terms in its high share of part-time jobs, with most women employed part-time. In 2005, 61 % of women were working in part-time jobs, as well as 15 % of men (SCP 2006, p. 145, based on data from the Organization for Economic Cooperation and Development—OECD). Typical female jobs are in personal services, mostly labor intensive and poorly paid. Schippers (1987) characterized the situation as one of "unequal pay for unequal work," and this segregation has continued. This is in contrast to Hakim's (2000, 2003) more positive take on Dutch women's part-time work as offering favorable part-time career paths. Although she is correct that women are protected in stable part-time careers, several researchers (e.g., Schippers 1987; Kalmijn and Luijkx 2006; Luijkx et al. 2006) demonstrate that there is no equality in the careers of Dutch men and women. This inequality and the resulting economic dependence become particularly problematic for women in the event of a divorce or death of a spouse, when they become economically vulnerable (Uunk 2004).

Education Level, Field of Study, and the National Education System

Education Level, Field of Study, and Fertility

The relationship between level of education and fertility has been a central focus within demography (Rindfuss et al. 1980, 1984, 1996; Balbo et al. 2013). Higher education (particularly of women) operates to postpone the timing of fertility and particularly the age at first birth (Bulatao and Casterline 2001). Longer educational enrollment can also limit the quantum of fertility by leaving a shorter reproductive period to have more children. Highly-educated women in the Netherlands are more likely than less-educated women to remain childless (CBS 2004). If they do have children, many postpone first births and compress higher-order births, or in other words "catch up" by having higher-order children at short intervals (Sobotka 2004).

Women in the Netherlands have made considerable gains in education, now exceeding men in higher education levels (Mills and Praeg 2013). An area that has received less attention is specific fields of study, which lead to particular occupational trajectories that may or may not be amenable to combining family and employment. A growing number of studies have linked educational and occupational fields to fertility (Hoem et al. 2006; Lappegård and Rønsen 2005; Martin-Garcia 2010; Van Bavel 2010; Begall and Mills 2013). This research generally shows a positive association between "classic" female educational fields—such as teaching and health-related studies—and higher fertility. Possible explanations may be either self-selection of women into jobs that offer working conditions supportive of work-family balance (Cook and Minnotte 2008; Begall and Mills 2011) or preferences of women with high family orientation for occupations with stereotypical feminine qualities such as contact and caring (Van Bavel 2010). Another explanation is that socialization and formative educational institutions infuse particular attitudes and values in girls and boys. Although it is difficult to distinguish these different processes, Begall and Mills (2013), examining Dutch cohorts born between 1940 and 1985, found that women who studied technical, economic, or cultural subjects had a significantly lower transition to first birth than women with a degree in educational studies (teaching). They likewise found that women in occupations with a higher proportion of women had a significantly faster transition to first birth.

Education System, Free Higher Education, Child Well-Being, and Fertility

Although education systems are a central topic within stratification research in sociology, they are often ignored in demographic fertility studies. Education prepares young people for the transition to the labor market, and the costs of education and level of competition are pivotal for the early life course. National education systems differ in many aspects, such as the number of school years required, how certificates and job training are valued, the costs of education, how the education offered matches the demands of the labor market, and how "easy" it is for young people to translate their skills into jobs and develop the stability often desired to start a family (Allmendinger 1989; Mills and Blossfeld 2005; Shavit and Müller 1997). In general, vocational training that allows more immediate entry into the labor market can give young people stability at an earlier age than other types of higher education.

The price of higher education is likely one crucial factor in parents' decision making about how many children they can afford. In some countries, parents or students need to take out personal or student loans to finance their education (Lebeau et al. 2012). In the Netherlands, very few children attend private, fee-paying schools. Until 2012, public education was virtually free through the university level, and students also obtained a monthly financial payment from the state. Thus, when weighing fertility choices, previous cohorts were not likely to view higher education as a prohibitive cost of having children, but rather as a right. A recently proposed change to move from free university education to a system of student loans, to be initiated in the autumn of 2014, will likely have far-reaching consequences in this respect.

Another aspect of the relationship between education and fertility is the position of children growing up, investments by parents, and children's well-being. The Netherlands is virtually free of any notion of "cramming" or the competitive preparation for school that occurs in some East Asian countries. This may be one reason why UNICEF (2013) recently ranked Dutch children as the happiest in the world in terms of material and educational well-being, behavior, housing, and environment. Dutch children start school at age four, are generally not required to do any homework until they finish primary school at age 12, and are often involved in extracurricular (non-academic) activities after school. At age 12, children take a nationwide test called the CITO, which determines their general academic level and streams them into higher or vocational education. The lack of competition even among high school students is also likely fostered by the fact that, until now, there has been no formal competition for admission to university. Nearly all tertiary-level studies (with the exception of medicine and other limited areas) are open to all students who finish a higher-level, university-streamed high school (VWO in Dutch), with no additional selection criteria for grades. Since Dutch universities are not formally ranked, there is likewise little pressure to enter the "right university."

Religion: Secularization of Dutch Society

Changes in cultural norms and ideation associated with secularization are one of the pillars of the second demographic transition (Lesthaeghe 1995). Previous research has shown a high correlation between religious variables and number of children across countries (e.g., Adsera 2006). One of the strongest predictors of family size has been shown to be church attendance (Adsera 2006). Others have even argued that religion is one of the main drivers of fertility and that "conservatives will inherit the Earth" (Longman 2006). Although the Dutch population tended to be religious in the past, the high level of secularization today, combined with a relatively high level of fertility, at least for Europe, seems to challenge the association of religiosity with family size, as noted by Frejka and Westoff (2008).

The Netherlands had one of the highest levels of fertility in Europe until around the early 1960s (see Fig. 9.1), comparable to countries such as Ireland. These high fertility levels were largely driven by the Catholics in the southern part of the country (Van Poppel 1985; Engelen and Hillebrand 1986). As Fig. 9.1 illustrates, there was a relatively dramatic decrease in fertility over the next decades, but the Netherlands remained a country with moderately high levels of fertility, with a TFR of 1.9 in 2009 (Max Planck Institute for Demographic Research/Vienna Institute of Demography 2014). Historically, the Dutch population consisted primarily of Christians who were geographically divided, with Protestants in the north and Catholics in the south, and with very limited intermarriage. In churches and religious schools, pro-natalist and pro-family Christian teaching was prevalent (Berghammer 2009). Regular social meetings and strong social networks among church members provided both instrumental and emotional support to parents raising children (see also Buehler and Philipov 2005). There was also strong appreciation of motherhood and particularly of the primary care provided by mothers to their own children.

Until the mid-1960s, Dutch society was characterized by what has been called "pillarization," which started at the end of the nineteenth century. This meant that Dutch society was divided by affiliation to Protestant, Catholic, or non-religious "humanist" beliefs, reflected in highly structured social institutions, from clubs and sports teams to schools (Bryant 1981; Dekker and Ester 1996). As Dutch society became secularized, many people shed these divided institutions, and now only remnants exist. Beginning in the mid-1960s, the Netherlands has become a highly secularized, non-religious nation (Need and de Graaf 1996), with around 40 % of the population not affiliated to any religion—one of the highest proportions in Europe (Statistics Netherlands 2007, p. 116). There has also been a sharp drop in church attendance, even among those who claim a religious affiliation (Berghammer 2009; De Graaf and Te Grotenhuis 2008). Religion has largely lost prominence in daily life and is rarely used today as a reference for behavior (see De Graaf and Te Grotenhuis 2008). Need and de Graaf (1996) argue that a central reason for secularization has been rationalization, which refers to the notion that the Netherlands is a technologically advanced society where scientific-based knowledge tends to undermine religious faith. The process of rationalization has been spurred by higher educational attainment over time. At the same time, the social-integration role played by religion has become weaker and less influential in shaping fertility behavior. Due to this secularization, denominational differences in fertility have become negligible since the mid-1960s (Somers and Van Poppel 2003).

Housing Regimes

Although often ignored, housing regimes can have indirect effects on fertility. Housing regimes are characterized by differences in levels of home ownership, difficulties in accessing mortgages, housing prices, and the availability of affordable rental housing (Mulder 2006; Mulder and Billari 2010). Housing markets may affect fertility by restricting the ability of young people to leave the parental home and establish their own home or cohabiting household with a partner. In the Netherlands, students leave home relatively early, often to study and live in small apartments. This is in contrast to their counterparts in Italy, for example, who often stay in the parental home considerably longer. The Dutch housing market has a fairly large and affordable rental sector for one-person or student living, which allows young people to leave the parental home to study at fairly young ages. In the past, however, there was a high unmet demand for other types of housing, and particularly an extreme shortage of affordable housing for families in the larger cities, such as Amsterdam. In recent years, the government has responded by building more single-family homes in urban areas (Mulder 2006).

The norm that access to a high-quality house is a necessary precursor for forming a union and starting a family remains strong (Liefbroer 2005). A common Dutch proverb for settling down is "house, tree, pet" (*huisje, boomtje, beestje*), which reflects a size and quality of housing not always possible in this very small and densely populated country. Several studies have demonstrated that the timing of childbirth is closely related to acquisition of a single-family home (Feijten and Mulder 2002; Mulder and Wagner 2001). Others have linked delayed childbirth in southern European countries to the low access to high-quality houses (Castiglioni and Dalla Zuanna 1994). Expensive housing could also affect a couple's decision to have two or more children, since a larger family would entail additional expenses or even a move to a larger house. Another theory is that high costs of home ownership might lower fertility by competing with the high costs of having and rearing children. In fact, studies in the United Kingdom have linked home ownership with low, rather than high, fertility. This is possibly because mortgages in the United Kingdom require a sizeable deposit, which means that individuals must accumulate savings before they can obtain a mortgage, whereas in the Netherlands, there is no need to accrue savings in order to obtain a mortgage (Hakim 2003; Murphy and Sullivan 1985).

A striking cross-national difference is the distribution of age at home ownership. Whereas the peak distribution of homeownership is in the mid-60s in Italy and Austria, it is 15 years earlier, at around age 50, in the United States, Canada, the United Kingdom, and Australia (Chiuri and Jappelli 2003). The authors attribute this to differences in financial systems and the availability of credit.

Housing markets have also been shown to affect family formation and dissolution. A tight housing market, for instance, has been shown to be related to divorce or separation, with homeowners less likely to divorce than renters (Mulder and Billari 2010). The causality is not straightforward, however, since a joint investment in a house may reflect the level of commitment in a relationship, with married individuals more likely to own a home than those in consensual cohabiting unions (Poortman and Mills 2012). Several studies have shown a positive relationship between union formation, particularly marriage, and home ownership (e.g., Clark et al. (1994) for the United States and Kendig (1984) and Mulder and Wagner (1998) for the Netherlands and Germany).

Mulder and Billari (2010) classify housing markets into various housing regimes according to the level of homeownership and the difficulty in acquiring a mortgage. The Netherlands is characterized as a "lower-level, mortgage finance: career homeownership regime." Other countries in this regime include, for example, Denmark, Germany, the United Kingdom, and the United States. Countries such as Austria,

France, and Portugal are characterized as "elite homeownership regimes," while the European countries with the highest fertility (Ireland, Iceland, and Norway) have an "easy homeownership regime." The most "difficult homeownership regimes" are found in Italy, Spain, and Greece, where mortgages are difficult and intergenerational transfers are the imperfect solution. Mulder and Billari (2010) show that just over 50 % of people in the Netherlands own a home, with the rest living in private rental, or more commonly state public, housing. The total amount of mortgage loans as a percentage of national gross domestic product (GDP) is extremely high in the Netherlands compared with the situation in other European countries due to state co-financing of mortgages (*hypotheekrenteaftrek*). There have been various public debates on whether the government should abolish this generous mortgage policy, which allows large low-income families and young people to buy homes.

Immigration: Do Migrants Sustain High Fertility Levels?

One hypothesis, often raised but rarely tested, is that the relatively high level of fertility in the Netherlands may be attributed to an increasing number of migrants with high levels of fertility. In 2011, about 11.2 % of the Dutch population was foreign-born, compared with 14.7 % in Sweden, 12 % in Germany, 11.2 % in France, 8.8 % in Italy, and 1.4 % in Poland (European Union 2011). This includes only foreign-born or first-generation immigrants. The Dutch population also includes a similar proportion of second-generation individuals who were born in the Netherlands to immigrant parents. The current stream of migration into the Netherlands began in the early 1960s, composed largely of labor immigrants or supposed "guest workers," mostly from Turkey, Morocco, Surinam, the Antilles, and Southern Europe (Italy, Greece, and Spain) (Triandafyllidou et al. 2007). An additional influx came in the 1970s from the same countries, largely composed of the families of the former "guest workers." In the late 1970s and early 1980s, Surinam gained independence from the Netherlands, which brought an additional influx of immigrants from that country. People from Morocco and Turkey still immigrate to the Netherlands, largely to marry Dutch-born individuals of Moroccan or Turkish descent.

Fokkema and colleagues (2008) argue that "migrant births account for a substantial share of all births in the Netherlands," with about 25 % of all births in 2004 to mothers with a migrant background. Whereas native Dutch people had a total period fertility rate (TPFR) of 1.6 births per woman in 1999, fertility was higher for immigrants from Iraq (3.4), Morocco (3.3), Somalia (4.4), Turkey (2.5), China (2.8), and Afghanistan (2.3) (De Valk et al. 2004). Garssen and Nicolaas (2006) show, however, that since 1980, fertility of second-generation immigrant women has come to resemble that of the native-born Dutch population. Although fertility among migrants from Turkey and Morocco still remains relatively high, even they have started to reduce fertility levels slightly. A central reason for higher fertility among these groups is related to religious norms, but younger ages at childbearing also plays a role as well as the fact that people tend to immigrate when they are at their peak childbearing years (Garssen and Nicolaas 2006).

In a more detailed analysis of fertility levels from 1995 to 2004, Fokkema et al. (2008) conclude that women with a non-Western or migrant background had only a limited impact on the TPFR of the population as a whole, increasing overall fertility by 0.06–0.08 children per woman, even though this was a period during which the migrant population was increasing. The TPFR was higher among all immigrant groups than among the native-born population, but the impact may have been limited because among the non-Western groups with high fertility (e.g., Somalis) there were fewer migrants and even fewer women of childbearing age. A second explanation is that many second-generation Turkish and Moroccan women are still less than 30 years old. Second-generation migrants tend to have children later in life, resembling the Dutch native-born population. Since these second-generation migrants are still of childbearing age, they may go on to have children and this may affect the TPFR, albeit less than the first generation (De Valk and Liefbroer 2007). One factor that has not yet been researched is the impact of recent Dutch emigration on fertility rates. Many of those who emigrate are of childbearing age. Just as with minority immigrants, however, emigration is likely to have a minimal impact on overall fertility levels.

Conclusion

Summary

The Netherlands appears at first glance to be a "fertility paradox" in the sense that it has maintained moderate levels of fertility despite concerns about a highly dense population, virtually no pro-natalist policies, and a largely non-religious society. The goal of this chapter has been to unravel this paradox by examining how various direct and indirect policies, institutions, and cultural norms and schemas have generated the Dutch fertility patterns we observe. Using a multilevel theoretical framework as a guide, we argued that the macro-level policies and cultural schemas of this country (e.g., family policy, welfare regime, housing, gender norms) affect individual-level decision making, including how individuals process or frame information and form fertility intentions and behavior. These micro-level processes, in turn, have generated the macro-level fertility trends that we observe.

In contemporary times, the Netherlands has always had a high population density, which produces underlying pressures to reduce fertility or maintain a stable population. Although fertility dropped from the late 1960s, the Netherlands has consistently maintained a TFR above 1.7, reaching even 1.88 in 2009 (Max Planck Institute for Demographic Research/Vienna Institute of Demography 2014). It also has one of the oldest ages of mothers at first birth in the world, but many couples with one child go on to have a second child immediately. Partnership legislation in the 1990s opened up new possibilities beyond marriage, and now more than one in five children are born outside of marriage. Ninety percent of these children are formally acknowledged by their fathers. The use of effective contraceptives is widespread, and, as a result, the Netherlands has one of the lowest levels of teenage pregnancies in the world (CBS 2010).

The only direct government policy that might be linked to fertility is child allowances, but these were not introduced to encourage fertility, and in recent years they have been reduced. In relation to family-related institutions, perhaps the most striking observation is the Dutch aversion to the use of formal childcare. The institutionalized system of formal childcare was only seriously introduced in the Netherlands in the mid-1990s, and since then the system has undergone many changes. The limited number of hours that children spend in formal care is related to the large number of female part-time workers and a strong cultural norm stressing the importance of childcare by mothers or other biological family members such as fathers or grandparents. Compared with other Western European countries, the Netherlands has a short—but fully paid—maternity leave of 16 weeks. Following childbirth, most women reduce their working hours. Most individuals disapprove of women with small children working full-time, similar to attitudes in Austria, Switzerland, and Germany.

In light of these strong cultural norms favoring childcare by the mother or other biological kin and disapproval of full-time working women, one might argue that there is no need to introduce any pro-family or pro-natalist policies in the Netherlands. What is striking is that these strong pro-family, traditional norms exist in a largely secular society. To understand how this apparent paradox might have emerged, we examined a constellation of inadvertent or indirect national policies that affect fertility.

The paternalistic welfare state was developed primarily to protect citizens, but it also prescribed the ideal life course and family constellation, with men considered the primary breadwinners and women responsible for the household. This stance has filtered down to Dutch households even today. Dutch gender roles remain traditional (Mills et al. 2008), with a one-and-a-half-earner model consisting of a male breadwinner and a woman working part time. Women's part-time work is often in marginalized positions, characterized as "unequal pay for unequal work" (Schippers 1987). Contrary to Hakim's (2000) positive view of Dutch women with part-time careers, in the event of divorce or death of a spouse many of these women fall into poverty and remain economically vulnerable (Uunk 2004).

Although fertility research often focuses on the impact of education levels, and particularly on women's gains in education, this chapter also explored education systems, the cost of higher education, and the impact of field of study on labor-market outcomes. Dutch women have high levels of education, but they are often streamed into fields of study that lead to marginal positions in the labor market. It may be that they are socialized into these positions or select themselves into this track, since they know that such an education will eventually lead to a job, such as teaching or healthcare, in which they can combine work and family relatively easily. State-sponsored higher education, with fairly open admissions and little ranking of programs or universities, has meant that parents do not have to limit the number of children they have because of worry about costs or other impediments to sending a child to university.

Dutch society has experienced extreme secularization over the past years and is now one of the most non-religious societies in Europe. Higher-parity births were previously attributed to Catholics in the south, but today religion only appears to play a role in fertility in very select, highly religious groups. It may be, however, that even after secularization, the highly engrained norms and values—as well as the policies enacted by a Christian-led government well into the 1990s—have maintained a strong focus on classic family and gender roles. In addition, generous government mortgage and co-financing policies have allowed young people to buy their own homes or qualify for affordable public housing. Finally, although some have argued that recent immigrants are responsible for relatively high levels of fertility, evidence shows that this is not the case.

What Can We Learn from the Dutch Case?

The first lesson we can take from the Netherlands is that direct family policy focused on fertility is not always necessary to promote moderate to high fertility levels. Strong norms and values are also important. Second, late fertility combined with rapid catching up and low levels of teenage pregnancies in the Netherlands reflect the strong emphasis on an individual's or couple's control over fertility, including the timing of pregnancies and number of children. The Dutch have a very open attitude toward sexuality both in the education of children and in daily debate and the public media. Although Dutch women score lower than women in some other countries on gender equity in the workplace and the division of household labor, younger cohorts, in particular, are more educated than their male counterparts and have a strong voice in the household and over their own fertility.

The third and perhaps the most important lesson is that a flexible labor market with part-time work opportunities for women has translated into relatively happy and healthy parents and children, in addition to higher levels of fertility. It is likewise important to note that Dutch men work fewer hours than many of their East Asian or European counterparts, and about 15 % work part-time. Some attribute both high fertility and children's well-being to their parent's high level of happiness. Psychologist Ellen De Bruin (2007) has argued that a focus on personal choice and freedom in partnerships, sexuality, and religion has played a strong role in the distinctly low levels of female depression in the Netherlands. This is likewise coupled with the "right to work part-time," which contributes to a favorable work-life balance. More recently, an article in the *Huffington Post* (Belkin 2013) entitled "What mothers really want: To opt in between" argued that most mothers would find working part-time an ideal option for work-family reconciliation. Other family caretakers beyond mothers can also play a role. For example, Dutch men with young children are increasingly taking off from work for what is termed a "daddy day" (Papa dag) 1 day a week when children are small. The structural use of grandparents to care for children also increases work-life balance and family ties.

Is the Dutch System Sustainable?

The focus on part-time work and the "good life," free education, support for unemployment and disability, co-financing of mortgages, and generous child allowances and support for childcare have also taken a toll on the state. The part-time work culture of Dutch women may become economically impossible. Dutch couples continue this one-and-a-half model of the division of labor because they can afford to, but recent cuts in government benefits may push more women into the labor market and both parents into longer working hours.

The controversial female politician and Minister of Education, Culture, and Science, Jet Bussemaker, has continuously worked to bring the gender inequality issue of Dutch women into the public debate. She has repeatedly argued that Dutch women should feel guilty because the Dutch state invests so much in their education and then they pull out of the labor market. There have been policy suggestions that Dutch women should pay the state back for their free education if they leave the labor market and do not use the training they received. Minister Bussemaker also sparked a nation-wide debate in 2013 when she argued that "Too many women live off of their husbands" (*Te veel vrouwen teren op hun man*) and "Women need to get rid of the eternal guilt about their family" (*Vrouwen moeten af van dat eeuwige schuldgevoel over hun gezin*) (Abels 2013).

The recent financial crisis has meant that many formally generous policies have had to be reduced. This includes cuts to childcare and also child allowances. A recently proposed change to move from free university education to a system of student loans, to be initiated in the autumn of 2014, also shows that there are increasing cracks in the system and limits to state generosity. Only the future will tell whether it was these generous policies, enabling Dutch women to remain in the home, that have sustained the Netherlands' relative high levels of fertility.

References

Abels, R. (2013, November 5). Minister Bussemaker: "Te veel vrouwen teren op hun man" [Minister Bussemaker: "Too many women live off their husbands"]. *Trouw*.

Adsera, A. (2006). Religion and changes in family-size norms in developed countries. *Review of Religious Research, 47*(3), 271–286.

Allmendinger, J. (1989). Educational systems and labor market outcomes. *European Sociological Review, 5*(3), 231–250.

Bail, C. A. (2008). The configuration of symbolic boundaries against immigrants in Europe. *American Sociological Review, 73*, 37–59.

Balbo, N., Billari, F. C., & Mills, M. (2013). Fertility in advanced societies: A review. *European Journal of Population, 29*, 1–38.

Beerthuizen, R. J. C. M. (2003). *Anticonceptie op maat: Van puberteit tot overgang* [Contraception to size: From puberty until menopause]. Houten: Bohn Stafleu Van Loghum.

Begall, K. H., & Mills, M. (2011). The impact of perceived work control, job strain and work-family conflict on fertility intentions: A European comparison. *European Journal of Population, 27*(4), 433–456.

Begall, K. H., & Mills, M. (2013). The influence of educational field, occupation and occupational sex segregation on fertility in the Netherlands. *European Sociological Review, 29*(4), 720–742.

Belkin, L. (2013, December 8). What mothers really want: To opt in between. *Huffington Post*. http://www.huffingtonpost.com/2013/08/12/what-mothers-really-want-_n_3744110.html. Accessed 24 July 2014.

Berghammer, C. (2009). Religious socialization and fertility: Transition to third birth in the Netherlands. *European Journal of Population, 25*, 297–324.

Bryant, C. (1981). Depillarisation in the Netherlands. *British Journal of Sociology, 32*(1), 56–74.

Buehler, C., & Philipov, D. (2005). Social capital related to fertility: Theoretical foundation and empirical evidence for Bulgaria. In *Vienna Yearbook of Population Research* (pp. 53–82). Wien: Verlag der österreichischen Akademie der Wissenschaften.

Bulatao, R. A., & Casterline, J. B. (Eds.). (2001). Global fertility transition. *Population and Development Review, 27*(suppl).

Castiglioni, M., & Dalla Zuanna, G. (1994). Innovation and tradition: Reproductive and marital behavior in Italy in the 1970s and 1980s. *European Journal of Population, 10*(2), 107–142.

CBS (Centraal Bureau voor de Statistiek). (2004). *Kinderloosheid en opleidingsnivea* [Childlessness and educational level]. http://www.cbs.nl/nl-NL/menu/themas/bevolking/publicaties/artikelen/archief/2004/2004-1469-wm.htm. Accessed 23 July 2014.

CBS (Centraal Bureau voor de Statistiek). (2010). *Veel Antilliaanse en Surinaamse tienermoders* [More Antiliean and Surinamese teenage mothers]. http://www.cbs.nl/nl-NL/menu/themas/bevolking/publicaties/artikelen/archief/2010/2010-3276-wm.htm. Accessed 8 Sept 2014.

CBS (Centraal Bureau voor de Statistiek). (2011). *Niet-gehuwd samenwonen in de Europese Unie* [Unmarried cohabitation in the European Union]. http://www.cbs.nl/NR/rdonlyres/38E09A54-93CD-4981-B618-E80017250A5A/0/2011k2b15p9art.pdf. Accessed 8 Sept 2014.

CBS (Centraal Bureau voor de Statistiek). (2012). *Kinderen van niet gehuwde ouders vaker erkend* [Children born from unmarried parents more often legally recognized]. http://www.cbs.nl/nl-NL/menu/themas/veiligheid-recht/publicaties/artikelen/archief/2012/2012-3719-wm.htm. Accessed 8 Sept 2014.

Chiuri, M. C., & Jappelli, J. (2003). Financial market imperfections and home ownership: A comparative study. *European Economic Review, 47*(5), 857–875.

Clark, W. A. V., Deurloo, M. C., & Dieleman, F. M. (1994). Tenure changes in the context of micro level family and macro level economic shifts. *Urban Studies, 31*(1), 137–154.

Coleman, J. S. (1990). *Foundations of social theory*. Cambridge, MA: Harvard University Press.

Cook, A., & Minnotte, K. L. (2008). Occupational and industry sex segregation and the work–family interface. *Sex Roles, 59*, 800–813.

De Bruin, E. (2007). *Dutch women don't get depressed: Hoe komen vrouwen zo stoer?* [How is that women are so tough?]. Amsterdam: Contact.

De Graaf, N. D., & Te Grotenhuis, M. (2008). Traditional Christian belief and belief in the supernatural: Diverging trends in the Netherlands between 1979 and 2005? *Journal for the Scientific Study of Religion, 47*(4), 585–598.

De Valk, H., & Liefbroer, A. C. (2007). Timing preferences for women's family-life transitions: Intergenerational transmission among migrants and Dutch. *Journal of Marriage and Family, 69*, 190–206.

De Valk, H., Liefbroer, A. C., Esveldt, I., & Henkens, K. (2004). Family formation and cultural integration among migrants in the Netherlands. *Genus, 55*, 9–36.

De Vries, M. R., & Wolbers, M. H. J. (2005). Non-standard employment relations and wages among school leavers in the Netherlands. *Work, Employment and Society, 19*, 503–525.

Dekker, P., & Ester, P. (1996). Depillarization, deconfessionalization, and the de-ideologization: Empirical trends in Dutch society, 1958–1992. *Review of Religious Research, 37*(4), 325–341.

Den Dulk, L. (2001). *Work-family arrangements in organisations: A cross-national study in the Netherlands, Italy, the United Kingdom and Sweden*. Amsterdam: Rozenberg.

Dorbritz, J., Höhn, C., & Naderi, R. (2005). *The demographic future of Europe—Facts, figures, policies: Results of the Population Policy Acceptance Study (PPAS)*. Stuttgart: Robert Bosch Foundation/Federal Institute for Population Research.

Duvander, A.-Z., Lappegård, T., & Andersson, G. (2010). Family policy and fertility: Fathers' and mothers' use of parental leave and continued childbearing in Norway and Sweden. *Journal of European Social Policy, 20*, 45–57.

Dykstra, P. A., & Komter, A. E. (2006). Structural characteristics of Dutch kin networks. In P. A. Dykstra, M. Kalmijn, T. C. M. Knijn, A. E. Komter, A. C. Liefbroer, & C. H. Mulder (Eds.), *Family solidarity in the Netherlands* (pp. 21–42). Amsterdam: Dutch University Press.

Engelen, T. L. M., & Hillebrand, J. H. A. (1986). Fertility and nuptiality in the Netherlands, 1850–1960. *Population Studies-Journal of Demography, 40*(3), 487–503.

European Council. (2002). *Presidency conclusions, Barcelona European Council, 15–16 Mar 2002*. Document SN 100/1/02 REV 1. http://ec.europa.eu/invest-in-research/pdf/download_en/barcelona_european_council.pdf. Accessed 9 Oct 2014.

European Union. (2011). *Eurostat: Your key to European statistics*. http://epp.eurostat.ec.europa.eu/portal/page/portal/eurostat/home. Accessed 22 Mar 2012.

Feijten, P., & Mulder, C. H. (2002). The timing of household events and housing events in the Netherlands: A longitudinal perspective. *Housing Studies, 17*(5), 773–792.

FNV Bondgenoten. (2014). *Bezuinigingen kinderopvang—feiten en cijfers* [Cuts in childcare—facts and numbers]. https://www.fnvbondgenoten.nl/themas/kinderopvang/wijziging_kinderopvangtoeslag_per_2013/437167/. Accessed 22 July 2014.

Fokkema, T., de Valk, H., de Beer, J., & van Duin, C. (2008). The Netherlands: Childbearing within the context of a "Poldermodel" society. *Demographic Research, 19*(21), 743–794.

Fokkema, C. M., & Esveldt, I. (2006). *Child-friendly policies* (Work Package 7). Wiesbaden: Bundesinstitut für Bevölkerungsforschung.

Fokkema, T., & Liefbroer, A. C. (2008). Trends in living arrangements in Europe: Convergence or divergence? *Demographic Research, 19*, 1351–1418.

Frejka, T. (2008). Birth regulation in Europe: Completing the contraceptive revolution. *Demographic Research, 19*(5), 73–84.

Frejka, T., & Westoff, C. F. (2008). Religion, religiousness, and fertility in the US and in Europe. *European Journal of Population, 24*(1), 5–31.

Garssen, J., & Nicolaas, H. (2006). Recente trends in de vruchtbaarheid van niet-westers allochtone vrouwen [Recent fertility trends of non-Western foreign women]. *Bevolkingstrends, 54*(1), 15–31.

Garssen, J., & van Duin, C. (2006). Bevolkingsprognose 2006–2050: Belangrijke uitkomsten [Population projections 2006–2050: Important outcomes]. *Bevolkingstrends, 54*(4), 85–92.

Government of the Netherlands. (1999). National Report submitted to the Regional Population conference, Budapest, December 1998. In: UNECE (United Nations Economic Commission for Europe) (Ed.), *Population in Europe and North America on the eve of the Millennium: Dynamics and policy responses* (pp. 131–136). Geneva: UNECE.

Hakim, C. (2000). *Work-lifestyle choices in the 21st century: Preference theory*. Oxford: Oxford University Press.

Hakim, C. (2003). *Models of the family in modern societies: Ideals and realities*. Aldershot: Ashgate.

Hoem, J. M., Neyer, G., & Andersson, G. (2006). Educational attainment and childlessness: The relationship between educational field, educational level, and childlessness among Swedish women born in 1955–59. *Demographic Research, 14*, 331–380.

ILO (International Labour Organization). (2013). *Working conditions laws report 2012: A global review*. Geneva: ILO.

Ivanova, K., Mills, M., & Veenstra, R. (2014). Parental residential and partnering transitions as triggers of adolescent romantic relationships. *Journal of Marriage and the Family, 76*(3), 465–475.

Jones, G. W. (2007). Delayed marriage and very low fertility in Pacific Asia. *Population and Development Review, 33*, 453–478.

Kalmijn, M., & Luijkx, R. (2006). Changes in women's employment and occupational mobility in the Netherlands: 1995 to 2000. In H.-P. Blossfeld & H. Hofmeister (Eds.), *Globalization, uncertainty and women's careers: An international comparison* (pp. 84–112). Cheltenham: Edward Elgar.

Kendig, H. L. (1984). Housing careers, life cycle and residential mobility: Implications for the housing market. *Urban Studies, 21*, 271–283.

Kohler, H. P., Billari, F. C., & Ortega, J. A. (2002). The emergence of lowest-low fertility in Europe during the 1990s. *Population and Development Review, 28*, 641–681.

Kontula, O., & Miettinen, A. (2005). *Synthesis report on demographic behaviour, existing population related policies, and expectations men and women have concerning the state* (Working Paper E 19/2005). Helsinki: Population Research Institute/Family Federation of Finland.

Kool-Smit, J. E. (1967). Het onbehagen bij de vrouw [The discomfort of women]. *De Gids, 130*(9/10), 267–281.

Lappegård, T., & Rønsen, M. (2005). The multifaceted impact of education on entry into motherhood. *European Journal of Population, 21*, 31–49.

Lebeau, Y., Stumpf, R., Brown, R., Lucchesi, M. A. S., & Kwiek, M. (2012). Who shall pay for the public good? Comparative trends in the funding crisis of public higher education. *Compare, 42*(1), 137–157.

Lesthaeghe, R. (1995). The second demographic transition in Western countries: An interpretation. In K. O. Mason & A. M. Jensen (Eds.), *Gender and family change in industrialized countries* (pp. 17–62). Oxford: Clarendon.

Liefbroer, A. C. (2005). The impact of perceived costs and rewards of childbearing on entry into parenthood: Evidence from a panel study. *European Journal of Population, 21*(4), 367–391.

Liefbroer, A. C., & Dykstra, P. (2000). *Levenslopen in verandering: Een studie naar ontwikkelingen in de levenslopen van Nederlanders geboren tussen 1900 en 1970* [The changing life course: A study of the development of the life course of Dutch persons born between 1900 and 1970]. WRR Voorstudies en achtergronden V107. Den Haag: Sdu Uitgevers.

Longman, P. (2006). The return of patriarchy. *Foreign Policy, 153*, 56–65.

Luijkx, R., Kalmijn, M., & Muffels, R. J. A. (2006). The impact of globalization on job and career mobility of Dutch men: Life-history data from the mid-1950s to the year 2000. In H.-P. Blossfeld, M. Mills, & F. Bernardi (Eds.), *Globalization, uncertainty, and men's careers: An international comparison* (pp. 117–144). Cheltenham: Edward Elgar.

Martin-Garcia, T. (2010). The impact of occupational sex-composition on women's fertility in Spain. *European Societies, 12*, 113–133.

Max Planck Institute for Demographic Research/Vienna Institute of Demography. (2014). *The human fertility database.* http://www.humanfertility.org. Accessed 6 June 2014.

Mills, M., & Blossfeld, H.-P. (2005). Globalization, uncertainty, and the early life course: A theoretical framework. In H.-P. Blossfeld, E. Klijzing, M. Mills, & K. Kurz (Eds.), *Globalization, uncertainty and youth in society* (pp. 1–24). London: Routledge.

Mills, M., & Praeg, P. (2013). *The role of gender in school-to-work transitions in Europe* (Short Statistical Report 4). Brussels: European Commission Directorate-General, Justice and Fundamental Rights.

Mills, M., & Täht, K. (2010). Nonstandard work schedules and partnership quality: Quantitative and qualitative findings. *Journal of Marriage and Family, 72*, 860–875.

Mills, M., Mencarini, L., Tanturri, M. L., & Begall, K. (2008). Gender equity and fertility intentions in Italy and the Netherlands. *Demographic Research, 18*(1), 1–26.

Mills, M., Rindfuss, R. R., McDonald, P., & te Velde, E. (2011). Why do people postpone parenthood? Reasons and social policy incentives. *Human Reproduction Update, 17*(6), 848–860.

Mills, M., Praeg, P., Tsang, F., Begall, K., Derbyshire, J., Kohle, L., Miani, C., & Hoorens, S. (2013). *Use of childcare services in the EU Member States and progress towards the Barcelona targets* (Short Statistical Report 1). Brussels: European Commission Directorate-General, Justice and Fundamental Rights.

Mooi-Reci, I., & Mills, M. (2012). Gender inequality and unemployment reforms: Lessons from twenty years of unemployment insurance benefit experiments. *Social Forces, 91*(2), 583–608.

Mulder, C. H. (2006). Home-ownership and family formation. *Journal of Housing and the Built Environment, 21,* 281–298.
Mulder, C. H., & Billari, F. C. (2010). Home-ownership regimes and lowest-low fertility. *Housing Studies, 25,* 527–541.
Mulder, C. H., & Wagner, M. (1998). First-time home-ownership in the family life course: A West German-Dutch comparison. *Urban Studies, 35*(4), 687–713.
Mulder, C. H., & Wagner, M. (2001). The connections between family formation and first-time home ownership in the context of West Germany and the Netherlands. *European Journal of Population, 17,* 137–164.
Murphy, M. J., & Sullivan, O. (1985). Housing tenure and family formation in contemporary Britain. *European Sociological Review, 1*(3), 230–243.
Need, A., & de Graaf, N. D. (1996). "Losing my religion:" A dynamic analysis of leaving the church in the Netherlands. *European Sociological Review, 12*(1), 87–99.
Poortman, A.-R., & Mills, M. (2012). Joint investments in marriage and cohabitation: The role of legal and symbolic factors. *Journal of Marriage and Family, 74*(2), 357–376.
Portegijs, W., Hermans, B., & Lalta, V. (2006). *Emancipatiemonitor 2006: Veranderingen in de leefsituatie en levensloop* [Emancipation monitor 2006: Changes in the living situation and life course]. Den Haag: Sociaal en Cultureel Planbureau.
Remery, C., van Doorne-Huiskes, A., & Schippers, J. (2002). Labor market flexibility in the Netherlands: Looking for winners and losers. *Work, Employment and Society, 16,* 477–495.
Rijksoverheid. (2014). *Kinderbijslag* [Child allowances]. http://www.rijksoverheid.nl/onderwerpen/kinderbijslag. Accessed 22 July 2014.
Rindfuss, R. R., Bumpass, L., & St John, C. (1980). Education and fertility: Implications for the roles women occupy. *American Sociological Review, 45,* 431–447.
Rindfuss, R. R., St. John, C., & Bumpass, L. L. (1984). Education and the timing of motherhood: Disentangling causation. *Journal of Marriage and Family, 46*(4), 981–984.
Rindfuss, R. R., Morgan, S. P., & Offutt, K. (1996). Education and the changing age pattern of American fertility: 1963–1989. *Demography, 33*(3), 277–290.
Schippers, J. J. (1987). *Beloningsverschillen tussen mannen en vrouwen: Een economische analyse* [Pay gap between men and women: An economic analysis]. Groningen: Wolters-Noordhoff.
SCP (Sociaal en Cultureel Planbureau). (2006). *Emancipatiemonitor 2006* [Emancipation monitor 2006]. Den Haag: SCP.
Shavit, Y., & Müller, W. (Eds.). (1997). *From school to work: A comparative study of educational qualifications and occupational destinations.* Oxford: Clarendon.
Sobotka, T. (2004). *Postponement of childbearing and low fertility in Europe.* Amsterdam: University of Groningen/Thela Thesis.
Somers, A., & Van Poppel, F. (2003). Catholic priests and the fertility transition among Dutch Catholics, 1935–1970. *Annales de Demographie Historique, 2,* 57–88.
Statistics Netherlands. (2007). *Statistical yearbook of the Netherlands 2007.* Voorburg/Heerlen: Statistics Netherlands.
Triandafyllidou, A., Gropas, R., & Vogel, D. (2007). Introduction. In A. Triandafyllidou & R. Gropas (Eds.), *European immigration: A sourcebook* (pp. 1–19). Aldershot: Ashgate.
UNECE (United Nations Economic Commission for Europe). (2014). *Statistical database: Mean age of women at birth of first child.* http://w3.unece.org/pxweb/dialog/varval.asp?lang=andma=04_GEFHAge1stChild_randpath=../database/STAT/30-GE/02-Families_households/andti=Mean%20age%20of%20women%20at%20birth%20of%20first%20child. Accessed 6 June 2014.
UNICEF (United Nations Children's Fund). (2013). *Child well-being in rich countries: A comparative overview.* http://www.unicef-irc.org/publications/pdf/rc11_eng.pdf. Accessed 22 July 2014.
Uunk, W. (2004). The economic consequences of divorce for women in the European Union: The impact of welfare state arrangements. *European Journal of Population, 20,* 251–285.

Van Bavel, J. (2010). Choice of study discipline and the postponement of motherhood in Europe: The impact of expected earnings, gender composition, and family attitudes. *Demography, 47*(2), 439–458.

Van Poppel, F. (1985). Late fertility decline in the Netherlands: The influence of religious denomination, socio-economic group, and region. *European Journal of Population, 1*(4), 347–373.

Visser, J. (2002). The first part-time economy in the world: A model to be followed? *Journal of European Social Policy, 12*(1), 23–42.

Visser, J., & Hemerijck, A. (1999). *A Dutch miracle*. Amsterdam: Amsterdam University Press.

Wielers, R. J. J., & Mills, M. (2011). The flexibilization of the Dutch labor market: The impact of globalization on the life course and inequality. In H.-P. Blossfeld, S. Buchholz, D. Hofaecker, & K. Kolb (Eds.), *Globalized markets and social inequality in Europe* (pp. 46–75). New York: Palgrave MacMillan.

The manufacturer's authorised representative in the EU is Springer Nature Customer Service Centre GmbH, Europaplatz 3, 69115 Heidelberg, Germany. If you have any concerns regarding our products, please contact ProductSafety@springernature.com

Printed and bound by CPI Group (UK) Ltd, Croydon, CR0 4YY
23/03/2026
02076671-0001